COCAINE

CHANGES

In the series
HEALTH, SOCIETY, AND POLICY,
edited by Sheryl Ruzek and Irving Kenneth Zola

COCAINE
CHANGES

The Experience of
Using and Quitting

DAN
WALDORF

CRAIG
REINARMAN

SHEIGLA
MURPHY

TEMPLE UNIVERSITY PRESS
Philadelphia

Temple University Press, Philadelphia 19122
Copyright © 1991 by Dan Waldorf, Craig Reinarman, and Sheigla Murphy.
All rights reserved
Published 1991
Printed in the United States of America

The paper used in this publication meets the minimum requirements of American
National Standard for Information Sciences—Permanence of Paper for Printed
Library Materials, ANSI Z39.48-1984 ∞

Library of Congress Cataloging-in-Publication Data
Waldorf, Dan.
   Cocaine changes : the experience of using and quitting / Dan
Waldorf, Craig Reinarman, Sheigla Murphy.
      p. cm. — (Health, society, and policy)
   Includes bibliographical references and index.
   ISBN 0-87722-863-9 (cloth : alk. paper)
   1. Cocaine habit—United States. 2. Narcotic addicts—United
States—Case studies. I. Reinarman, Craig. II. Murphy, Sheigla,
1949–   . III. Title. IV. Series.
   [DNLM: 1. Cocaine. 2. Substance Abuse. 3. Substance Dependence—
psychology. WM 280 W166c]
HV5810.W24   1991
616.86′47—dc20
DNLM/DLC
for Library of Congress   91-664

Coke makes you use your senses more. It's a very sensual drug. This makes your body feel good. . . . It makes you think. It just makes you feel good. . . . It stimulates you.

—*Case #902, a 33-year-old white female snorter*

It makes you hyper and smarter, faster and better; . . . you know, sort of like the Six Million–Dollar Man.

—*Case #636, a 25-year-old black male freebaser*

Cocaine, it's a demon drug, man. It's ridiculous, it's insane, and we all know it is. . . . The shit is so strong, it raps you out of your mind, goes into your pocket, grabs your dick, and says, "Hey, you're *mine*."

—*Case #606, a 28-year-old Latino freebaser*

CONTENTS

CONTENTS

PART IV
CONCLUSIONS

ACKNOWLEDGMENTS

M*ost books* have few authors but many contributors. This one is no exception. It is based primarily on a study funded by a generous two-year grant from the National Institute on Drug Abuse, which allowed us to pursue our research wherever it led. Dr. Michael Backenheimer, the NIDA project officer, and Patricia Simmons, the financial officer, gave us sage advice and kind assistance. Of course, our findings and interpretations may not reflect the views of NIDA or its staff.

The grant was administered by the URSA Institute in San Francisco. Among the URSA staff members who facilitated our work, we would like to thank Jeffrey Fagan, Kenneth (Woody) Wodrich, and Betty-Jean McNeil. The study drew directly on the skills of many project staff members. Those who worked longest include Graciela Rivera-Perata, Della Rushing, Patrick T. Macdonald, Natasha Nicholson, and Frank Myers. At various stages in the research, others made valuable contributions as well: Maureen Alioto, Connie Fishman, Dan Hart, Ron Lembo, Doug McDonnell, Sherry Michalske, Toby Marotta, Stephanie Riegel, Frank Smith, Julian Torres, and Sylvia Virsik. Carol Sowell, the copyeditor, also did an excellent job of making us say what we meant in the final manuscript.

The most important contributions came from our respondents. Interviews that might have been arduous were instead delightfully educational. We could not have done the study at all without the time, tolerance, and truthfulness of the participants. They let us into their homes and their worlds. They allowed us to ask prying and often impertinent questions about their private lives and their experiences with cocaine. They were untiringly generous in their responses.

We owe a special debt of gratitude to a small subsample of respondents whom we had first interviewed in 1974 and 1975. Many of them had left cocaine behind and were not interested in thinking or talking about it again. Yet all agreed to extensive follow-up interviews. Their generosity and openness about their past and present is greatly appreciated.

We must also note that the book draws upon material from the study that we previously published in scholarly journals. Chapter 4 summarizes data on cocaine and work, some of which appeared in *Research in Law, Deviance, and Social Control* (Reinarman et al., 1988). Part of our data on cocaine-related sexual problems that appears in Chapter 8 was published in the *Journal of Drug Issues* (Macdonald et al., 1988). An earlier version of the eleven-year follow-up study reported in Chapter 11 appeared in the *British Journal of Addiction* (Murphy et al., 1989).

Finally, four people provided service above and beyond the call of collegiality. Throughout our research, Janet Francendese of Temple University Press encouraged us to write this book. She unfailingly gave us her scarce time and ample editorial talent, and somehow managed always to nudge and never to nag. Professor Peter Adler of the University of Denver provided us with a series of insightful and inspiring comments very early in our writing. The series editor, Professor Irving Kenneth Zola of Brandeis University, caught numerous errors in a later draft and provided many helpful suggestions. Last but not least, Professor Harry Gene Levine of Queens College, City University of New York, gave us a brilliant line-by-line critique that helped us figure out what it was that we had figured out. All authors should have such help, for it gives real meaning to the oft-cited yet rarely realized phrase "community of scholars." Each of these people contributed to whatever is worthwhile in this book, although none is responsible for flaws caused by our failure to listen to them carefully enough.

CHAPTER 1

CHANGING PERSPECTIVES ON COCAINE:
AN INTRODUCTION

In the spring of 1986 politicians and the mass media launched a "war on drugs," the latest in a long line of such wars. This time, cocaine was cast as the core villain in a chorus of claims about an "epidemic" or "plague." As President Reagan put it in a nationally televised address, cocaine is "killing a whole generation of our children" and "tearing our country apart."[1] In July 1986 alone, network news programs aired more than seventy segments on drugs, most on cocaine (Diamond, Acosta, and Thornton, 1987). In addition to thousands of newspaper stories, *Time* and *Newsweek* each devoted five cover stories in 1986 to the cocaine "crisis." Politicians in both parties engaged in a competition over new "get tough" anti-drug laws from 1986 through 1989 and even challenged each other to take urine tests. It was a conservative historical moment. Politicians took strong stands. The media reported scary stories. Cocaine became the scourge of America in the 1980s.

This book is about heavy cocaine users, the humans behind the headlines. The study from which it emanates was conducted between 1985 and 1987, just as crack or rock cocaine was coming into vogue. Most of the people we describe, therefore, are "snorters" who used the drug intranasally. However, we also interviewed a good number who smoked cocaine in "crack" or "freebase" form and a smaller number who injected cocaine intravenously.

1

All the people you will read about in this book are or were serious cocaine users, not those who merely experimented with or casually used cocaine. In order to be included in our study, a person had to have used a minimum average of two grams (about $200 worth in 1986) of cocaine per week for at least six months, or have used at least some cocaine every day for a minimum of one year.[2] Many of our respondents used considerably more than these minimums. Thus, the voices heard here are of those who regularly used substantial amounts of cocaine for a substantial period of time. Compared with representative national samples surveyed by the National Institute on Drug Abuse (NIDA), our respondents fall easily within the most extreme 5 percent of the 24 million Americans who have tried cocaine (NIDA, 1986b; Adams et al., 1989). Indeed, NIDA surveys from the early 1970s through 1988 show that less than 1 percent of those who have ever tried cocaine use it on a daily basis, as many of our subjects did. At the peak of the cocaine scare in 1988, less than 1 percent in a national household survey used cocaine once a week or more, as did virtually all our respondents (see, e.g., NIDA, 1989; Shaffer and Jones, 1989). It is safe to say, then, that the people we interviewed are among the United States' heaviest users of cocaine.

Initially, our study emphasized the processes of cessation from cocaine abuse, what treatment professionals call "recovery." But we found early on that in order to understand how people stopped, we had to look at how they got started and at all the processes of use and abuse. So we decided to explore the natural history of cocaine use—initiation, the uses to which the drug is put, controlled as well as uncontrolled use, cocaine in the workplace, cocaine selling, the various types of problems associated with cocaine abuse, and motivations to stop as well as strategies for doing so.

We began our research during a period when most drug researchers, treatment professionals, and drug policymakers had come to believe that cocaine was an extremely dangerous, addictive substance. This view has been reinforced by the more recent proliferation of crack smoking among the urban poor, but cocaine's current reputation reflects a major shift in perception over the last fifteen years. During the 1970s when cocaine reemerged in the United States, many researchers who studied short-term or casual users believed cocaine hydrochloride did not live up to its early twentieth-century reputation as a dangerous drug and was relatively innocuous as drugs go (much the way marijuana was then viewed). Most drug researchers who studied intranasal cocaine users at that time found that the majority engaged in recreational or moderate use, that relatively few reported negative effects, and that even these effects were rarely severe (e.g., Ashley, 1975; Grinspoon and Bakalar, 1976; Phillips and Wynne, 1980).

In the 1980s this position began to change dramatically. As more people began to use the drug in larger doses for longer periods, and as people began to smoke freebase and crack, more physical and psychological problems were reported and more people sought help. Treatment programs tailored for cocaine abusers began to proliferate, and the clinician-entrepreneurs who founded them began to warn all who would listen of the terrible powers of cocaine, claiming that its use quickly led to myriad problems and eventual addiction.

If these new concerns about cocaine were exaggerated, that does not mean they were unwarranted. More users were having difficulties with the drug, according to the evidence on drug-related hospital emergencies and deaths from the Drug Abuse Warning Network (DAWN), a monitoring project of the National Institute of Drug Abuse. For example, between 1979 and 1985 emergency room episodes in which cocaine was "mentioned" increased nearly fivefold, from 1,931 to 9,403. Three years later in 1988, the number of such "cocaine-related" emergency room episodes had grown nearly fivefold again, to 46,020. Similar DAWN indices on "cocaine-related" deaths rose sixfold, from 99 in 1979 to 615 in 1985, and more than doubled to 1,589 by 1988 (DAWN, 1987; Adams et al., 1989). Medical emergencies and deaths continued to increase into 1989.[3]

It should be noted, however, that these types of data do not easily lend themselves to causal inferences. Although cocaine is often mentioned in emergency room reports, alcohol is also involved in a large proportion of such episodes, as are other drugs used in combination with cocaine. Moreover, any drug can be mentioned whether or not it is actually related to the emergency or death. For example, the presence of cocaine in the blood of victims of traffic accidents and gunshots warrants a "mention" whether or not it played any causal role in the incident that led to the emergency (see Reinarman and Levine, 1989).

Notwithstanding such qualifications, both problem indicators and the tone of public discourses about cocaine are different today from what they were a mere decade ago. Cocaine has developed a very negative reputation, and more and more clinicians and researchers have chronicled the problems associated with its use. Much of this change coincided with the spread of the riskier rapid-delivery methods of cocaine use such as freebasing and crack smoking. The 1988 NIDA household survey showed that while overall cocaine use continued to decline, an estimated 2.4 million people in the United States had at least tried freebase or crack, and nearly one in five of them (484,000) once a month or more.

Because such modes of ingestion get more cocaine, in a purer form, into the brain far more rapidly, they provide a more potent high with greater abuse potential than intranasal use. Crack use also spread rapidly among already troubled urban poor, who have always been particularly vulnerable to drug problems. And some of the change in attitudes toward cocaine was related to the growing number of cocaine users showing up in treatment. Many of these were not new crack addicts but long-term snorters and shooters whose problems developed slowly over years of heavy use.

The prevalence of cocaine use increased rather sharply in the latter half of the 1970s, and reports of problems also increased. By the 1980s, the social base of users had shifted from mostly middle-class and affluent whites to encompass a broader segment of the population—particularly the unemployed, impoverished blacks and Latinos of the inner cities (e.g., Washton and Gold, 1987). Once the new, more dangerous mode of ingestion, crack smoking, was linked to a new, vulnerable user population which was already seen as a "dangerous" or "criminal class," the change in cocaine's reputation from recreational stimulant to national scourge was assured.

The message today from most research about cocaine is that it has very high addiction potential and that most people who use it are risking grave physiological and psychological harm. Beyond what is known from research and clinical findings, however, the moral entrepreneurs who mobilized the nation for the war on drugs made many questionable claims about cocaine being the root of a host of preexisting social problems. Everything from delinquency and school dropout rates to poverty, prostitution, and work productivity declines has been attributed to cocaine (see Reinarman and Levine, 1989).

The accumulating evidence of cocaine problems—particularly the sometimes harrowing tales told by our own respondents—has persuaded us that this drug can no longer be considered innocuous. At the same time, we believe that the prevailing view of the connection between cocaine (and crack) and the nation's ills is distorted. We expect that as this war on drugs fades, public discussion about cocaine will move to a middle ground. In this book we have tried to explore some of that terrain, to describe in detail the dangers of cocaine while avoiding hysteria. To posit the existence of this middle ground, however, is to have a point of view (some might say a bias), so we should sketch out some of the reasons behind our stance.

Americans historically have exhibited a peculiar anxiety about consciousness-altering substances. In a deeply Protestant culture rooted in the individualism of "self-made" men and women, self-control has always been the social glue of society. And where self-control looms this large, its loss is a much-feared phenomenon (Levine, 1990). We suspect that this is why drug scares, during which a wide range of fears are projected onto one chemical bogeyman or another, are a recurring feature of American life.

During the temperance crusades of the early nineteenth century, for example, alcohol was the central focus of struggles over self control. Demon drink was blamed for virtually every evil, every personal and social problem found in America from the dawn of industrialization in the 1830s through Prohibition nearly a century later (Levine, 1984). In succeeding scares various other drugs have had to shoulder more than their share of blame for social problems (Reinarman and Levine, 1989). Cocaine is one such drug and the current scare is but one in a long history of scares that have scapegoated alcohol, morphine, heroin, methamphetamines, barbiturates, LSD, and marijuana. On the other hand, there has never been any shortage of real drug problems in the United States. Our point is that little progress can be made toward resolving the real problems if they are not distinguished from the contrived ones.

— We believe that people use legal and illegal drugs for discoverable reasons and that these reasons do not necessarily entail either social or psychological pathology. Nor does drug use always lead down the road to ruin. Humans have ingested drugs for purposes of consciousness alteration throughout history (Weil, 1972). Barely out of the caves, our ancient ancestors learned of the joys of intoxication (and probably the woes of hangovers) from birds and other animals who ate fermented fruits (Siegel, 1989). Thousands of years ago, during the transition from hunting and gathering societies to primitive agriculture, great care was taken to brew beer, which was valued for its savage-taming and nutritious qualities (Levine, forthcoming). The ingestion of chemical substances to alter consciousness has continued in virtually all cultures and across all epochs.[4] The recent waves of drug use and abuse in the United States are not unprecedented and should therefore be kept in perspective.

Consider alcohol and cigarettes. These legal drugs are widely advertised and readily available. Yet each of them causes far more deaths, health problems, and economic losses than all illicit drugs *combined*. Alcohol users behind the steering wheels of cars kill nearly ten times the number of people who die from all illicit drugs in the United States. More people die of lung cancer and heart disease related to cigarette smoking in a week than die of cocaine use in a year. More than one thousand people died of "cocaine-related causes" when we were interviewing in 1986; but as tragic as this is, it pales in comparison to the three hundred thousand who died from "tobacco-related" causes the same year. Put another way, for every cocaine-related death in the United States in 1987 there were approximately one hundred alcohol-related deaths and three hundred tobacco-related deaths. Yet politicians' speeches and media coverage might lead one to conclude that cocaine was by far the greatest killer.

Even a cursory comparison of licit and illicit drugs shows little relationship between the dangers or social costs of a drug and its legal status. To keep drug problems in perspective, then, we need to remind ourselves why society has developed its perceptions and policies and to examine them critically.

A vast complex of police and government control agencies and a multibillion-dollar, for-profit treatment industry exist in the United States. However humane and well-intentioned may be the people who earn their living in such institutions, they have a vested interest in drug scares and drug wars. Because of the nature and social location of their work, treatment workers and police tend to see "drug problems" everywhere they look, even when what is there is merely the *use* of a drug that some define as deviant by human beings who are troubled in other ways. Moreover, since the nineteenth century, the media's dramatic tales of ruin and redemption from one drug or another have sold a lot of newspapers. And politicians have long found it useful to scapegoat drugs for a wide array of public problems that may not have much to do with drug use, but which their policies seldom seem to alleviate. As a consequence, the mere use of an illicit drug is routinely equated with drug abuse and assumed to be problematic.

Despite the expenditure of billions of tax dollars and the best efforts of police at all levels of government, law enforcement has never been able to disrupt seriously the supply of illicit drugs. Because huge profits are possible when desired commodities are criminalized, suppliers are persistent and daring; it would take draconian efforts to stop supplies. If tomorrow we built a twelve-foot wall around the entire United States, the next day drug smugglers would have their thirteen-foot ladders at the ready. And while most police officers are honest and risk their safety in this ever-futile battle, others are corrupted by the big money involved. In short, attempts to repress drug use with prohibitionist policies have resulted in many costs but few benefits (Nadelmann, 1989).

Hundreds of thousands of Americans have been arrested for drug offenses. One in four young black males are in prison or otherwise under the control of the criminal justice system, most on drug-related charges. Despite such massive attempts at deterrence, drug sales continue to grow, for understandable reasons. In a context in which prohibitionist policies have created a black market with huge potential profits, drug sales offer what is arguably the best chance many poor or minority youths will ever have to live the "American dream."

The recent expansion of crack sales in ghetto communities is an example of how illicit drug markets have been operating in poor neighborhoods for seventy years. Furthermore, the crack industry has been "investing" in inner-city neighborhoods precisely when legitimate industries have been moving out and taking jobs with them. Unlike most legal industries, the illicit drug business is an equal opportunity employer offering good pay to the unskilled. At the same time, federal, state, and local governments have all cut spending on employment and social-service programs that might have eased some of the socioeconomic suffering that is at the root of much drug abuse.

While we are skeptical about current popular discourse and public policies regarding drug problems, we must also admit at the outset that we, too, have modified many of our views about cocaine. Users' current problems with cocaine have forced us to take a less sanguine view of it. Our initial research in the 1970s suggested that cocaine was not an especially dangerous drug for most recreational users (Waldorf et al., 1977; Reinarman, 1979). As in other research at that time, the cocaine users we studied simply did not report or exhibit many problems. It is now clear, however, that many more cocaine users have developed difficulties than we would have imagined then.

In calling this book *Cocaine Changes,* we are referring to more than the changes in our views of cocaine. The number and types of people using cocaine have changed, as has the mode of ingestion employed by many of them. And, as most of our users noted, the nature of the cocaine high itself changes over time—from energizing to depressing, from a social experience to an isolating one, from a sexual enhancement to a cause of sexual dysfunction. And just as the effects of cocaine change from the first year of use to the tenth, users also experience diminishing returns from the first snort to the tenth.

Our title is also intended to suggest that the consequences of cocaine use have changed some users (as several of them put it, "Cocaine put me through changes"). While we found little evidence of the violence and crime that media accounts of cocaine users imply are inevitable, many of our respondents did report bizarre behavior which they attributed to cocaine. Many long-term heavy users who tell their tales in these pages have changed their minds about cocaine and decided to quit using it. We are still not sure that cocaine is always as damaging as it is being made out to be, but the testimony here clearly suggests that our earlier assessment of the risks must also be changed.

So, while we maintain a certain skepticism toward the excesses of the war on drugs and some doubts about the effects of repressive policies, our interviews have led us to share many of the new concerns about cocaine. Our data do not, however, provide unequivocal support for the war effort. Our findings disconfirm as many stereotypes about heavy cocaine users as they confirm. Although TV documentaries

display bejeweled black brutes "pushing" death on the install-
ment plan to helpless victims, we found people of all races and
classes "turning on" their friends (and often "shutting them
off" if they began to abuse). About half of our heavy users
reported at least some of the serious problems found in clinical reports, but the other half reported few, if any, such problems. Although many of our interviewees escalated their use
from experimentation to abuse and addiction, many others
did not. Some felt they were enslaved by cocaine in the stereotypical way; but most were simply making choices about how
to juggle productivity and pleasure while trying to fashion
meaningful lives in modern America.

Perhaps our most striking impression was the gap between
the image of cocaine users as amoral hedonists blindly pursuing indulgence and excess and the reality of our heavy users.
They are by and large "normal" folks, quite like all the other
ordinary citizens one encounters in everyday life, save for their
consumption of a disapproved drug. They work hard. They
care for their families. They vote and play softball. And this
normality turns out to be theoretically crucial. For we will
argue that what keeps many heavy users from falling into the
abyss of abuse, and what helps pull back those who do fall,
is precisely this *stake in conventional life.* Jobs, families,
friends—the ingredients of a normal identity—turned out to
be the ballast that allowed many of our users to control their
use or to return from abuse to occasional, controlled use.

In the end, our respondents forced us to relearn an old
lesson. While many spoke of the pharmacological prowess of
cocaine, we found precious little evidence that heavy cocaine
use eventually turns people into muggers or murderers. This
reminded us that *however powerful a drug may be, its effects
are always mediated by the norms, practices, and circumstances of its users.* Such a finding does not lend itself to
simplistic slogans about the dangers of drugs. Nor will it lead
to simple solutions to our drug problems. But if it forces us to
think in more complicated ways about drug use and its cultural context, then we will be in a better position to develop
rational public policies toward drug problems.

A NOTE ON METHODS

This book is based on in-depth, life-history interviews with people who used a lot of cocaine. We interviewed 267 current and former heavy users from northern California. Most of what follows is based on 228 of these, a group we call our main sample, which is comprised of 122 current users and 106 quitters; all tables are based on this group. We interviewed the remaining 39 people in the course of two subsidiary studies: a long-term follow-up of a small network of users we first studied in 1974–75 (Chapter 11), and a group of crack users and freebasers (Chapter 6). When respondents in these substudies fit our criteria for the main sample (see Appendix), they were included in it. Half the follow-up group and four-fifths of the crack and freebase group were part of the main sample of 228.

We located all our subjects via "snowball" or chain-referral sampling techniques, in which one respondent recommends others, who in turn recommend others and so on (Biernacki and Waldorf, 1981; Watters and Biernacki, 1989). Such a strategy allows researchers access to deviant, hidden, or otherwise hard-to-reach populations who could not otherwise be studied. Of course, a group of heavy cocaine users identified in this way cannot be considered rigorously representative of all cocaine users in the United States, or even of all heavy users. In order to draw such a random representative sample, the parameters of the total population at issue must be known, which is impossible with people who engage in criminalized behavior. Yet, by using snowball sampling strategies, we were able to tap into different networks or chains of cocaine users and to exercise some control over how many of each types of person we would interview. This technique allowed us to maximize diversity and to avoid overrepresenting some types of users while missing others.

Two of five respondents were female, and three in ten were racial minorities. One in six were African-American, and about half that many were Latino. Our respondents ranged in age from 18 to 53 years, with the average age being 30. Their average level of education was a high school diploma plus 1.2

years of college; one in three were college graduates. About
two in five were married or living with a lover. Two in five
were white-collar workers, one in eight held professional or
managerial occupations, and a quarter were in skilled or unskilled working-class occupations. About three-fourths had
been regular users of marijuana and many had at least experimented with other illicit drugs, although less than a quarter
had ever been convicted of a crime as an adult. (See Appendix
for more details on the sample.)

In one important respect our respondents are unusual.
Unlike many of our colleagues in drug research, we deliber-
ately did not go to treatment programs or prisons to find
respondents. We knew that such "captive samples" might
make our work easier, but we also knew it would skew our
findings. Those whose cocaine use leads them to treatment or
jail are different in many ways from users who do not end up
in such places. This is important because the number of cocaine users, even heavy users, outside of treatment or jail is far,
far greater than the number inside. In this sense, our respondents were drawn primarily from the ranks of the great, un-
studied "silent majority." Thus, by interviewing cocaine users
in the more natural settings of their homes and communities,
our "sample" may well be more representative of serious
cocaine users than most others drawn randomly from institu-
tional populations. We have no way of proving this, but we do
know that we ended up with a fairly diverse group.

From these different data we describe the ways people use
cocaine; how some manage to control and moderate their use;
how others develop abusive use patterns, serious health problems, or become socially dysfunctional; and how surprisingly
large numbers overcome their problems or successfully struggle to stop their cocaine use with common-sense cessation
strategies.

Unlike most people who write about cocaine users, we did
not observe and interview our respondents with any intent of
helping, treating, controlling, or otherwise changing them. We
did not wish to make them over or otherwise affect their lives.
Our principal intent was simply to understand them better—

to learn from them what they did and why, and to try to tell their stories. This is the stance we took into the field and, we suspect, the reason so many serious cocaine users were willing to talk with us so candidly about illegal and often embarrassing behavior.

In addition to increasing the likelihood of cooperation, this approach has other distinct advantages. When observers with agendas (conscious or unconscious, trained or untrained) approach other people to treat, assist, change, or control them, the observers tend to assume that the behaviors they are observing are "destructive," "immature," "pathological," "undesirable," or "against the common good." Whether or not such assumptions are warranted matters less than the fact that they both frame and color what is seen. Treatment or control agendas, for example, often lead observers to the further assumption that they are in some way superior to the often troubled people they are observing. Without necessarily recognizing it, those who take even a subtle stance of superiority smuggle into their accounts one-sided, negative, and often moralistic judgments about the people and behaviors under study. Such judgments are typically framed in the scientific jargon of psychiatry, clinical psychology, social work, or chemical-dependency treatment. The descriptions that result are likely to reflect the views of the observer while too often neglecting the point of view of the subject.

In this book we have tried to avoid such problems and simply to describe cocaine users and their behaviors—not so much from our point of view as from theirs. We have sought to study cocaine users from within their culture rather than from outside it and to present their world as they see it. In general, we have tried to withhold judgments about the appropriateness or inappropriateness of drug-using behaviors so that we might reach some understanding of the cultural meaning of those behaviors for the individuals involved.

Such an ethnographic approach has deep roots in both anthropology and sociology. Cultural anthropologist Clifford Geertz (1973; 1983) has written of this method as "thick description." He argues persuasively that because human beings are suspended in webs of significance and meaning that they themselves have woven, one can comprehend their behavior best "from the native's point of view." Sociologists have drawn on similar theoretical and methodological traditions to produce some of the landmark studies of drug use: Alfred Lindesmith's classic study of opiate addicts in (1947); Howard Becker's study of the processes of becoming a marijuana user (1953); and Ed Preble's and John Casey's analysis of life in the New York heroin scene (1969). More recently, the same approach was used to great advantage in Patricia Adler's ethnography of cocaine smugglers (1985) and Patrick Biernacki's study of untreated recovery among heroin addicts (1986; see also Waldorf, 1980).[5]

The ethnographic approach is not particularly popular; the natives whose points of view we attempt to render here have been defined as deviant by the dominant forces in society. Nevertheless, we have adopted it because we believe it can offer greater understanding of drug users, of what the experience of cocaine use means in the context of users' lives. This is crucial because past attempts to "solve" our nation's drug problems have seldom succeeded and have almost always had unintended negative consequences. We do not entertain the utopian hope of solving, once and for all, these problems. We do believe, however, that only by struggling to understand drug use from the point of view of drug users will we develop a solid foundation on which to build public policies that can reduce the harm that drugs can do.

PART I

USING COCAINE

CHAPTER 2

GETTING INTO COKE:
INITIATION AND STYLES OF USE

Rochelle, a 19-year-old black woman who lives in a ghetto in Oakland, told us in one of our first interviews that she was introduced to cocaine at age 16 by friends of her older sister. She freebased the first time she used the drug. Rochelle enjoyed the high immensely and continued to freebase every day for two weeks. During that initial period her boyfriend gave her the drug. After that relationship ended she did not use again for two months. Her second cocaine run (episode of use) lasted a year, during which time she used about four grams a week.

To our surprise, Rochelle's was not a typical initiation. In fact, her early experience was exceptional; most people we interviewed snorted for long periods before trying freebase or crack. Most did not particularly enjoy or appreciate their first experience with cocaine and only continued use after some months of experimental or very casual use. (See tables in Chapters 5, 8, and 9 for precise details.)

The first use of cocaine, as in beginning use of cigarettes, alcohol, or any illicit drug, is nearly always initiated by friends as a part of some social situation. It is a rare case indeed in which one's first use of cocaine is occasioned by a stranger. This only stands to reason, for the practice of sniffing a white powder up one's nose, even if it were not a heavily stigmatized drug, is utterly foreign to most people.

17

Typically, a friend offers another friend a line of cocaine at a party, a dinner, or some other get-together. The second friend snorts the drug intranasally and is surprised because the high is nothing special. In fact, many people reported that they did not get high at all the first time they used cocaine and had to learn how to recognize what at first seemed a subtle euphoria. They had to learn how to discern the drug's effects much the way marijuana users do (Becker, 1953).

These initiates are usually intimates whom the giver knows well, trusts, and wishes to treat or favor. The giver usually views the drug as a luxury to be shared with a valued friend. A good illustration is this account of a 36-year-old black investment officer who had used cocaine for six years when we interviewed him.

> RESPONDENT: The very first [time] was with a bunch of friends. I had heard about it long before I used it; it had a certain mystique for me. The situation was, I'm sitting with friends at a party, and a friend that I really know was talking and he says, "Do you want to get high?" I say, "High off what?" And he says, "Well, I got a little blow." And that's basically how it started.
>
> INTERVIEWER: What were the first effects?
>
> RESPONDENT: None. . . . I was looking for bells to ring and stuff. I mean you hear so much about cocaine—cocaine this, cocaine that—so, you know, being ignorant of [what] its effects were, I thought that well, shit, it'd have to be something really spectacular. It has to be something that's really gonna move me, I'm gonna be devastated by it. And all I felt was something going up my nose that had a slight bite to it and no noticeable change in my functions or anything. . . . Later I felt I had to go to the bathroom to urinate. (Case #609)

Often boyfriends or lovers initiate girlfriends as was true with Jean, an energetic, red-haired 31-year-old white office manager who used cocaine for five years. Her heaviest use was twenty-eight grams a week for six months, an extraordinarily large amount. At the time, she was living with a rock and-roll music promoter who supplied most of her drugs.

RESPONDENT: I had this boyfriend and he used to do cocaine, right, and like I used to sit and watch him. . . . I would say to him, "How could you do that?" The thought of snorting that up your nose used to make me cringe, you know, because I just could feel it and it used to make me sick. And so he did this regularly, you know, and so one night we stayed up real, real late and we had to go to work the next morning. So I was complaining that I was really tired and he kept saying, "If you try this, it will wake you right up," and I kept on saying, "No, I don't want to." Then I finally did and I didn't really feel anything, but I wasn't scared to do it anymore.

INTERVIEWER: You didn't get high though?

RESPONDENT: No. If I was it didn't knock me over or anything . . . or I didn't get that extreme rush or anything like that. All it served was I knew what it felt like to snort this, but I wasn't high or anything. (Case #114)

In most instances the initiates took one or two lines on the first occasion and declined second offers because they were not impressed with the initial effects. Initiates often had an established image of and expectations for the drug. They often saw cocaine as a "glamorous" party drug that was relatively safe and not "addicting." With these big expectations, they were usually somewhat disappointed by the subtle qualities of the effects. This was illustrated by Sandy, a rather suave, middle-class white man who described himself as a "rah, rah" fraternity type when he first used the drug.

RESPONDENT: The first time was the end of the winter quarter of my freshman year in college, so I was 18 years old. It was at the fraternity house that I was then rushing. I had gone to that house several times to party with some of the guys who were at the house. I was smoking a lot of marijuana and shared it with [a friend]. At one point I was in this guy's room and he chopped a couple of lines and says, "Why don't you do one of these?" I knew what it was but I had never done it before. Without hesitating, I said, "Sure." I look back on it now and find it really amusing. It didn't even cross my mind not to do it.

INTERVIEWER: You were just at an experimental stage, 18?

RESPONDENT: I can see in retrospect that I bought into the fact that this was supposed to be the ultimate drug. It was supposed to be not harmful, safe, can't hurt you, nonaddictive, no after-effects, your eyes don't get red and you don't fall down or slur your words, and [it] is supposed to make you feel like a million bucks.

INTERVIEWER: How did you feel the first time?

RESPONDENT: It didn't really affect me that much. There was a slight tingling sensation in my nose as I snorted it, but the euphoria that really attracted me later on . . . I don't remember it hitting me that way. (Case #117)

Some users did recognize the effects the first time—a freeze at the back of the throat, a subtle awareness of euphoria, a sense of increased energy, and more animated conversation. Yet this recognition was not typical when first use was intra-nasal. With the more direct modes of ingestion, the effects are much harder to miss. Brook, a white, middle-class, 25-year-old computer operator, reported that his first "hit of base" made him feel "hyper and smarter, faster, better; you know, sort of like the Six Million–Dollar Man" (Case 636).

A good number of our respondents literally had to learn how to recognize the effects of snorted cocaine and how to experience the high. Andy, a white 23-year-old aspiring actor, is one example.

RESPONDENT: No effect, it didn't affect me at first, the first couple times that I did it.

INTERVIEWER: How long was it before it started to affect you?

RESPONDENT: I guess after the third try, but I really can't describe it much. It just made me feel real good. (Case #427)

A minority of the respondents even disliked their first experience with cocaine. A white, middle-class chef in one of the fashionable restaurants in San Francisco described her first experience as negative.

INTERVIEWER: How old were you when you first used coke?

RESPONDENT: I was in my senior year of college.

INTERVIEWER: So that would make you about 20 or 21?

RESPONDENT: Yeah, 21, I think. I didn't really feel it. A house that I was living at in Berkeley . . . I think they bought a gram to split between five or six people. There was a whole ritual involved with it and eating this really good dinner beforehand and everything. Then we had some wine, but I didn't really feel [the cocaine]. We ended up having to take this trip to the airport and all I felt was really restless in the car, and it was like I couldn't wait to get out of the car.

INTERVIEWER: So you didn't like it?

RESPONDENT: Um, I just thought, "What is this?"; you know, I didn't feel it. It wasn't strong and I just felt kind of anxious. So that was the first time. (Case #207)

Another graduate student at a nearby university reported that he never enjoyed the effects of cocaine even though he used it for eighteen months while he was a gram seller. He reported that cocaine made him feel continually depressed and isolated, and the accounts of his activities during this period support his statements. A typical day for this man was to wake up about 11:00 A.M., begin using cocaine immediately, and use all day. He stayed home continually, watching television and selling grams of cocaine to regular visitors. His only forays out of his apartment were to buy junk food and beer. After he stopped selling and using he was pleased at how active he became—going to movies and concerts, hiking in the Sierras, visiting friends.

The rest of this young man's life history led our interviewer to suspect that he was severely depressed even before he began using cocaine, and that cocaine exacerbated this condition and caused him to withdraw from social relationships. His account is unusual, however; most of our respondents used less cocaine, particularly during the early stages of their careers, and reported that it made them feel more energetic, euphoric, active, and sociable. But, as with other types of drug use, both legal and illegal, individuals bring their own unique psychological sets and physiologic or metabolic characteristics to the experience. Such individual factors often have profound effects on users' perceptions of the experience and, we think, help account for the variability in both reports of first effects and subsequent use patterns.

Although no one process of initiation was uniformly experienced by all our respondents, some themes were common to most accounts. First, the vast majority of the people we interviewed did not, metaphorically speaking, lose their virginity on cocaine. Most were seasoned drug users, first of alcohol and later marijuana. They took it for granted that "getting high" had some positive meaning, so it was not a giant step for them to indulge their curiosity about a new high. Second, almost none sought out cocaine on their own the first time. Rather, it was offered by a trusted friend in a setting that both found comfortable (typically a private space in which no one who might be offended was present). Third, because the initial effects most often had to be learned and were experienced as more subtle than expected, few emerged from their first experience with any definite desire or plan to use it again or to buy their own supply.[1]

In looking over our respondents' accounts of their first use, we were struck by how poorly they fit with the popular image of cocaine as a highly addictive, "hard" drug. Aside from Rochelle and a few other younger users whose first cocaine experience was smoking crack or freebase, most users we interviewed simply were not "moved" in any profound way at first. Very few reported a negative first experience either, and so they were left with an inchoate openness or willingness to try cocaine again if it happened to be offered.

This particular kind of openness was consequential in at least one important way. Many of the people we interviewed had heard, prior to their first few snorts, about the dangers of cocaine—that it is often lumped with heroin as an addicting narcotic. Once they experienced the drug firsthand, however, that aura tended to fade. One member of the long-term follow-up group made the point this way: "I had the narcotic paranoia, I guess from the official line. I thought it was in the heavy-duty class like junk so I was wary. After my friends tried it I tended to side with them. Once I tried it I knew it was all right if you watched yourself. It was fun, but no big thing." (Case #907).

Once users discovered that cocaine was not such an over-powering high or "instantly addicting," they tended to discount the "official line." What our subjects took as extreme antidrug warnings did not "check out" with their experience. Ironically, this disparity seemed to inoculate them against such warnings, leading many to throw out the proverbial baby with the bathwater. Thus, instead of keeping our respondents away from cocaine, warnings that got discredited by personal experience helped leave many neophyte users open to further use.

ESCALATION

The majority of our respondents increased their use of cocaine gradually. Most, not particularly impressed with their first experience, did not go out of their way to seek out the drug. If they were in a situation where cocaine was offered they might use it again, but most made no effort to secure supplies of their own. Joyce, the chef quoted earlier, recalls:

RESPONDENT: It was a long time before I used it again. I went back East and I lived back there and it was years. . . . Then I came back to California.

INTERVIEWER: So a big hiatus between the first time and the second time?

RESPONDENT: Right, actually no, wait a minute. I remember one other time in between; . . . this is good for me because now I'm remembering all this. My brother must have already been getting into it. He went to Stanford and he said that for my birthday he would either give me a present or a quarter of a gram of cocaine. I guess he was dealing at the time and I said I would take the cocaine. I think this was probably '81. So I took it and I had it in Philadelphia and I don't even remember. I think I did it with my boyfriend, and I don't even remember at all.

INTERVIEWER: So it was not a big occasion?

RESPONDENT: No. Then when I moved back to California my sister and her boyfriend were living in the Castro and they were into it by then.

INTERVIEWER: This is your older sister?

RESPONDENT: Yeah, who unfortunately is still into it. They were doing it a lot, and that's when I first started doing it on any kind of regular basis. I remember still not really liking it too much or feeling like I only wanted to do a little. The main thing I noticed about it, which is still really striking to me, is that, in conversations with people after I got high to a certain point, I felt like I couldn't connect or relate and I would just be so wired up. After a certain point in time I didn't give a shit and I just wanted to do it.

INTERVIEWER: So you didn't have particularly good experiences then early on?

RESPONDENT: I liked it but it wasn't that great, and I definitely didn't want to go way out with it. I wanted to keep it, you know, in control. We had some real good conversations and I remember sitting around with my sister and her boyfriend.

INTERVIEWER: But then there would be a certain point when that would stop?

RESPONDENT: For me I would just want to keep it at this one level; otherwise, I would just feel too hyper. They would do it and do it and do it and couldn't stop. (Case #207)

We suspect that this pattern of slow, gradual escalation had to do partly with the general availability of the drug and with an individual's access to sellers or personal contacts who would give them cocaine. For example, many of the older respondents, who began experimenting with cocaine in the late 1960s and early 1970s when it was much less available, used very infrequently during the early years of their cocaine careers. This was less true for those who began their use in the late 1970s and early 1980s when cocaine was much more widely available. Younger users often escalated their use more rapidly than the modal pattern. Jean, the office manager, is an extreme example, reporting a pattern of rapid escalation that appeared directly related to her boyfriend's pattern of regular supply and heavy use.

RESPONDENT: The pattern of use after that [initial experience] was every Friday we would buy a gram for the weekend. Also he did a lot of recording work and he would get paid with drugs. But pretty much the pattern remained that I would do a gram on the weekend.

INTERVIEWER: So you're using it to party?

RESPONDENT: Right, and it was strictly from Friday to Saturday, and Sunday I would rest up, do my nails, and get ready for work the next week, and it wasn't a problem.

INTERVIEWER: How long did you go with that pattern, that weekend pattern?

RESPONDENT: A month.

INTERVIEWER: One month?

RESPONDENT: And then after it was just real accessible, you know, I graduated to buying an eighth [of an ounce] for the weekend. I convinced myself this was cost-conscious, you see, and so what I would do is buy an eighth and split it up into three and a half grams, and it would be one gram for Friday and one for Saturday and one for Sunday and then, you know, left-overs. And this pattern probably continued for a month or two months. But as this was going on it started varying and like sometimes I would get him to get a gram in the middle of the week. It stayed standard that Friday absolutely there had to be an eighth but, you know, if something came along on the week-day that was cool too.

INTERVIEWER: So it slowly spread over the week?

RESPONDENT: Yes, . . . and then it reached a point where it was every day, every day a gram a day. And I pretty much did it mostly myself.

INTERVIEWER: And you said you used heavily for roughly three or four years?

RESPONDENT: Well, it got worse, you see.

INTERVIEWER: Okay, tell me about it.

RESPONDENT: Well, after a while it's like I had to have a gram a day, I had to, and no ands, ifs, or buts.

INTERVIEWER: That's having a wake-me-up in the morning?

RESPONDENT: Yeah.

INTERVIEWER: And nipping a few times during the day?

RESPONDENT: Oh no, not a few times. There were times when I would snort an eighth [of an ounce] by myself and start in on it at about ten o'clock at night.

INTERVIEWER: And do that within a day?

RESPONDENT: Yeah, and that was pretty consistent. And this was like on a daily basis.

INTERVIEWER: How long did you do that?

RESPONDENT: I was so caught up in it that I lost track, but probably a good six to eight months or maybe longer. (Case #114)

Joyce's use of a gram a day was considered a large amount by most of the others. Although the majority of our subjects neither escalated their use as rapidly as did Joyce nor ended up using so much or so often, most agreed that availability is a key ingredient in escalating use. With Joyce, living with a person who had ready supplies clearly was a factor. Generally, when cocaine became more available, most users tended to use larger amounts and use more often. This is particularly true for cocaine sellers (see Chapter 5). Sellers typically consumed greater amounts, more frequently than nonsellers. Similarly, those who had ready sources—men and women who lived with sellers or who had close relatives who sold—used more cocaine more often than others who did not have such ready access. Users and sellers tended to agree that if you sell cocaine you will use it. Thus, a story of a long-time large-scale dealer who was said never to use his own product was considered remarkable by our respondents. But his strategy for exercising such control proves the importance of availability: whenever he received supplies he packaged them in standard amounts for resale and then placed them in a vault to which he had limited access. He went to the vault only to get the cocaine for delivery. On the rare occasions when he did use cocaine, he would go to another dealer friend and purchase grams at a regular gram price. In this way he kept his use within strict limits despite its easy and inexpensive availability.

Two other factors were often cited as contributing to escalating use: a slow increase in tolerance for the drug, and the seductive and rather insidious nature of the drug itself. Tolerance is a tricky concept when applied to cocaine use. It is generally defined as a state that occurs after repeated use of a drug when a given dose produces a decreased effect, or when larger doses are required to achieve the same effect. Many of our heavy users reported increasing their doses (snorting longer "lines," thicker lines, more lines, or more often). Curiously, however, unlike opiate users, few actually stated that they got a decreased effect from each dose. Rather than *needing* more of the drug to get the same "jolt," they reported simply *wanting* the jolt again and again. Moreover, in contrast to classical tolerance, many of our respondents maintained stable, albeit heavy, use patterns over many years without increasing doses.

If few of our heavy users reported decreasing effects and if many did not raise their doses, then there is probably more to the escalation we observed than classical tolerance. We suspect, without having any expertise in the area, that this is where the unique neurochemistry of cocaine comes into play. For example, in the human brain cocaine both facilitates the release of norepinephrine and dopamine and prevents their reuptake at nerve endings (e.g., Langer and Enero, 1974; Van Dyke and Byck, 1982; Mule, 1984; Gold and Verebey, 1984;

Gold, Washton, and Dackis, 1985). The result, in short, is that dopamine and norepinephrine are found at higher levels for the first few minutes after use, and at levels lower than normal shortly thereafter when neurotransmitters decrease. This physiologic action helps account for why users feel positively stimulated or euphoric, and yet soon thereafter not only feel less than euphoric as they drop back down to "normal," but actually dysphoric or below normal. While this process is not the same as, say, tolerance to opiates, it does help to account for why many of our heavy users increased the size or frequency of their doses as time went on.

The word *insidious* recurred in several transcripts, and not just those of the most troubled heavy users. *Webster's New Collegiate Dictionary* defines insidious as "awaiting a chance to entrap: treacherous" or "harmful but enticing: seductive." This seems to be precisely what our respondents had in mind when they used the word. Most agreed that cocaine's euphoric effects offered not only a sense of well-being, but a feeling of mastery or power that was so reinforcing it often led them to use more frequently than they planned or expected. Casual weekend use for pleasure can, as in Joyce's case, slowly lead to use during more and more days of the week. As we will show in Chapter 3, even those who initially limited their use to specific situations—long hours at work, parties, or sexual activities—gradually found themselves using in more and more situations as well as more frequently. Those who used cocaine only in weekend party situations sometimes would feel that they deserved a little treat during the week. People who went on periodic binges sometimes found their binges stretching over longer periods at higher dosages. And, as Chapter 3 will show, the uses to which cocaine's stimulating and euphoric effects were put tended to multiply. All this helps to explain why many users escalated their use over time. It is also important to note, however, that such escalation was far from inevitable; about as many of our respondents maintained stable use patterns as escalated.[2]

TYPES OF USERS

Our users' reports on amount and frequency of use point to four patterns of use. One is typified by Joyce's pattern— consistent, very heavy daily use. In general, users do not have a term that describes this heavy, daily pattern except for occasional derogatory designations such as "coke hog," "a million-dollar nose," or "taking it to the max." Such coke hogs are more often found among cocaine smokers and shoo- ters, who generally use more often and more heavily. But there are snorters like Michelle (Case #112) who also fit this pat- tern. Her boyfriend introduced her to the drug, and she used moderately (a few lines or a quarter of a gram per day) for a six-month period. After her father died and she experienced profound emotional difficulties, she steadily increased the amount and frequency of her use. At one point she used an ounce (twenty-eight grams) in seventeen days. The day she bought the ounce she literally put her nose into the bag of cocaine and snorted with both nostrils in a frenzy of use. She reported that she did not eat or drink anything in the whole seventeen-day period. Her craving and need for cocaine was so strong that she spent all her salary on coke, took out loans totaling $30,000, and even traded sex for coke. Michelle's pattern of cocaine use after her father's death could easily be characterized as addictive. She obviously had no control over her use and seemed to be using heavily to handle her emo- tional problems.

Those who smoke freebase or crack and those who inject cocaine also frequently fall into the coke hog category. Both methods of use cause more dramatic effects, greater compul- sion, marked "comedowns" that are experienced as painful, and depression. Peter, a freebaser, is a good illustration (Case #103). He is an only child from a family of lawyers. His father was a prestigious Montgomery Street attorney in downtown San Francisco and his mother a prosecutor; both had great expectations for him. He lived up to their expectations for a time, selling real estate and attending law school on a busy schedule. Snorting coke assisted him in these activities, particularly in the beginning, and he states to this day that he would not have passed the bar exam without cocaine. He said that passing the exam while using cocaine confirmed all of his early beliefs that cocaine was a wonderful drug.

Freebasing, however, was his downfall. He began to freebase because he liked it and because he was having physical problems with his nose and throat as a result of snorting. Once he began to freebase he lost control. During a six-month period, he used nearly an ounce a week, and at his peak he used two ounces a week for a month. At one stage he rented a studio apartment near his law office where he could be alone and freebase every day. During seven months of freebasing, he managed to alienate his family, break up his marriage, and embezzle sizable sums of money from three of his clients. Surprisingly, he did not experience severe physical problems while freebasing. His decision to quit resulted from the general deterioration of his personal relationships and his professional and criminal conduct. He made three attempts to stop—once at a hospital treatment program, once at a short-term residential program, and then a seventy-two hour stay in a hospital, followed by regular visits to Cocaine Anonymous meetings. When we interviewed Peter he had been "drug-free" for eighteen months, was repaying some of his old debts, had given up law practice, and was working as a counselor in a drug and alcohol program.

Roger typified shooters, or intravenous users, who often display similar patterns of protracted uncontrolled use (Case #403). He used cocaine for three years, snorting for a year and then shooting for two years. In his peak period he was shooting eleven grams a week for what he estimated was a solid year and a half. At that time (1976 and 1977), cocaine was cheaper than it was at our interview. He was paying $400 for a quarter of an ounce (seven grams), and, because he was well-to-do, money did not become a big problem for him until the end of his cocaine career. During the peak period, he used daily and described his life as being "like a hermit in a cage." At one point he was injecting LSD with cocaine because he liked the "rush" of the combination. Roger stopped using coke after the death of his lover (a prominent businessman in the San Francisco Bay area) and the business they shared went under. At the time of the interview he had not used cocaine in five years but had used marijuana and alcohol on a recreational basis.

At the other end of the continuum from "coke hogs" are "nippers," people who use regularly, often every day, but only in relatively small amounts (e.g., two or three small lines a day). These users generally are in control of their drug use and manage to maximize positive effects and minimize negative effects. Nippers keep their cocaine use subordinated to their work and family responsibilities, and it almost never gets out of control or interferes with their ability to function in daily life. They use regularly but are able to avoid the negative physical or psychological effects often associated with heavier use. They usually do not see their cocaine use as problematic and periodically stop using cocaine for short or long periods.

Unlike most coke hogs, nippers often maintain very specific routines or rules about their cocaine use—using only at certain times of the day and not at times when they have to "take care of business." These are men and women who use cocaine with a specific activity in mind—for instance, to work, to party, or to have sex—not always to feel high or to handle emotional problems or stressful situations. Such controlled users are discussed at greater length in Chapter 7.

Between nippers and coke hogs are the "bingers" who use heavily for short periods and then lay off cocaine for several days or a week or two. This binge pattern is common among "weekend warriors"—persons who may abstain during the work week but treat themselves to cocaine at party times, particularly on weekends. Our illustrative case of a binge user is a 44-year-old dentist named Stewart who began his cocaine use by ordering pure cocaine from a pharmaceutical company for the unusually small sum of $40 an ounce. Stewart began using cocaine in 1971 and was not impressed with the drug the first time; he took it four or five times before he got high. In 1973 he bought his first supply and then used regularly for four years. He described his pattern of binge use.

INTERVIEWER: So when did you . . . start using heavily?

RESPONDENT: I started living with a lady and she was into it and she loved it, and we had pharmaceutical around. We would do it all weekend long.

INTERVIEWER: Did it ever affect your work? Did you ever take days off?

RESPONDENT: No, I didn't, but I was often fairly burnt-out come Monday. I would just be real drained and not have much emotional reserve. I can remember once when I realized that things had gone out of hand. It was on a Monday and I was working on someone, and I looked up and looked out the window at some trees and I noticed that the trees started moving. At that point I said, number one, that cocaine could be a psyche-delic or could have some psychedelic effects and that, two, even though I felt straight, that was only a relative term. I was ob-viously not straight and should not be working. The usual effect was that I would come to work . . . well, I would have come down on a Sunday night. . . .

INTERVIEWER: Using a Valium?

RESPONDENT: I first got into using barbiturates to come down and then I got into using Valiums because it was much more readily available. It wasn't a controlled substance and it was just everywhere. So I would come down and coming to work on Monday was a little bit of a chore. I would just be kind of frazzled come Monday, and by Tuesday I was starting to feel human again. Monday was just one of those days that you just got through, Tuesday I was starting to feel human, Wednesday I really felt like I was under control and I had the world by the tail again, by Thursday I was looking forward to Friday so that I could start again. By Friday . . .

INTERVIEWER: But you had longer weekends than you did work weeks sometimes?

RESPONDENT: Well, I would usually stop working on Friday afternoon, and I can remember really looking forward to getting home and getting the first weekend line, you know. I might be going somewhere that weekend or doing something, and in that case it would be more of a binge thing than straightening back up for Monday. It seemed to go on like that forever. (Case #428)

Many bingers kept their cocaine use quite separate from their work or from other activities where one has to be "straight" or relatively drug-free. Binge use is often regulated or constrained by personal finances (supplies run out and the user does not have the money to continue) or by the experience of prolonged negative effects (becoming "overamped" [hyper-stimulated], nervous, exhausted, or depressed). Other bingers, however, found their binges getting longer and more intense. Sandy is a good illustration of someone who used very heavily during short and long binges but after a while was not able to control or compartmentalize his use.

INTERVIEWER: So did you use coke to go to work in the morning?

RESPONDENT: No, I used at work maybe only five or six times.

INTERVIEWER: So cocaine is associated with partying?

RESPONDENT: After a while it wasn't fun and it was just part of the activity but it was definitely what I considered to have partied.

INTERVIEWER: Sociable things and going out with the . . .

RESPONDENT: Well, not even that. Most of the time it was partying with my dealer or my dealers.

INTERVIEWER: So sitting there and talking?

RESPONDENT: Right, and playing backgammon or watching TV or playing cards. Basically mindless stuff. More and more during that winter I saw the activities that I was . . . going wrong and becoming much more isolated and doing things by myself and wanting to spend less time talking with friends and less time at the dealer's house and more time by myself.

INTERVIEWER: Were you using more then?

RESPONDENT: No question, my consumption started going up. I had a big party night at the end of the winter. And that night in fact I got into my car and drove to Santa Barbara to the girl that I was seeing. We took three or four days for vacation. I felt real bad and I told myself that it had to stop. Once again I said that. So I came back and I switched into my superhuman mode and said okay, no more partying. I would be running, lifting weights, eating well, and doing all those things. I stayed on this . . .

INTERVIEWER: Physical fitness?

RESPONDENT: It was a Jekyll and Hyde situation. So I stayed on my Dr. Jekyll kick for about two weeks. I remember that vividly. I partied once and I said, oh I deserved that. About a week later that's when my real big binge started. Then it was about six weeks and it was either every day or every other day for about six weeks solid. I stole $1,000 at least or even maybe $1,500 out of an account that I had access to that was my dad's. I drained all kinds of money and of the money I was making at work I spent several thousands of dollars on cocaine those weeks. I didn't do anything at work. (Case #117)

Sandy tended to use in short binges with intervening periods of remorse, soul searching, and active attempts to quit. He generally used until he ran out of money. He also tended to work on an on-and-off basis during this period. Eventually Sandy went to private therapy twice. He lied to his first therapist about his cocaine use, then out of desperation attended a short-term residential program followed by a year of aftercare.

The fourth type of cocaine user we call "ceremonial" or occasional users. These men and women do not binge or nip daily. Cocaine is used by this group at special social occasions—a night out dancing, a major party or celebration, a special occasion for sex, or a wedding. For our follow-up study we interviewed a young boutique manager who at one time during the 1970s used regularly. But she told us that during the past few years she and her husband had bought cocaine only one time, for their wedding anniversary. They also took one or two lines at parties or other social occasions, but that use was unplanned and infrequent. Both enjoyed their cocaine experiences, but they chose to use their money to buy a house and simply decided to regulate their use. An added benefit of this type of use was that on those ceremonial occasions when they did snort some cocaine, it remained pleasant and enjoyable and they did not experience negative physical or psychological effects.

To judge from the NIDA surveys of the incidence of cocaine use, the majority of users in the United States fall into the category of ceremonial user. They use the drug occasionally, but do not abuse it. They experience pleasant effects and avoid unpleasant effects. Above all they are very moderate in their use patterns. They do not lose control, go on heavy binges, use it every day, or experience cocaine-related problems.

We were surprised to learn that many people who had previously used cocaine heavily could return to occasional or ceremonial use and not lose control. Indeed, more than half (52.6 percent) of the seventy-six untreated quitters we interviewed had done just that. They did not hold abstinence values, and once they got over the problems they were having with the drug they found they could use it on special occasions, enjoy it, and not return to an abusive pattern.

Another type of user, which may represent the largest group of all, is the experimenter. Experimenters are those who use the drug once or perhaps a few times but who for any number of reasons—particularly lack of availability or because they did not experience any positive effects—never use it again. Generally, one or two experiences satisfy any curiosity they had about the drug. Because our study was designed specifically to examine heavy users, we did not gather data on this group.

HOW MANY COCAINE ADDICTS? A NOTE ON ADDICTION

Of the four types of users we have described, coke hogs and bingers generally reported the heaviest use and the most cocaine-related problems (see Chapter 8). These use patterns and problems are commonly taken to be essential characteristics of cocaine addiction. Surely many of our heavy users would fit a commonsense definition of "addict," and some even described themselves with the word "addicted." However, not all hogs and bingers can be considered addicts, for there are a variety of definitional difficulties with the very concept of addiction.

In the early stages of our study, we grappled with the question of how to identify the cocaine addicts among our interviewees. We quickly discovered two things. First, few of the people we interviewed fit into neat categories; if there was a typical use pattern it was a changing one that did not always include the same sets of problems. Second, over the course of the twentieth century the definition of addiction has been repeatedly jury-rigged to cover an ever-shifting behavioral terrain. Indeed, to judge from the recent proliferation of Twelve-Step groups, addiction has become the metametaphor for all the troubles of our epoch. There are now Alcoholics Anonymous–like groups not only for narcotics and cocaine addicts, but also for workaholics, overeaters, credit card addicts, "shopaholics," gambling addicts, adult children of alcoholics, sex and love addicts, and even "codependents"—those who find themselves "hooked" on unhappy relationships (see Reinarman and Phillips, 1991). If virtually every human trouble can be defined as an addiction, then it becomes difficult to wring real meaning from the concept (see, e.g., Peele, 1989).

E. M. Jellinek, the inventor of the modern disease concept of alcoholism on which so much addiction research is based, made careful distinctions among types of alcoholics. He also noted the impossibility of determining whether this addiction was primarily physiological or psychological, and in fact argued that social and economic factors were crucial aspects of addiction (Jellinek, 1952). Although Jellinek went to great lengths to identify an orderly progression of "phases" of alcoholism, subsequent research has not found unequivocal empirical support for a discrete disease entity with uniform symptoms and a linear progression of stages (e.g., Cahalan, 1970; Room, 1983). Ultimately, the disease concept of alcoholism was promoted not on scientific grounds, but rather on moral and political grounds: to name alcoholism a disease allowed Jellinek and the alcoholism movement to use the prestige of medicine to displace moralistic condemnation of the drunkard with the idea that problem drinkers deserved treatment (Seeley, 1962; Room, 1978; Schneider, 1978).

When the disease concept of addiction was applied to other drugs, it fared little better. When first applied to opiates like heroin, addiction meant something quite concrete: physiological dependence as evidenced by classical tolerance and withdrawal symptoms. Mere craving was impossible to define scientifically and in any event connoted moral weakness as much as physical dependence. By the 1950s it was clear that not all drugs were physiologically addicting in this classic sense, harmful though they may have been. Researchers hunted for a more elastic concept and added "psychological habituation" to the addiction vernacular (Zinberg, 1984). A few years later drug scholars moved beyond this term, too, because of the difficulty of distinguishing physical from psychological dependence. They then substituted different types of "dependence," but the criteria remained ambiguous and laden with moral values.

These conceptual acrobatics were necessitated by the same sorts of empirical complexities of drug-taking behavior that we found among our heavy cocaine users. The old notion that dependence inevitably results from regular use of even heroin simply was not borne out by research on real heroin users in noninstitutionalized settings (e.g., Zinberg, 1984; Hanson et al., 1985; Blackwell, 1983; 1985). Nor could more commonsensical strategies solve the problem. The simple criterion of persistent use despite harm to self or others may be therapeutically practical, but such harm is not always attributable to the drug alone. It almost always depends on the user's psychological set, the social setting of use, as well as dose, chronicity of use, health of the user, and a variety of other factors (Zinberg, 1984).

More recent attempts to nail down operationally what is

meant by the term "addiction" have led to still more elastic definitions. For example, in 1972 the American Psychiatric Association moved away from "addiction" toward "drug abuse," which they defined as the nonmedical use of drugs that alter consciousness in ways that "are considered by social norms and defined by statute [as] inappropriate, undesirable, harmful . . . or culture-alien" (cited in Zinberg, 1984, 39; see also Jaffe, 1985). But this definition speaks only of abuse rather than the narrower phenomenon of addiction, and the terms are moral rather than medical. There is also a troubling circularity to this version: while lawmakers have usually justified their drug-control laws in terms of medical evidence, these medical experts framed their definition of drug abuse in terms of laws.

Recent World Health Organization (WHO) definitions of addiction have not solved the problem either. In WHO's 1969 formulation, addiction is a compulsion to use a drug; yet this criterion need not entail even continuous use, much less tolerance and withdrawal. As reformulated by WHO in 1981, addiction became "dependence," defined in terms of a syndrome in which drug taking is "given a much higher priority than other behaviors that once had a higher value" (cited in Shaffer and Jones, 1989, 42). While no more precise, at least these redefinitions acknowledge that "addiction" is a moving target.

Perhaps the most recent and widely used definition is that found in the American Psychiatric Association's *Diagnostic and Statistical Manual of Mental Disorders* (1987). The DSM-III-R, as it is known, lists nine criteria for "dependence" that range from using more of a drug than intended to classical tolerance and withdrawal. To be diagnosed as officially dependent, however, requires only that *any three* of the nine criteria be present.[3]

The advantage of these definitional shifts is that the falsely discrete *category* of "addiction" has been replaced by a more complex *continuum*, though unfortunately it remains difficult for even skilled clinicians to say with certainty what addiction is. At the extremes, it may seem a simple matter to see who is and is not an "addict," and we interviewed many heavy cocaine users whose use pattern would fit almost any definition of addiction. The problem is that many of the new, looser definitions of addiction can fit almost any regular cocaine user—even one who never develops tolerance, exhibits withdrawal symptoms, harms himself or herself, or sacrifices other important things in the pursuit of cocaine.

As we have said, all our respondents were heavy users and many experienced serious cocaine-related problems of some sort. But aside from the most extreme cases, we cannot be facile or glib about categorizing most of them as "addicts." Their use patterns were not always compulsive and dysfunctional and were more often complicated and changing. During a given episode, some bingers, many hogs, and most crack smokers or freebasers could resemble the stereotypical desperate dope fiend. Then, however, they could go for several days or weeks without using at all. Although many of our subjects increased their use, this was not necessarily simple tolerance. And while many of our quitters reported feeling "low" or craving cocaine after cessation, few reported classical withdrawal symptoms.

Our solution to these definitional dilemmas will disappoint readers looking for a head count of addicts or an addiction rate. Even if a precise profile of cocaine addicts existed and even if there were true consensus criteria, we would have had difficulty measuring them. We were not privy to clinical data, and we could not mount a frontal assault on the addiction question in our interviews. Given the vagaries of the concept in the scientific literature, we simply could not ask drug users, "Are you an addict?" and get valid data about anything other than self-perception. Even if we asked, some who might be addicts would deny it, while others who might not be would say they were. Moreover, given the surprising degrees of control exhibited by many of our respondents, we did not feel justified in assuming that mere quantity of use, apart from its qualitative aspects, was a valid proxy for addiction.[4]

We will not, therefore, be able to say anything definitive about cocaine addiction per se. We chose instead to disaggregate the various elements of "addiction" into concrete cocaine-related problems, which we could ask about more directly. This approach offers clearer and cleaner methods and measures and allows us to assess a diffuse range of cocaine-related problems that might have been missed had we searched only for some underlying disease entity. Our assumption, then, is that not all of the troubles that heavy cocaine use can create are mere manifestations of addiction, dependence, or disease (cf. Room, 1983).

CHAPTER 3

THINGS GO BETTER WITH COKE:
THE USES OF COCAINE

For years cocaine has enjoyed a reputation as a "party drug." Its psychoactive effects fit this image well: central nervous system stimulation that leads to euphoria, exhilaration, increased energy, and reduced fatigue. Once users learned how to recognize these effects, most found them to be fun, and this sort of stimulation does, as one of our respondents put it, "keep the party going a while longer." There are perhaps other situational reasons why cocaine is considered a party drug. Initial use usually occurs in some partylike setting, and many of our respondents continue to associate the drug and its effects with activities that go on in such settings—friends, music, dancing, animated conversation, feelings of well-being that facilitate candor and humor, a sense of intimacy.

But parties are not the only situations in which cocaine is used. There is, of course, great diversity in individual reaction to the drug, but such differences usually are not pronounced. Many users emphasize its energizing effects, some its euphoria, and others the more subtle sexual effects. In general, our interviews suggested that cocaine's ability to boost energy and enhance mood made it a welcome treat on almost any occasion. Further, unlike alcohol, marijuana, and hallucinogens, cocaine did not diminish a person's basic competence in daily life—unless and until it was used in excess. In contrast, marijuana and LSD, for example, are valued by users precisely because they render the ordinary extraordinary and make the accomplishment of routine tasks into amazing feats. Cocaine does not alter consciousness in this fashion, but rather is said to energize, amplify, and enhance one's experience and competence. Thus, our users spoke of cocaine as a general pick-me-up in a rich variety of circumstances: cleaning one's house, conversing with small gatherings of friends, writing or studying, bringing one back "up" from an alcohol or marijuana high, etc. Our respondents reported at least ten uses for cocaine.

> To party in varying private and public situations
> To socialize in small or large groups
> To enhance sex
> To open up and talk through problems
> To work
> To entertain clients or work associates
> To diet
> To fortify themselves for arduous tasks such as long car trips
> To get high
> To be alone

We should note that smoking crack or freebase and shooting did not appear to have as many uses as snorting. Because of the mechanics of these rapid-delivery methods and the intense highs that result, there are limits on where and when users can employ them. Freebasers, crack smokers, and injectors usually do not use the drug at work or to work. Indeed, our freebasers and crack users agreed that they could do little else when smoking (see Chapter 6). Shooters told us much the same thing.

In this chapter we will use individual case illustrations and interview excerpts to describe three of the major uses of cocaine: to party, to enhance sex, and to work.

SNORTING TO PARTY OR SOCIALIZE

Anita, an attractive 18-year-old mestiza, is a cashier in a quick-stop grocery. When we interviewed her she had been snorting cocaine for four years and smoking crack occasionally for two years. In her peak period she used four grams a week for four months. According to her own description she is a "party girl," but she also uses cocaine at work. She was introduced to it by a boyfriend when she was fourteen years old. After her initial experimentation she began within a matter of weeks to use it regularly on weekends: "I was going to school at the time . . . and we did it on weekends and we used to go out to the beach, snort coke, listen to tunes, smoke weed, and party."

Most often Anita consumed cocaine in small groups of friends. She seldom paid for the drug. A group of three or four would often snort an eightball (eighth of an ounce) in an evening. She also reported using at concerts.

INTERVIEWER: What about your recreation?

RESPONDENT: I enjoy it at the beach, just kicking back, drinking wine, and smoking cigarettes. And concerts—I get loaded at concerts definitely, that's a must.

INTERVIEWER: Who did you see last?

RESPONDENT: Survivor and REO, and I go to the Coliseum all the time they come and I bring my blow with me. (Case #605)

Such activities are not limited to young or working-class people. A dynamic 39-year-old white female advertising executive who has used cocaine for fifteen years described her preference for using in party and social situations.

I can't imagine how horrible it would be to sit at home and do coke by yourself. If I have coke I want to find someone to do it with. . . . I want to have fun. . . . I enjoy it with other people. . . . I can't work and do coke, and in a creative business you definitely can't do it. Later in the evening I would do it like partying with clients because in my business cocaine is expected. You are expected to treat your clients with dinner, cocaine, champagne, and booze. (Case #501)

Patty, a white 36-year-old economist who has used for fourteen years, described her pattern in the 1970s.

INTERVIEWER: So you were using in '74 and '75?

RESPONDENT: We were into going and hearing music, doing drugs, and going dancing. We were all single except for Gloria, but she managed to get out once in a while. We were into partying, drinking a little, and doing coke, and it was fun.

INTERVIEWER: But you were not using daily then?

RESPONDENT: No, just on weekends. (Case #437)

Patty maintained that pattern for a number of years until she began to sell the drug. After that she became a daily nipper.

Some of our respondents, particularly bingers, restricted themselves to weekend/party use exclusively, but others found this pattern difficult to maintain. As they discovered new situations or activities in which the cocaine high was pleasurable, many users found themselves using on weekdays. The dentist we quoted earlier tried to restrict his cocaine use to weekends because he felt that using during the week interfered with his work.

INTERVIEWER: Did you work while using it?

RESPONDENT: The only person that I worked on when I was under the influence of cocaine was you! Really, I remember. But I didn't like to work under the influence of cocaine. It's very distracting and it interferes with your ability to concentrate. No matter what anybody says you're not sharper with cocaine. (Case #428)

He maintained a heavy weekend pattern (Friday to Sunday) for four years while he was "experimenting with a whole new life-style. I was making new and different friends, most of whom, if not all, were into drugs, and some of them were smuggling or dealing drugs." Over a weekend he would use three or four grams, then remain clean Monday through Thursday while he worked.

Harv, a young black bass player in a rock group, had a similar rule about cocaine use at work. He preferred to use in social situations.

When I go to play [bass], I don't like to use it. It messes up my time. . . . People say, "Oh, I can be more creative," but, hey, I can't even play when I'm doing it. . . . Some people can come up with something creative but I can't. When I do it I basically just want to sit back and rap and have a good time. Doing it by yourself is a drag and it's a social thing for me. I want to do it with people around me. (Case #552)

Cocaine use was not limited to the sort of social gatherings that Harv preferred. Many of our respondents used it to enhance sexual activities or to work. However, they mentioned using cocaine at parties far more frequently than for any other activity. The euphoric and energizing qualities of cocaine, particularly early in users' careers, were especially valued in social situations.

Snorting to Enhance Sexual Relations

Like marijuana, Ecstasy, or MDMA and many other drugs, cocaine is reputed to enhance sexuality. Many people attribute unusual erotic powers to the drug, saying that it can create strong sexual drives, instant erections or multiple erections, multiple orgasms, intensified orgasms, and even priapism. Most such attributions, however, are made by persons who use the drug only occasionally. Heavy users presented a mixed picture on this score; some used it for sexual enhancement, others did not (Macdonald et al., 1988). Freebasers and crack smokers reported highs that they likened to orgasm, but rarely had sex while on a "run." Snorters more often told us they found increased sexual pleasure with the drug, but this tended to be early in their careers.[1] Many reported that cocaine's sexual effects changed and waned with time, especially with heavy or daily use.

Let us begin with positive descriptions. Josey is a 29-year-old black woman who works as a systems analyst. She used cocaine for four years. During her peak period when she was freebasing, she consumed about six grams a week. She created quite a stir among her "baser" friends when she continued to freebase while she was pregnant,[2] nearly up to the end of her term. Those risks notwithstanding, Josey and others told us that cocaine made sex more intense, more gratifying, less inhibited, and more varied and unconventional.

> RELAXATION: My major thing was being able to relax and getting into it.

> MORE INTENSITY: The buildup [the foreplay] is increased and that adds to the intensity and also the other body sensations, so it did add to it.

> LESS INHIBITION: I think I became more in tune with my sexuality in that I was more aggressive instead of passive. . . . It was just a good feeling, I just felt good. . . . It kind of enhanced the foreplay, that's what it was, which made it more fun.

She also felt that she had more endurance and was more innovative and unconventional.

> There would be times after one orgasm—and that's when I'm basically through for the night kind of thing . . . but after cocaine and especially with freebasing it may not be. . . . It may be a span of three hours or something of having an orgasm . . . a long foreplay, orgasm, resting, and then just waking up with this urge and the energy and the tingle just to do it again. I would do it, you know, like that for like five times, which I thought, wow! So I thought that was interesting.

She reported that she was more unconventional and more likely to explore different kinds of sexual situations.

> INTERVIEWER: Did you ever have sex on cocaine that you would call unconventional?

> RESPONDENT: Yes.

> INTERVIEWER: What kinds of things?

RESPONDENT: I would say unconventional where there would be things that I would never have dreamed about or even read in books. . . . Things I thought I wouldn't do even under the influence.

INTERVIEWER: So here's a list of a few things and you can respond to them as much or as little as you want. Group sex— more than two people is a group?

RESPONDENT: That I would have to say yes, but they weren't always good. I like either a one-on-one or a group of people just as friends hanging out. I feel real uncomfortable when it becomes a sexual freak show. Yeah, it's not my thing at all. You know, I'm not bi[sexual].

INTERVIEWER: Okay, how about rough sex?

RESPONDENT: No.

INTERVIEWER: How about masturbation?

RESPONDENT: Yeah.

INTERVIEWER: The use of mechanical devices?

RESPONDENT: Yes, and yes to the next one.

INTERVIEWER: Anal sex?

RESPONDENT: Yeah.

INTERVIEWER: How about sex in risky places?

RESPONDENT: No.

INTERVIEWER: Sex that you regretted or shameful sex?

RESPONDENT: Oh yes, but at least I had the excuse that I was under the influence.

Josey saw distinct differences between the sexual effects of snorted cocaine and those of smoking freebase.

RESPONDENT: Say with the snorting it was . . . it's really different. Snorting was more of a mellowness only because all the effects of that upper was on me. With freebase and sex it would be almost . . . the rushing of it was frantic at times. Like, "Hurry, I really need to get off" or something like that. With tooting [snorting] it would just always be part of the foreplay kind of thing. I think snorting in that way is mellower and people have more control when they aren't behind the pipe. The actual sex I would say was slower and mellower at times. Snorting was more of an enhancement and an aphrodisiac with sex being the main thing, where base was the main thing and sex was secondary.

INTERVIEWER: Is one better than the other?

RESPONDENT: They are both good.

INTERVIEWER: Have you ever had an orgasmic sensation when basing, when you got a real good hit?

RESPONDENT: No, I heard rumors before that basing was better than a nut kind of thing and I disagree. The sensations are totally different and I think I would always prefer an orgasm. I mean I've had great hits but it's never done that to me. Who needs a man around then, right?

INTERVIEWER: So then you've never thought of basing as a sex substitute?

RESPONDENT: Oh no, I'm very nasty. I like sex. (Case #607)

Our interviewer had known Josey for years and stated that she tends toward understatement and was not inclined to boast about her sex life. Nonetheless, Josey was unusual among respondents in that her sexual experiences under the influence of cocaine have nearly always been positive and that her husband, who was her principal partner, did not have the erection problems reported by many men and their partners, especially the heaviest users and freebasers.

A male respondent reiterated Josey's interest in cocaine and foreplay when he described his sexual experiences.

INTERVIEWER: Okay, let's talk about sex.

RESPONDENT: What I like about sex on cocaine is basically . . . I don't like so much foreplay per se, but I like the foreplay when

I'm on coke a good deal. . . . Foreplay is wonderful and especially cunnilingus.

INTERVIEWER: Okay, so basically you really get off on the foreplay?

RESPONDENT: Yeah, the touching and the slow movement and the subtlety of the woman's body. (Case #543)

Some male respondents used cocaine to help them meet and seduce women. A white marijuana seller who found that cocaine facilitated his sex life made it a rule never to sell cocaine because he believed that having a supply around would lead him to use more. He used it for about eight years. He generally snorted the drug but estimated that he had free-based about one hundred times.[3]

INTERVIEWER: When you first started using who did you like to use cocaine with?

RESPONDENT: It would be a very easy way to pick up ladies and that's something you learn real quick. You got this around and boy, they love you and they love you literally. It just makes things so much easier socially. . . . But as the years go by, you know, you want some because your girlfriends want it . . . and especially the ladies, they love it. If you have a lot of powder, they'll spread a lot of legs. It keeps your lady happy. . . .

INTERVIEWER: What effect did cocaine have on your sexuality? Tell me the differences between snorting and freebasing.

RESPONDENT: You could almost come when you were smoking the stuff.

INTERVIEWER: So sex and freebasing were really intertwined for you?

RESPONDENT: Oh yeah.

INTERVIEWER: What about snorting and sex?

RESPONDENT: Yeah, I did a lot of that.

INTERVIEWER: Did you have trouble getting an erection ever?

RESPONDENT: No.

INTERVIEWER: And what about having an orgasm?

RESPONDENT: Yeah, that would be a problem when I would snort.

INTERVIEWER: What about when you freebased?

RESPONDENT: Not at all.

INTERVIEWER: Okay, what did you like best about coke?

RESPONDENT: I guess the fact that it got you a lot of ladies. There was a link between that and an easy good time. It was something that everybody wanted and especially the fact that it improved your sex life. . . . There would be people doing video-tapes of the orgies taking place and stuff like that and we would get into it. We had a real good time for everybody and sometimes too much of a good time. (Case #578)

Other heavy users offered similar positive reports. A for-tyish black man named Cecil, who had snorted cocaine for nearly twenty years, noted that cocaine and sex went together very well. He told us it helped him be less inhibited, to over-come his earlier guilt about sex, and to be more innovative.

Cecil began to use cocaine in 1967 but did not use heavily until 1970 when he owned a popular jazz nightclub which had both black and white clientele. At the time he was having some financial difficulties maintaining the bar (some of the groups were expensive and occasionally the patrons were sparse). He began to sell cocaine on the side to satisfy his own and his wife's propensity to use the drug and to help pay the bills. Many of the nightclub's customers were also cocaine customers so his drug sales meshed with the bar scene. His general position about cocaine and sex was that it brought out people's true nature (his own included): "What I have always said about drugs, and particularly cocaine is it brings out whatever is there. It doesn't put anything there but it just brings out your true nature. My true nature, I'm an animal."

Cecil was generally aggressive about his sexuality and contrived to arrange encounters with one or more women at a time. He explained this behavior in terms of his life-style and his cultural milieu at a particular moment in history.

RESPONDENT: I was living a life-style and a situation and an environment that was conducive to that. Like waitresses and groupies and all of that and musicians and customers and hitch-hikers! [They laugh.] It's funny now, but it sure was nice. That was before all of this insanity and paranoia about AIDS and fear. . . . It was a free and open and beautiful society.

INTERVIEWER: Yeah, free love.

RESPONDENT: Yeah, the free love. This was from the love generation and the Haight-Ashbury [in San Francisco] and that whole period, right. So again I always say it was a part of the time and the coke was a part of that.

Even though he no longer uses it regularly, Cecil still equates cocaine with sex.

INTERVIEWER: Did you ever reach a place when you couldn't have sex when you didn't have coke? The absence of coke meant the absence of sex?

RESPONDENT: Let me put it this way . . . even today I find it hard wanting to get into sex . . . unless coke is there. Because of habit or whatever, coke is part of the whole sexual experience. . . . The two just go together. (Case #591)

As might be expected, reports about cocaine and sex varied by gender—more than by frequency or quantity of use, mode of ingestion, or even career stage—suggesting that pharmacological effects on sexuality were mediated by nondrug factors. Men made positive claims like Cecil's far more often than women. Men's statements tended to be about assertiveness, endurance, and numbers or combinations of partners. This leads us to suspect that at least some men's comments about cocaine and sex may be attributed to their desire to appear macho or sexually active and aggressive. Women more often described cocaine and sex in neutral or negative terms. For example, a 30-year-old black woman snorter told us, "I don't like it when men are high on it. They always say, 'Oh I can last forever,' but I hate it. . . . [Sex] gets very mechanical and not very loving" (Case #555). When women did make positive statements about sex and coke they often spoke of intimacy, closeness, communication, and feeling comfortable and sexy. For example, Phyllis, a 37-year-old white geographer who used cocaine for seven years (two grams per week on weekends for two peak years), spoke of the relationship between cocaine and sex in terms of open communication.

> I think the biggest value of coke in my life has been that it helped me straighten out my personal life, which was telling John [her long-term lover] things that bugged me and to make us closer than we could have ever been. I don't think I would have ever had the guts to tell him some of the things. . . . I had some near rape experiences, that if they weren't rape I couldn't have explained, and figured out what happened to me, why I got into those [situations], things I had to resolve that come up continually in our careers, continuous temptations, even fantasy. I think that's the area we've gotten into now that really makes me think that we have a real mature relationship. We have gotten to the point where we can tell each other [our] fantasies and we don't get angry. . . . I think coke has really aided in that.
> I wasn't raised in an environment [she was brought up as a Mormon] where we could talk about sex. So I think that was the most important thing, and that really enhanced sexuality because I felt that for once I could talk to someone in depth about everything that was related to sex. And that was something I felt was a freedom, a freedom that I never knew before. I never expected it and I never thought it could happen. So that was positive, very positive. (Case #592)

Finally, some respondents of both genders offered negative reports of cocaine's effects on sexuality. Nancy, a meteorologist turned stockbroker who had two long episodes of controlled use, generally did not see sex on cocaine as a big deal: "I never could understand the relationship between coke and sex. For me it was nothing. Now take weed [marijuana], that is something else. Now that is the *real* sex drug" (Case #559). A 30-year-old male international banker was more specifically negative. He had used cocaine over an eight-year period, at his peak using three grams or more a week for three months, sometimes snorting several grams in day-long binges. He and his wife used cocaine on their wedding night with bad results.

> So we got married and we planned this very large wedding and it was a real fluke to everyone involved. We got married in Santa Barbara and we ended up doing coke at our wedding. That's kind of weird and it kind of fucks things up, you know. It kind of makes you kind of cold to each other. . . . And on your wedding night that's bizarre. (Case #122)

For many other users, cocaine's effects on sexuality was a function of the way they ingested the drug. One 34-year-old white woman who snorted early in her career and then moved to smoking captured this point well.

> You really can't have sex when you freebase. Your nerves are so, so tense. I just find that you really can't. I feel no emotion for my husband when I freebase, no emotion whatsoever. It was different when we were snorting. . . . We were able to come down and have sex. But with freebasing, no, you can't. I can't at all, personally, and my husband cannot. (Case #615)

In short, while most of our respondents had something good to say about sex under the influence of cocaine, most were more equivocal than Cecil. There was great individual variation on this subject, but the majority would probably agree that sex on coke could be enhanced after limited doses, early in their using careers, or when snorted; sex tended not to be enhanced after large doses, late in a heavy use career, or when smoked (e.g., Macdonald et al., 1988).

Using at Work or to Work

Over a century ago, Sigmund Freud, then an unknown young Viennese physician, conducted self-experiments on the effects of cocaine and reported that under its influence "one feels more vigorous and more capable of work" (Freud, 1884, 60; cited in Erickson et al., 1987). Despite cocaine's reputation as a "party drug" and a sex enhancer, many of our respondents also found it useful for work purposes. As a central nervous system stimulant, cocaine often made repetitive or arduous tasks, late shifts, or long work hours more bearable, indeed pleasurable. A psychology professor we interviewed found that cocaine helped him be a more disciplined and productive writer, able to sit at his computer screen composing for hours longer than mere coffee would have allowed. A factory operative reported that cocaine allowed him to concentrate better during the wee hours of the graveyard shift. Many of his coworkers had the same experience, he said.

Some of our subjects got into cocaine through work, often buying it at work rather than bringing it to the workplace (see "The Company" Chapter 4). For example, a 34-year-old white man, a private investigator at the time of our interview, described his cocaine use on a previous job as an elevator repairman at a downtown office building.

> Um, I don't remember being really that impressed with it [the first few times], but then later, about 1977 and 1978, I started working in San Francisco in a big office downtown and just about every coworker I had was doing it, even my supervisor and my boss. . . . At that time I was working as an elevator mechanic and making excellent wages and that was when I started doing about a gram a day. It didn't seem to hinder my work at all.

Later in the interview he described a typical day.

> I'd get up about six or seven because I didn't have to get to work until eight, and I only lived five blocks away from the office. The

work up there was pretty lackadaisical. I would walk in at eight. . . . Breakfast was always my favorite meal so I would have a good breakfast at the cafeteria. The food was cheap and you can get a really good breakfast. Then by ten o'clock there was a mandatory coffee-break time and everybody would be hiding out in the men's room to get ready to start the day, and I'd do a quarter or a half [gram] and then I wouldn't do some until noon. Like if I had a quarter I would spread it out over maybe like from twenty to thirty minutes and that was the usual time we had for the coffee break. I would then do some more at noon or I wouldn't even bother, and then do some again around three and that would keep me going until the evening. I didn't do any more in the evening but the times that I did I would do some around five or six or seven, shortly after I would get off work, and I would try not to do any more. (Case #309)

This respondent generally felt energized by cocaine and reported that when he wasn't working he was active riding his ten-speed racing bicycle on long trips and mountain climbing.

Janet, a waitress at a rock-and-roll bar in San Francisco, observed that cocaine use was an "occupational hazard" in her line of work. She reported both positive and negative effects on her work, though she mentioned the positive effects first.

INTERVIEWER: Okay, tell me what it's like to work on cocaine.

RESPONDENT: Well, at a certain point for the first couple of months it gives you this nice little lift, and you kind of get focused in on all the things that you have to accomplish in order to start the night out. And then you're more friendly; I'm more friendly. It makes me a little more outgoing; I'm more chatty, which of course, helps you get better tips. . . . I found coke to be very functional for me. That's one of the problems I have dealing with it, I can function on it. . . . One of the things that I always wanted was a line at the very beginning of the night just to sort of get going, and if we got busy enough, a lot of times I would never do another line. It would work out fine. . . . I would spend $7 [sharing a quarter of a gram with two or three other employees].

She continued to use at work in a controlled manner for roughly four years. She then began to escalate her use during nonwork hours with her boyfriend and her coworkers (she claimed that all but two of ten employees in her club used cocaine). Eventually her use stopped giving her that "lift" and began to have a different effect: "It can take on the opposite effect of course where then you're instantly tired, constantly tired, yawning, you know, no matter how many lines you've had. And also you don't want to talk anymore because you're too uptight" (Case #551).

At the time of our interview Janet was concerned about her escalating use, but she continued. She stopped during a two-week vacation, and a month later stopped again for three weeks to try to get her coke use at work under more control. She estimated that at the time we spoke to her she was using one and one-half to two grams a week, costing approximately $150 a week. During periods when she worked less she generally used less.

Janet's story suggests that, whatever the biochemical attractions of this drug, the setting of use—in this case the workplace—can also be an important factor in cocaine's allure. We interviewed eight other waiters, waitresses, and chefs and heard similar accounts of employees pooling funds to buy small amounts to use at work. For them, too, hard work, constant activity, and long, late hours seemed instrumental in their cocaine use (see also Chapter 4).

Many of our respondents successfully managed to nip small amounts of cocaine to enhance mood or productivity for work. But not all controlled their use even as well as Janet did. On the contrary, Joyce, the highly skilled chef at a fashionable nouvelle cuisine restaurant in Berkeley, also found cocaine functional in her job but had much more difficulty with her use. (Case #207)

Joyce was an attractive, ebullient, 30-year-old when we interviewed her. As noted in the previous chapter, she first used cocaine when she was 21 and attending a large university in the suburbs. She was not impressed by her first experience and did not use again until she was 24. When she was 25 she returned to the San Francisco Bay area from the East Coast where she had learned to cook. Upon her return she began to use sporadically with her older sister and the sister's boyfriend. She took a job in an expensive restaurant in San Francisco and began to use cocaine at work with other employees. In general, Joyce kept her use under control, using a quarter to a half a gram a week for two years.

Then she was asked to join a group of other employees from the grill who wanted to open a new restaurant. She undertook the job with considerable enthusiasm and dedicated herself to making the new endeavor a success. Like many of the other employees, she used cocaine to help her get through the fourteen- and fifteen-hour days. Under those conditions her use increased to a gram a day and she continued at that rate for six months. During the fourth month of this episode her work performance began to suffer and soon her boss talked to her about getting help for her cocaine problem.

She went to Alcoholics Anonymous accompanied by one of the bosses for three months and managed to stay off the drug. But when she stopped attending meetings she resumed using cocaine at her previous level. Six months later she was fired from her job and was emotionally devastated.

Our purpose in this chapter has been almost purely descriptive: to illustrate some of the principal uses for the cocaine high among our heavy users. It is important to note that the mere fact that cocaine had so many different uses in so many important spheres of daily life may be a clue for understanding why so many users escalated their use. Whether used to extend or intensify parties, to enhance or prolong sex, to boost mood or productivity for work, or simply as a treat to make an occasion a bit more special, cocaine for these users was experienced as *functional* as well as fun.

Many other recreational drugs are valued precisely because they temporarily interfere with everyday functioning. Some observers have argued that such drugs are used to "escape" reality. While this argument should not be accepted uncritically (e.g., Preble and Casey, 1969), it provides a useful contrast. We got the distinct sense from our respondents that cocaine—particularly when used intranasally at low doses and early in careers—immerses users more intensely *into* their realities. There is a paradox here that was captured nicely by Janet the waitress: "That's one of the problems I have dealing with it, I can function on it." The concept that "things go better with coke" helps account for why so many users found so many uses for cocaine, and why ultimately so many of them either regulated their consumption or got into some kind of trouble.

CHAPTER 4

COCAINE AT WORK:
A CASE STUDY OF "THE COMPANY"

Prior to the mid-1970s, cocaine use was concentrated among relatively small circles of illicit drug users, bohemians, and members of a few affluent, high-pay, high-pressure professions. Cocaine first made headlines because of its association with Hollywood celebrities, rock stars, Wall Street "yuppies," and professional athletes. Comedian Robin Williams once quipped, "Cocaine is God's way of telling you that you make too much money." Cocaine users became much more heterogeneous as cocaine use spread through the population. By the time the sharpest increase occurred in the late 1970s, cocaine use was occurring across the occupational spectrum and in all sorts of workplaces to enhance productivity as well as pleasure.[1]

Among those respondents who mentioned using cocaine at or for work during at least part of their cocaine careers, there were: attorneys of various types; business executives including the owner of a diamond business, a national sales manager for a multinational corporation, a vice-president of finance for a Silicon Valley high-technology firm, an executive recruiter, a vice-president of a holding company, a restaurant owner, and an advertising executive; and other professionals such as a dentist, a psychologist, and a stockbroker. There were other white-collar respondents who used cocaine at work: a bookstore owner, a commercial photographer, a computer operator in a big law firm, a research assistant, a tennis club manager, a music producer, a film industry prop master, a real estate office manager, several secretaries, and an art gallery owner whose clients and patrons often expected cocaine as an accoutrement to showings and parties.

Respondents in high-skill working-class occupations also used cocaine at or for work on at least some occasions. These included a mechanics inspector in a plastics factory, a machinist who worked in the nuclear power industry, a house painter, a yacht maintenance and repair worker, two carpenters, a limousine driver, two stagehands, an oil refinery mechanic, a telephone installer, a prostitute, a bus driver, an auto mechanic, an elevator mechanic, a cook, and two bartenders, both of whom noted that cocaine use was something of an occupational hazard for people who worked late hours making good times for customers.

Our sample was not limited to those who earned high salaries or even good hourly wages. Many were poorly paid, low-skilled members of the working class who were struggling to get by: a porter for a produce company, a warehouseman, a quick-stop market clerk. This category included two assembly-line workers, one of whom told us that in his plant several low-level suppliers sold cocaine to many of their coworkers to help them "get through the shift" from midnight on. Other working-class respondents found cocaine functional in their jobs. Restaurant workers (like Janet in Chapter 3) often pooled money for cocaine because it reduced the chronic fatigue that came with long hours on their feet, aided their productivity, and improved their dispositions (and thus their tips). There were also housewives who valued cocaine for its ability to help them manage a multitude of complex tasks simultaneously, and unemployed workers who enjoyed escaping ennui.

Some of those who used at or for work reported problems at work that they attributed to their cocaine use, but others apparently never let their use affect their jobs at all. Most of our respondents generally did not use cocaine at or for work.

Of those who did, all we can safely say on the basis of our data is that it is possible to have cocaine-related work problems without being an extremely heavy workplace user, just as it is possible to be a regular, heavy workplace user and still perform one's job in a satisfactory manner. Here, too, individual differences such as personal problems and networks of supportive people are probably important, as are workplace characteristics such as stress and alienation (Reinarman, Waldorf, and Murphy, 1988).

To provide a picture of the various ways cocaine might or might not affect work, we will present data from a series of interviews and field observations conducted at one workplace.

A Case Study of "The Company"

Pursuing one of our networks of respondents we interviewed nine people who worked in the same engineering consulting firm near San Jose, which we will call "The Company." Eight had used enough cocaine for a long enough time to qualify for the study. One had used too infrequently to be included but had worked at the firm for ten years and knew all the actors. From their accounts we learned that about half of the company's fifty employees had used at least some cocaine at some point. Of these, thirteen used it heavily, and five of them experienced serious problems with the drug. Only one employee was ever approached by the owners of the company about his cocaine problems. During a six-month period of heavy use his work performance fell off drastically. After the managing partners confronted him, he resigned. Unfortunately, we could not locate him for an interview, but we learned about his problems from other respondents at The Company.

In some respects one of the senior partners in The Company, Nick, set a precedent for cocaine use there. He began to use the drug heavily after the death of his wife. The interviewer, who knew Nick well, believed that his cocaine use was in part an effort to overcome his bereavement. After two years of heavy use he had drifted into selling the drug. He became forgetful and paranoid, and he began to have moral doubts about selling cocaine, particularly to his son, who had experienced even more difficulties with the drug than Nick had.

Nick gave up selling, but continued to use for six more months. During this period he became disenchanted with work and decided to sell his share in the business and travel. He went to Asia for thirteen months. Upon returning he married his previous lover. At the interview he claimed that both decisions—to sell the business and to get married—were made suddenly, and that cocaine had impaired his judgment about selling the business.

Another employee, Stephen, had problems with cocaine that began while he was with The Company, though these problems affected his personal life far more than his performance at work. Stephen sensed that he was using too much, wasting money on the drug, and feeling powerless about quitting despite his declining productivity on his private writing.

Stephen joined The Company after he earned a Ph.D. in psychology. He had used cocaine recreationally for a time when he lived with a friend who had ready access to the drug. But then when he moved to Los Angeles to work on his Ph.D. he did not have the money to buy and used only a half dozen times in as many years. When he took a job with The Company he suddenly had more money than he had earned in years as a "starving graduate student," as he described himself.

At that point Stephen began to buy the drug (one of his sources worked at The Company) and to use it for his private work writing a book. He felt he needed a little pick-me-up after his day job so he could get to the task of writing in the evening. Arriving at home, he would "lay out a few lines" on the mirror in his desk drawer and set to work. At 9:00 or 10:00 P.M. he would stop writing, eat dinner, "smoke a little weed," watch an hour of television (he was a devoted viewer of "Hill Street Blues"), and go to bed. Slowly he built his book.

Stephen continued to use in this manner for nine months. When he changed his schedule of work at The Company to afternoons, he began to use cocaine in the mornings to work on the book. However, despite his rules about confining cocaine use to his private writing, he also began to use at The Company. He was still using moderately, albeit regularly—four or five lines a day or perhaps a gram per week. This pattern continued for six months. He was then offered a postdoctoral fellowship and a part-time teaching job at a university some distance from his home, and left The Company. He had finished the first draft of his manuscript.

With this job change Stephen's pattern of cocaine use also changed. He used a few lines to make the drive to his teaching job and a few lines to rewrite his manuscript, but did not use at the teaching job. During that year he managed to make everyone of his teaching assignments, conduct a new study for his fellowship, and complete part of the next draft of his manuscript. But in the process his cocaine use escalated and this worried him. At our interview he described his changing pattern of use.

RESPONDENT: It went from very social and very occasional and gradually changed to much less social although also social, then to principally work, then to only work.

INTERVIEWER: So the focus of it changed?

RESPONDENT: Right, and for a while it really was an aid to productivity, there was no question. I could sit at my desk and be less distracted and have more energy and more focus, longer than I could without it. . . . So I started using it more frequently and then the lines were a little bit longer and then I began bringing it to work. . . . It became something I could do to get me through the drive. Yeah, I would do it there [at the university] if I were cramming to get a lecture written and I had some on me. Gradually I almost always had some on me. . . . By the end of '84 and beginning of '85, I was doing probably a dozen lines a day . . . sometimes one every half hour.

INTERVIEWER: So you were becoming more aware then that this thing had you by the tail?

RESPONDENT: Right. I'm going out at night at ten o'clock and taking $100 out of the money machine and making deals! Instead of being productive it started becoming counterproductive in two ways. One, I spent a lot of time chasing around and trying to make connections to get it so I could keep the supply around; and the second thing was I would come home and do it and I would do so much that I couldn't focus anymore. Sometimes I'd read one paragraph fifty times. In the beginning I was snorting in order to write. By the end of '84 I was sitting there trying to write in order to snort. I got less and less done instead of more and more done. I would use more to the point of getting so wired that I couldn't really do anything. I couldn't deal with people and I used to hate it when the phone rang and I used to hate it when somebody would come over. Yet I would come right home from work and do another line.

In the long run, then, Stephen suffered for this attempt to increase his productivity but not necessarily in physical terms. Throughout his cocaine-using career he made sure to eat well and get a reasonable night's sleep. His suffering was psychological; beginning in the middle of 1984 he began to struggle to get control of his use. After three months he made a decision to stop buying.

I made a decision not to buy it and not to have it around and I just sort of stopped. I had known for six months or so that eventually I'd have to quit [but] the date got stretched to suit my, quote, addiction, end quote. In the middle of January of '85, I just stopped buying. Two dealers were out of business and I didn't bother going back to the third, and I wasn't going to the city every day [where he had another source at The Company] so that helped. (Case #439)

For a month or so after stopping, Stephen felt a little low on energy, but gradually he began to feel that he was getting more done. Working at his new computer served as a diversion; he had to learn how to use it for his revised manuscript. As one might expect, he experienced some craving from time to time. But he taught himself to "appreciate feeling 'normal,'" which he defined as "not feeling overamped," not having tight muscles, not grinding his teeth, not being so impatient. Today Stephen is a full-time faculty member at a university on the East Coast, and a very prestigious press has published his book. He never buys cocaine and uses only on one or two special occasions per year when it is offered to him.

Another problematic user who worked at The Company, Alberto, a rather dashing Latino economist, did not buy or get the drug from sources at work, but he did use it regularly at work. He had a lover who sold cocaine in sizable quantities and she was his primary source. He estimates that he used an eighth of an ounce (seven grams) of cocaine a week for about twelve months. Eventually he had problems with insomnia, recurrent back pains (which he diagnosed as liver problems), depression, and sexual impotence. Alberto described his heavy use period.

INTERVIEWER: What was a typical day for you? Did you use it at work?

RESPONDENT: Yeah, all day long. . . . It was like cigarettes, I noticed. I see people that smoke cigarettes that have this reaction. They get up in the morning and the first thing they are going to do is have a cigarette, and then they'll take a shower, and then they'll have another cigarette. . . . The same thing with cocaine. You'll get up and do a line because your nose is fucked up from the night before. So you have a line and you feel better and take a shower . . . and you had to do it all day long so that nobody would know, or at least you thought nobody knew.

INTERVIEWER: And so all day long you would . . . ?

RESPONDENT: All day long, every day, and then I would go home and really get crazy.

Alberto's lover did not use at the same level as he did; she would regularly stop using for one or two weeks while she attended college. Early in their relationship she used it much the same way he did. He described this period.

> We went out all the time and danced or listened to music, or we were out to the opera or to the symphony or go roller-skating. And no matter what we were doing we were high doing it. We couldn't do anything unless we were loaded. . . . It was to enhance everything that we did together. I was doing about an eighth [of an ounce] a week and I was having a great time for a year. But then I started to feel run down and literally started to hurt. (Case #415)

After some effort, Alberto stopped using for a short period when his lover went to college in Los Angeles. Then he began to get control of his use. At the interview he said he had not used heavily for a year but was still using approximately a gram a month, a dramatic reduction from his previous pattern of a gram a day. It should be noted that even during his period of heaviest use he was able to meet his responsibilities at work. When The Company underwent a retrenchment after finishing a big project and staff members were laid off, Alberto was retained as a reasonably productive employee.

Another valued employee, Frederick, used and sold cocaine at The Company. A slim, athletic type, he has a personality much like a Marine Corps drill sergeant. As director of operations at The Company, he shouldered considerable responsibility. Frederick described for our interviewer, a long-term friend of his, how he started to use at the office.

> RESPONDENT: And then in the office people wanted to have it around . . . and they were all going through their initial stages as users. . . . Basically, everybody in the office was going through the same stage that I was and instead of having a coffee break we would have a toot. I can't tell you how long it took me to realize that I was surrounded by people who either worked with me or friends of people who worked with me who wanted to have a little here and there, and [that] by being a person who could present them [with] a cleaner and better product than they were getting on the streets, I could suddenly have income . . . and have as much [cocaine] as I wanted for recreational purposes.

> INTERVIEWER: So you made a conscious decision that you were going to sell it because you wanted better stuff?

RESPONDENT: I wanted better stuff and I wanted my friends to have better stuff. (Case #408)

Frederick had sold and used at the office for approximately two years when he began to feel that he was losing control over the drug. He had been using a gram a day for three months. He feared he might be stretching his luck by selling so much (at his peak five ounces a week), and he noticed that friends at the office were moving away from him because of his heavy coke and alcohol use. Frederick also experienced regular sexual impotence, various nasal irritations, and had a general sense that he was abusing his body even though he took care to eat well, avoid dehydration, and get regular sleep. He quit using cocaine when he stopped selling it, and substituted food and alcohol for one or two months.

It should be noted that Frederick was not the only person who sold cocaine at The Company. Four other people sold the drug informally at one time or another, although none sold on the scale Frederick did. By the time we conducted our last interviews for this substudy only one person was selling cocaine there, and he was selling only grams and parts of grams. After about four years, demand for cocaine at The Company peaked and began to subside as one person after another cut back or quit. We suspect that as the heaviest users came to have problems, many of them quit or cut down on their use, and that they stood as living lessons in the office folklore so that other, more casual users also cut back on their use.

To round out the picture of The Company, we should emphasize that most of the employees who used cocaine were ceremonial users who exhibited nothing like the patterns of Frederick or Nick. There was also a small group of controlled users who had no problems with the drug. One such person is Haven, at one time a close friend of Frederick who used nearly as heavily as Frederick did. During Haven's heaviest period he used two grams a week for twelve months, but that was only for a short segment of his twelve-year cocaine-use career.

Haven is a particularly conscientious and competent employee. Always affable, he knows everything that is going on at the office and has a reputation for getting more done than most others. He is particularly skilled at maintaining good relationships and goes to great lengths to be helpful to both employees and outsiders. He was universally liked and respected at The Company. He also used cocaine every day. At our interview he reported that he had used every day during the previous seven days and consumed one and one-half grams in that week. He was primarily a nipper and regulated his use to minimize negative effects. He seldom used after 8:00 P.M. so that he could be asleep by midnight. Although Haven generally used at work, it was usually in small amounts. He felt that the drug made him more productive.

> RESPONDENT: I do a lot of detail work with economic projections, and also the fact that I've been working there for a number of years [ten years] and it's quite boring now. Sometimes just to get through something I need something.
>
> INTERVIEWER: Do you work a lot of late hours and stuff?
>
> RESPONDENT: Yeah, . . . cocaine will get me through the day or get me through working late, and when I go home I don't do any more and I'm ready to go to sleep.
>
> INTERVIEWER: How many years have you been in that pattern?
>
> RESPONDENT: A maximum of three. (Case #536)

Haven reported no physical problems associated with his cocaine use, and most who knew him affirmed that he handled his cocaine use better than other regular users in the office.

From our observations and interviews at The Company, it appears that the peak period of cocaine use occurred during 1984 and 1985, and then tapered off. Many people were using casually as early as 1979, but after an initial period of moderate use with minimal negative effects, at least a dozen began to use the drug more heavily. Five of these people subsequently developed one or another cocaine-related problem at least briefly before use receded markedly within the group.

We know of no simple way to explain this pattern of waxing and waning use. No one feature of the zeitgeist or characteristic of organizational culture at The Company explicitly encouraged or discouraged drug use. As we mentioned, several of the partners used cocaine, one abused it, and a director also was known to use the drug on occasion. However, none of these leaders encouraged others to use or was indiscreet about his or her use. Another partner was known to be opposed to nearly all drug use and did not indulge. Yet despite his "hands-on" management style and daily presence in the office, he remained unaware of the drug use that was occurring under his nose, so to speak.

The pattern of cocaine use in this setting may have been indirectly affected by the general managerial style that had evolved at The Company. After listing the various psychological problems and managerial misdeeds of several high-level managers (a sleazy lawyer, a spendthrift director), one partner observed, "Everybody decided not to confront anybody else about drugs because they never wanted to be confronted about their own problems. . . . There was a mutual tolerance of everybody else's weaknesses.

Management did express concern about cocaine on at least two occasions. One employee was approached about the effect his drug use was having on his productivity after he had failed to finish a project. Some time later, one of the authors was asked what management might do for persons who were having problems with cocaine, and he offered what advice he could. We never learned to whom they were alluding or whether the advice was acted upon.

As for the staff, almost everyone we interviewed expressed a laissez-faire attitude about coworkers' drug use. Some were inclined to overlook drug use and other pecadillos among those with whom they socialized outside of work. The employees and even many of the partners of The Company were on the whole a fairly young, liberal, and heterogeneous lot. They seemed to share an unwritten understanding about the importance of tolerance, which meant, among other things,

that what people did on their own time was their own business. For the most part, this tolerance served The Company
well. The Company was able to thrive most of the time by
drawing on the talents of a diverse staff, who seemed to thrive
on working at a place that respected their differences and their
privacy. Work schedules were flexible; supervision was relatively democratic. Many if not most of the staff members had
at least experimented with some form of illicit drug use, which
did not affect their performance. So if management had attempted proactively to impose a "clean and sober" ethic on
everyone—particularly on these sorts of talented professionals who valued autonomy—it would have been perceived as
unnecessarily heavy-handed and might well have bred resent-
ment and resistance. Aside from the few individuals who
overindulged (two on alcohol for a long time, five on cocaine
for a short time), there was no compelling reason to develop a
more disciplinarian work culture for everyone.

The general availability of cocaine may have facilitated use
at The Company. As we have shown, staffers got cocaine
several ways. Some brought their own from outside, some
bought it inside, some shared their supplies. But there were
few arrangements where people pooled money to buy large or
small amounts, as often occurred in downtown office build-
ings or bars. Cocaine was used in a variety of ways, but these
did not seem to help spread its popularity. Some used almost
exclusively for work, others only for fun after work, and still
others only irregularly in both spheres.

Our life history interviews offered a few other bits of data
that may help to account for the spread of cocaine use at The
Company. First, a majority of the employees were children of
the 1960s and held morally libertarian attitudes about most
drug use. Most had at least experimented with illicit drugs
in the past and some still used marijuana on occasion. In
their view, consciousness alteration was a valued part of human experience, not something to be condemned unless it
adversely affected work, health, or family. When cocaine
came onto the scene in the mid- to late 1970s, many em-

ployees found it both pleasurable at parties and functional at work. Moreover, their salaries were generally good, so they could afford to use cocaine without serious financial strain.

Second, the nature of the work at The Company helped camouflage the use of cocaine. As is typically the case for professionals, working hours were defined by the individual and responsibility was diffuse. The work itself was done privately in individual offices, and productivity was not easily measured in terms of finished inventory. As a result, neither the occasional cocaine use of many nor its deleterious effects on the few abusers visibly affected productivity.

Third, The Company was a highly competitive and stressful business. The office ethos was often hectic, with frequent deadlines demanding long hours and extra creativity. For some people this work style was somewhat pressured and alienating. Large groups would often stay in the office late at night writing proposals and finishing projects. Before cocaine came on the scene, a few staff members used methamphetamines in pill form to work the late hours and meet the deadlines, and almost everyone at The Company made regular use of the large bags of fresh-roasted, gourmet coffee beans on hand for grinding. When cocaine spread into these social circles it sometimes became the preferred drug for certain work purposes under these conditions. Sellers at the office provided regular supplies, and most users managed the effects well. At office parties, and particularly at Christmas, cocaine was sometimes discreetly available.

Most workers at The Company remained relatively productive throughout the peak period of use. Even those whose work may have been hampered at times by excessive cocaine use could usually hide it from the others. Unlike alcohol, marijuana, and psychedelic drugs, cocaine did not produce very obvious effects, except for the occasional extreme user who would sometimes appear pallid, anxiety-ridden, or "burned out." Whenever there were problems with productivity, cocaine was not singled out as the reason because many other, well-known problems were thought to cause angst and alienation at The Company. Employees who were having problems were sometimes thought to have burned out on stress, to have become unable to produce or keep up with the pace. But most workers were far less apt to be troubled by cocaine use than by inequalities in salary or power, or by the failure of partners to consult with them on key financial decisions.

Occasionally, someone would notice a problem. For example, one senior male staffer who never used cocaine had a severe drinking problem. He eventually deteriorated to the point where he could do no work at all. After being asked for a long-overdue report that he had not even started, he had a breakdown and left The Company. Another woman, who had a long-standing reputation as "high-strung," experienced a "minor nervous breakdown" as the result of work pressure and her own psychological problems. She had used small amounts of cocaine on some occasions outside of work, but no one believed that this had anything to do with her crisis. And as we mentioned earlier, one staffer was confronted about his cocaine use.

In general, all of our respondents at The Company believed that, while a number of people were using cocaine regularly during a two-year period in the mid-1980s, it caused surprisingly few workplace problems. Occasionally someone came to work with a drug hangover, and there was some absenteeism; but these problems were not seen by workers or management as serious. During the period of heavy use The Company was relatively prosperous and had a large staff. Eventually, most of the heavy use subsided and The Company continued to prosper despite a short fallow period. But even when we consider the five most problematic users, it remains clear that there was a *natural cycle* of cocaine use at The Company. Much as it has done in the culture at large, cocaine spread through this organizational setting from experimental to regularized use to abuse by some. Then, after the few problem users demonstrated that cocaine did not always improve productivity and that one would burn out if one used too much too often, there was a clear diminution of use throughout The Company.

We have a hunch about why this cycle took the shape it did, rather than leading deeper and deeper into individual and organizational ruin. The jobs at The Company were demanding, and we think this accounts for some of the initial appeal of cocaine there. By the same token, these jobs *mattered* to the people who held them. Company staffers had to succeed in graduate-level training in order to be hired, then had to work hard on every project to stay in business. Thus, ironically, the stressful jobs which in some ways facilitated cocaine use also seemed to serve as anchors against abuse. While no respondent said so explicitly, all spoke of their work as vitally important and of careers they aimed to advance. So even when the anchor did not hold well enough for some, they were moved to solve their cocaine problems, in order to hold onto their hard-won and highly valued professions.

We want to avoid the temptation to draw neat conclusions from such a variety of individual experiences in a complex organization. Yet we do not think it is stretching our data on The Company too far to suggest that cocaine seems to have had a particular appeal for 1960s young people turned professionals in the 1980s. They were socialized into adulthood at a point in history when consciousness alteration was seen as an exciting, even enlightening experience, when popular culture urged people to indulge rather than renounce the impulse to enjoy life. Two decades later they were ambitious, hardworking professionals in a competitive industry who had mortgages to pay and families to feed. Unlike other drugs, licit and illicit, cocaine seemed for a time to be tailor-made for their circumstances. It allowed them, in Freudian terms, to find some balance between the pleasure principle and the reality principle (Marcuse, 1955). With cocaine, most of the users, most of the time, managed to get high *and* to get things done—the best of both worlds, youth and adult, 1960s and 1980s. This was the reward in which the risk was embedded.

If this case study is any guide, then, understanding cocaine use and abuse in the workplace will require attention to the myriad ways that the characteristics and culture of workers interact with the structure and organization of work.

CHAPTER 5

SELLING COCAINE:
DRIFTING INTO DEALING

No *American* who has watched television or glanced at a newspaper since 1986 could avoid getting the impression that drug dealers are the very embodiment of evil, now that communism seems to have collapsed. The stereotype has become a staple of popular culture: a bejeweled, brown-skinned, BMW-driving, machine gun–toting brute being hauled off in handcuffs. Above him are the even viler villains of the so-called Colombian cartel, who rake in billions of dollars from the suffering of millions of people. Rapacious, greedy, routinely violent, indifferent to the human toll their transactions exact—Americans have been bombarded by such images of cocaine suppliers.

We have no doubt that some such characters exist at the highest levels of the illicit drug trade and that the crack trade in particular has spawned violence among dealers. Our experience indicates, however, that the cast is far more varied than prevailing images would lead one to believe. Because crack selling began after our research was well under way, we did not have much opportunity to interview large-scale crack distributors from the inner cities on whom recent media caricatures are based.[1] We did interview a number of middle- and working-class people, most of them white, involved in cocaine sales. We emerged from our interviews with a rather less dramatic picture of how cocaine gets distributed across the

United States and by whom. The cocaine sellers we met were not from a different gene pool, not very different from the rest of the users we talked to, who were not very different from ordinary citizens struggling through daily life. If our interviews are any guide, then beneath every big-time dealer who may approximate the stereotype are hundreds of small-time sellers who do not. In large part what we found were people buying from and selling to friends, usually in relatively small quantities, and often for little or no profit.

Those who did sell for profit expressed few moral qualms about it, yet there was a specific "moral economy" (Thompson, 1971) in the cocaine world that constrained commerce. Both sellers and buyers distinguished between "righteous" and "rip-off" dealers; customers generally expected that sellers would not misrepresent the quality or quantity of their product. Most sellers operated according to certain rules; for example, cocaine would not be sold to kids, to individuals who "couldn't handle it," or to those who were having cocaine-related problems. Many sellers we interviewed had "cut off" customers who were "using too much" or who got in trouble with the drug. One 24-year-old white woman quit dealing in part because, "I felt like I was making it too easy for some people. . . . I think they did more than they would have" (Case #569).

While even money-making dealers did not operate solely on the basis of profit maximization, few sellers we spoke to expressed moral qualms about the enterprise in general. This is not altogether surprising, for the idea of making money by purchasing a desired commodity at a low price and selling it at a high price has been a central feature of American culture since at least the nineteenth century. Indeed, as Charles Dickens observed in his *American Notes* (1842), "the love of 'smart dealing'" in America "gilds over many a swindle . . . and enables many a knave to hold his head up with the best" (cited in Coser, 1972, 508).[2] Moreover, the historical context our subjects inhabited was the post-Watergate world of the Iran-Contra scandal, the junk bond and merger mania fiascos, the exposure of massive bribery in President Reagan's Department of Housing and Urban Development, and the high levels of corruption involved in the savings and loan scandal. In such a world the mere selling of a desired drug might well seem to those involved a pale transgression. That the government had seen fit to criminalize some commodities such as cocaine and not others such as tobacco and alcohol was seen as pure politics, so the law had no great moral legitimacy for these dealers.

In this chapter we will describe what we learned about cocaine sellers and sales. One reason is to show that cocaine sellers in their natural settings appear rather different from media images. It is also useful to illustrate different types and styles of dealing to flesh out our picture of heavy cocaine use and to give readers a sense of the circles in which our subjects moved. Of most importance is what the cocaine sellers among our respondents can tell us about cocaine use—specifically, how unlimited access to relatively cheap supplies of cocaine affects users.

DRIFTING INTO DEALING

Almost anyone who uses cocaine with any regularity becomes involved in sales or distribution to some degree. Users often sell to defray the costs of their own supplies, to get better quality drugs, or to assist friends and associates in buying higher quality drugs at quantity prices. Distribution can take a variety of forms. Groups of friends or associates may pool funds to buy larger amounts of the drug than any individual might want in order to get lower prices. We heard several accounts of waiters and waitresses in bars and restaurants who each put $10 or $15 into a common fund to buy small quantities to be shared. The member who had a good connection made the buy as a favor for the group and more often than not took no profit. The same thing went on in very different circles. A woman executive in a large Silicon Valley company, for example, bought two or three ounces every few months, which she distributed to her friends at cost with no idea of making any profit. She did not even consider herself a seller; she was simply using her connection to assist her friends in getting better quality cocaine at a lower price. She had done this for three years when we interviewed her.

A number of individuals regularly bought and sold cocaine simply for their own supplies. Many called this "dealing for stash." This type of seller would buy small supplies—a sixteenth or an eighth of an ounce—and sell grams or parts of grams to friends for small profits. By adding $10 or $20 to the cost of a gram or $5 and $10 to parts of grams whenever they sold it, they would cover or subsidize the costs of their own supplies. Over a week or two they might realize $75 or $100 worth of cocaine. Very often they did not attempt to make any more profit than the defrayed cost of their own "stash."

In some instances a series of small transactions for friends at low levels of profit over a protracted period might lead a stash dealer to consider buying larger supplies with the objective of realizing real monetary profits above the cost of his or her own supply. The regular availability of supplies, a network of user friends, a modicum of start-up capital, with perhaps a higher-level dealer willing to "front" or consign are some of the preconditions for becoming a profit-making cocaine dealer. Escalation of their own use also seemed to push some stash dealers toward a more commercial operation. When such conditions fell into place, some users who had been merely dealing for stash seemed to "drift" into dealing. By "drift" we mean, borrowing from David Matza, that these people were "neither compelled nor committed" (1964, 28) to dealing. Nor did most ever decide to abandon law-abiding society or self-consciously adopt deviant values or an outlaw way of life. They seldom set out to become illicit businessmen or women; most simply seemed to fall casually into distributing a drug that they had long been familiar with (for a more detailed account see Murphy, Waldorf, and Reinarman, 1991; cf. Reuter, 1990). In some cases they became retailers to users or low-level sellers; in a few instances they became whole-

salers who sold "weight"—ounces, pounds, and kilograms—
primarily to other sellers.

In the San Francisco Bay area during the period of our
study (1985–87), cocaine sales were generally organized into
seven levels (see Table 5.1).[3]

Before describing the different types of dealers, we must
note some limitations in our data on sales. Initially we did not
ask respondents specific questions about cocaine sales because
we wanted to minimize their anxieties about our research.
Our study was primarily about use and cessation. Good rapport with respondents was essential, so we did not want to
raise suspicions that we had another agenda that might be
linked to law enforcement. We also wanted to assure our

TABLE 5.1
Levels of Cocaine Selling

Seller Level	Buying Units	Selling Units
Smugglers and various helpers	Multiple kilograms	Kilograms Pounds Half pounds Multiple ounces
Pound or kilogram dealers	Kilograms or pounds	Pounds Half pounds Multiple ounces
Ounce dealers	Kilogram Pounds Half pounds Multiple ounces	Ounces Part ounces Grams
Part ounce dealers	Ounces Part ounces	Part ounces Grams
Gram dealers	Ounces Part ounces	Grams
Half and quarter gram dealers	Quarter ounces Eighth ounces	Half grams Quarter grams
Street crack dealers	Quarter ounces Eighth ounces	Small units of crack

interviewers that they would not be put at risk by asking about the criminal activities of sellers who might be fearful if they believed they were being investigated. On the other hand, if respondents themselves brought up the topic of selling and seemed comfortable talking about it, we gave interviewers the latitude to ask about it further. In many instances respondents (usually quitters) were quite candid about their drug sales. Whenever someone was reluctant we avoided the subject completely. This strategy helped ensure both interviewer safety and good rapport. But it also means that our data on the incidence of cocaine sales among our respondents is not systematic, although it is clearly no less so than data on, say, dealers who are arrested.[4]

Despite these limitations we learned a good deal about selling. For a sizable percentage of our sample cocaine sales were seen as a good strategy to offset the costs of their own cocaine use. In most instances these users sold only small amounts to a limited clientele—grams or parts of grams to close friends or associates. We also had a few respondents who dealt in large amounts and managed to make considerable sums of money through these transactions. To illustrate the structure of cocaine sales we will describe briefly some sellers at each level of the hierarchy, starting at the top.

SMUGGLERS

Smugglers buy large quantities (multiple kilograms) from foreign suppliers, smuggle them into the United States, and sell kilograms, pounds, half pounds, and multiple ounces. We interviewed only two persons who fell into this category; both were runners. One runner, who carried cocaine smuggled from Colombia to various U.S. locations, decided to retire when things started to go wrong. This ex-runner, whom we have named Ralph, was not particularly comfortable talking about his selling activities and did not speak at length about them, but he did tell us how he got started and how he stopped selling cocaine.

RESPONDENT: In '82 we moved out here and I met this fellow from Colombia in a training class for work. We became fast friends and within a few months we were snorting a little bit of coke together, and we got involved with sort of a dealing partnership. That extended through '83 and we both were doing quite a large volume. He initially got me involved per se in the family I dealt with, a Colombian family, and I went to Miami several times.

INTERVIEWER: How much would you make?

RESPONDENT: Two or three thousand dollars a week.

INTERVIEWER: And how would you carry it?

RESPONDENT: In a suitcase.

INTERVIEWER: So just in a suitcase from Miami to here?

RESPONDENT: Well, wherever they wanted it. . . . I would go to Miami and New York, Boston, Chicago.

INTERVIEWER: Ever take any to Canada?

RESPONDENT: No, never crossed any borders with it. I wouldn't do that.

INTERVIEWER: Ever get paranoid about it?

RESPONDENT: No, I know how to wrap it so it's virtually undetectable. I always had complete confidence in my ability to deal with a situation like that. One time I got ripped off for some of the cash on one trip.

INTERVIEWER: So what did you do? Give them the money to stay alive?

RESPONDENT: I didn't have any choice about it. I was ripped off from the luggage by the airlines; and it was almost a quarter of a million dollars. At first they thought I had something to do with it . . . but my friend stuck up for me and . . .

INTERVIEWER: And they just wrote it [the loss] off?

RESPONDENT: Yeah, they just wrote it off.

INTERVIEWER: So how much would you carry at a time?

RESPONDENT: Four or five kilos. Six kilos sometimes; that was the most, I guess.

INTERVIEWER: So you saw a lot of it?

RESPONDENT: I used to occasionally sell a kilo and sometimes would even sell ounces, quarter pounds, or half pounds. I was making a lot of money and living a good ol' life: driving around in limousines, beautiful women, $125 bottles of champagne. I could go through ounces in a day and it got to be just out of hand. The people around me were getting paranoid because they were doing too much. It became a very unstable and unhappy situation. Then my friend got killed and I got ripped off for a serious amount of cocaine, and I decided to just get out of it. I said the hell with it. It wasn't worth risking my life and it wasn't worth my friend's life. He was dead and there was no reason to wait until I was dead too. . . . My friend got shot, murdered, and I got ripped off badly. I quit the whole scene and I just dropped out of sight from the Colombian family that I was doing business with. They were under a lot of heat from their home country and a lot of heat from this country. I was just tired and fed up, discouraged, and broke. (Case #433)

This career trajectory appeared typical of many dealers, especially those at the upper levels whose lives were fully immersed in a high-stakes, high-rolling scene in which cocaine supplies were plentiful. Access to low- or no-cost cocaine could become a use problem for any seller; at the highest levels, dealers could hardly use enough to affect their profits seriously. As Ralph put it, his use just got "out of hand." Ralph's case also led us to suspect that when dealing becomes one's full-time job, one is less apt to be constrained by conventional roles and responsibilities, and thus less apt to be a controlled user.

POUND OR KILOGRAM DEALERS

Pound or kilogram dealers usually buy in multiple pounds or kilograms and sell pounds, half pounds, and multiple ounces.

Four of our respondents fell into this category, but only three of them would talk about it in any detail. One was 45-year-old restaurant manager, Edie, who had sold cocaine with her husband, Steve, as a team. Steve and Edie began selling cocaine as a spin-off of their long-time marijuana business. For the first six months, they traded marijuana for ounces and parts of ounces of cocaine, and sold grams and eighths of ounces to their marijuana buyers. At that point they met a new customer who had particularly good contacts with a wide network of cocaine users, and they increased their level of sales to ounces. The quality of their cocaine was said to be good (Edie estimated it to be 85 percent pure) and they had no difficulty selling the drug. After another eight months of steady ounce sales they started to buy kilograms and sold on average one and one-half kilograms a week for four years.

When they began to sell cocaine, law-enforcement crack-downs were changing the marijuana market and the couple welcomed a new product. Edie explained:

> Weed was becoming harder to find in large quantities, was more expensive, and it was bulky. The economics of doing a smaller, less bulky more rewarding product like cocaine had a certain financial appeal to the mercantile mentality. . . . The profit margin was much higher [for cocaine], while the margin of profit was steadily declining for marijuana.

Their suppliers were a group of unusually well-organized Colombian smugglers who had strict operating rules. All transactions were on a cash basis only; customers could not be "fronted" cocaine or defer payment. They set strict prices for the various units of sales and expected these to be maintained to avoid squabbles between dealers who might go to each other for emergency supplies. They also regulated the amounts that their customers could sell. Dealers in the network were expected to work full-time as sellers and not to engage in other illegal or legal occupations. Edie thought that the purpose of this rule was to maintain a steady sales volume by ensuring that dealers did not treat drug sales as a part-time, casual activity they could retire from if they felt some pressure from police or family. Money and lawyers were provided to sellers in the network who were threatened with arrest. One member of the group was given a long vacation to the South Pacific when he was being investigated by the U.S. Drug Enforcement Agency.

Women were excluded from the network, but our couple circumvented this rule. Apparently Steve had an abrasive personality and could not maintain good relations with their customers, so they developed a rather strict division of labor. He conducted all the transactions with the supplier and collected most of the monies. Edie weighed and packaged all the sales units and delivered them to a small group of dependable, long-term customers. She was particularly skilled at maintaining relationships and "cooling out" her husband. They usually bought one and one-half or two kilograms a week and sold them in five or six transactions. A half kilogram was sent to Chicago every week to be sold by an old friend of Steve's, and the rest was sold in ounces or multiple ounces in the San Francisco Bay area.

Their style was generally low-key, and they did not encounter violence or threats of violence. They sold only to a small group of persons they had known for a long time. New customers were accepted only after they were vouched for by an old, trusted customer. Initially, they sold small units to buyers who came to their home. Edie explained some of the problems entailed in this type of selling.

RESPONDENT: We were picking up ounces and breaking them down and selling them in quarter ounces, eighths of ounces, or grams. Grams quickly became a pain in the ass. You don't know how many people will call you up at three in the morning wanting a quarter of a gram; some even expect you to deliver it!

INTERVIEWER: So they make a lot of demands on you too?

RESPONDENT: And screaming everything under the sun on the telephone.

INTERVIEWER: So they were quite outrageous. How did you calm that stuff down?

RESPONDENT: Simply refusing to cooperate and not selling them anything. I required that people make appointments, not speak about cocaine over the telephone. And setting business hours. (Case #436)

They changed these arrangements when they began to sell larger amounts known as "weight." At that point they allowed no one to come to their home but rather delivered the drugs on a weekly basis. On some occasions they would front drugs (for deferred payment), but this was not a regular practice. In the five years they sold cocaine they had only one scare: a customer of Steve's informed the police of their activities and their house was raided. Edie was only charged with possession of marijuana because the police did not find the cocaine (it was hidden in a bag of dog food that the police felt but did not pour out). She pleaded guilty to possession of marijuana and was placed in a diversion program. Shortly thereafter, they moved to a new neighborhood and continued dealing. They broke contact with the person they suspected had informed on them. Two years later they moved a second time when they began to suspect that the police might be observing them. When they decided to stop selling cocaine they were required by the smuggler to pass on their customer network to one long-standing customer trusted by the suppliers.

Steve and Edie made good money selling cocaine, but they did not become rich. When they decided to stop selling they each had about $30,000, which was invested in the stock market. There were telling differences between the two, however. Steve was a full-time coke dealer who did little else and enjoyed being a "high roller." He was also a very heavy binger who used large amounts every week. Eventually, his cocaine use led to mental and physical health problems that interfered with both his business and their relationship. On the other hand, while she was dealing, Edie worked successfully at her regular job and cared for her three children. Her use of cocaine remained moderate throughout her dealing career, and she never experienced cocaine-related problems.

OUNCE DEALERS

As Adler (1985) notes, some ounce dealers cut their supply by mixing it with a nondrug substance and some do not. The former tend to operate on restricted capital and try to maximize short-term profit. The latter are persons who have larger capital reserves and operate with long-term goals. They generally believe that by selling uncut or reasonably high-quality drugs they can maintain a good profit for long periods.

A dealer couple who tended to cut their cocaine told us that they bought and sold a kilogram a week for four years. Their arrangement was different from Steve's and Edie's, who dealt in parts of kilograms. The other couple did not have enough capital to buy a kilogram so were generally fronted part of the kilogram by their supplier every week. They sold ounces only for cash to seven customers.

> At our peak we were up to a kilo a week, which is 2.2 pounds. The people we sold it to were rarely fronted; it was mainly cash and carry. We were usually being fronted for part of the amount that we got; for example, giving them money for a pound and paying for the second pound when we sold it. (Case #520)

This couple claimed to have strict rules against selling the drug to heroin users, those who injected cocaine, and freebasers. These rules caused them to lose some customers as several moved from snorting to freebasing. The reasons for these restrictions were that freebasers "were too much hassle, because they acted like heroin addicts. They were too dependent on the drug and they often couldn't keep themselves together. They would bring heat on themselves because they were so loaded and . . . desperate for the drug" (Case #520).

Another cut-ounce dealer whom we will call Janis had a

somewhat different style of dealing. She began selling even before she used cocaine regularly, which is very unusual, and continued for three years. Our interviewer asked how she got started.

RESPONDENT: Um, what happened was I went to a couple of friends of mine's house and they were gonna buy an eighth [of an ounce] of cocaine from this guy. I told them, let me get it for you, I know I can get it cheaper because I knew the guy kinda liked me. Prior to that I only used it a few times. So I go up there, I get it cheaper, and as it ends up the guy starts fronting me stuff and I start doing a lot of work for him. And when I was somewhere with him making a buy of a half ounce of coke I knew the guys that were selling it to us from prior relations with my brothers, so um, when Alfredo left the room, that's the guy I went with, . . . they told me that I could get it straight from them, so they started fronting me half ounces. And then it went on from there until I was . . . I never had to, um, pay for anything up front but I turned [sold, over the course of her selling career] two kilos of cocaine, at least twenty-four different pounds and at least fifty quarter pounds, and ounces every day.

We considered her a cut-ounce dealer because she diluted her supplies regularly.

INTERVIEWER: You would put some stuff in it?

RESPONDENT: Yeah, lactose.

INTERVIEWER: You would put a gram in a quarter [ounce]?

RESPONDENT: In a quarter [ounce], shoot, when we had ounces we didn't put any in it at Christmastime. It was like little Christmas presents for all the customers.

She generally sold ounces and portions of ounces, but on some occasions she sold pounds and kilos.

INTERVIEWER: What did you usually buy, what size?

RESPONDENT: In the beginning, a quarter ounce, fronted.

INTERVIEWER: And then you began getting into it more and more heavily?

RESPONDENT: And I would at least have a quarter pound on me all the time.

INTERVIEWER: When you started getting heavy?

RESPONDENT: Right, there would be at least a quarter pound in my trunk. Until I got, well [ripped off], I had a half pound in the trunk and I . . . sold one ounce and I got seven ounces ripped off. So that's when I decided to quit for sure, I have to get out of this business.

INTERVIEWER: How much was that worth?

RESPONDENT: Two thousand apiece, fourteen grand, I paid for half of it. And then they gave me their price on the rest; they gave it to me for seventeen [hundred] apiece and I worked it off.

INTERVIEWER: So did you usually sell large amounts, quarters, at the beginning, in the middle, both periods?

RESPONDENT: The middle, ounces.

INTERVIEWER: Ounces, you were an ounce dealer? But in the beginning you just started selling quarter ounces?

RESPONDENT: An eighth, never really any half grams or anything that small, never. Maybe if, you know, a good friend bugged me I would give them . . . like when I would cut out that gram, maybe I would sell half, you know. . . . I turned quarter ounces once in a while. I didn't really have any clientele after I quit doing heavy things. After I got busted I didn't do things for a while and I lost a lot of clientele. I tried a half ounce just for personal use, and I was trying to clean myself off it because I knew I was going away and I wanted to change my life style and I figured it was a good time.

We asked her what a typical day was like while she was using and selling drugs.

RESPONDENT: Get up around eleven, go out to a real expensive breakfast, you know, brunches, all the time, [because] that would be the only meal we would have. Then I would usually wait about twenty minutes because if I did a line right afterwards it would seem like it [the meal] wouldn't digest properly. I was a vegetarian at that time, too. I was a health nut going to nutritionists and stuff and trying to balance everything out. But, um, I would do a line but it would be little lines consistently through the day without really getting real high at any time. You know, not any real ropes [large lines].

INTERVIEWER: Just keeping it going all day with little ones? Then at night?

RESPONDENT: Usually I would quit at midnight. I always went to sleep. (Case #101)

In our typology of users, Janis would be considered a nipper, or someone who uses small amounts every day and does not indulge in heavy binges. Her concerns about her physical health while she was using cocaine seemed to pay off because she was in good health when we interviewed her. Despite the availability of essentially free cocaine for personal use, her health-conscious values and her plans to finish college and go on to law school seemed to help her maintain a moderate use pattern.

We should note that Janis's initial involvement in sales was most unusual. In effect she used her sex appeal and attractiveness to get initial supplies of cocaine even before she began to use regularly herself. She knew potential buyers from her group of friends, her only other asset for selling cocaine at that time. For most large suppliers these assets would not be enough to warrant the kind of trust involved in selling cocaine.

Part Ounce Dealers

At this level individuals buy ounces or parts of ounces and sell parts of ounces. For example, they may buy an ounce or a half ounce and sell quarters or eighths. Our best description of a part ounce dealer is Patty. At the time of the interview she was a 36-year-old economist with two adolescent daughters to whom she was devoted. Patty began to sell cocaine after her separation from her husband because she needed the money. She had sold cocaine with her husband four years earlier, but he took over that business when she had her first child. At her separation she was saddled with her husband's drug debt to his supplier, overdue credit card accounts, car payments, and the mortgage on their modest house. She worked regularly at the time but did not earn nearly enough to meet her debts and take care of her kids. At that point Patty asked her connection to front her cocaine so she could get back in the business.

RESPONDENT: So I decide that I'm gonna deal, right, so I go to Farley and say, "I'll pay you back the two grand if you start fronting me. I'll pay you within two or three months what Tom owed you." So I start dealing myself.

INTERVIEWER: What level were you selling at?

RESPONDENT: I had two people selling eighths of an ounce every two days so I had these deliveries I was making.

INTERVIEWER: So you were fronting them?

RESPONDENT: Yeah, I'd front them and they would go sell the drugs. So I had those guys so they were good for an ounce a week between the two of them, and then I was selling another ounce a week myself. That period of time I was selling quite a bit of cocaine.

INTERVIEWER: So you had car payments, house payments, and all the debts?

RESPONDENT: Plus Mastercharge and Visa debts, so I had about $10,000 worth of debt to clear up, which I did in about six or seven months' time. I didn't use very much so I was making a lot of money. . . . I went pretty nuts [using] that first year and then I got my shit together and realized I was going to be a single parent. . . . So I cooled it, cut back a lot, but kept dealing. Farley wasn't upset because I was making good money for him.

INTERVIEWER: So he was leaning on you?

RESPONDENT: He wanted me to deal more, you know, and he kept on tossing me customers and stuff. Plus he was fronting me and charging me the front; he would charge me like $100 per ounce more than the cash price. Which means if I was doing two or three ounces in a week, which I was during that time, he is making $300 more than he's making with anybody else. (Case #437)

We were struck by how poorly Patty fit the stereotype of a cocaine dealer. She is conscientious at her "straight" job, a responsible and loving parent, and an active community member. At one point during her cocaine-selling career she was a Girl Scout leader; she regularly took her children and their troop on camping trips, sold candy and cookies, and engaged in all the other all-american activities of the Girl Scouts. At the same time she regularly gave guest lectures to students at her children's schools. Within her own large, extended family she remained a hub of activity throughout her dealing years. How can these sides of Patty be reconciled with her involvement in cocaine sales? Interestingly, she did not seem to feel that any reconciliation or moral rationalization was necessary. She sold cocaine for a period in her life because she *could*—she knew both users and sellers—and because she *needed to,* for she could not sustain her family on her legal earnings alone.

GRAM DEALERS

Gram dealers were the most ubiquitous in our group of sellers. In general, they bought quarters and eights of ounces (known as eightballs) and sold grams and multiple grams. Most worked out of their homes or places of work, selling cocaine to pay for their own stash and realizing only small profits. Others, like Hillary, took a more businesslike approach. Her first husband had sold cocaine and other drugs for several years, so she knew a large number of users and a few people who had regular supplies. Like Patty, she began to sell drugs to supplement her small income because her ex-husband did not contribute any money to support her son.

> RESPONDENT: I realized that I had to start selling coke in order to make enough money to support me and my son. I was working regularly, but it did not pay very much and I had contacts with both users and a few people who had good coke. I of course used it, but never let it get out of hand. I sold coke for the money and was not going to let my own use deter what little I made.
>
> INTERVIEWER: How much would you sell in a week?
>
> RESPONDENT: I bought a quarter [ounce] a week.
>
> INTERVIEWER: And how much money would you make?
>
> RESPONDENT: I always allowed myself like half a gram and that was what I would keep for myself. . . . I didn't make a whole bunch of money off it, like $150 a week.
>
> INTERVIEWER: How many customers on average would you have?
>
> RESPONDENT: Probably eight or ten rotating . . . maybe even as many as twelve, but some of these people only came once a month or once every few months and some came every week.

Hillary continued to sell at that level for two years and then stopped selling for approximately five months when she got married a second time. When she was first dating her husband-to-be she continued to sell, but, as with many sellers, the constant availability of inexpensive cocaine led both of them to snort up most of their profits. She was married in September and became pregnant with her second child in January. Interestingly, her pregnancy functioned as an anchor against cocaine use so that she could safely resume selling to save money for a down payment on a larger house.

> I was pregnant and I couldn't do any drugs so I figured this was a perfect opportunity. So I told Paul I wanted to start selling coke again and he really did not want me to. I said there is a way and

I'm going to do it. I did the same thing that I did before: I bought a quarter [ounce] a week and I put $200 cash a week into a special account, and I saved $6,000 in nine months by keeping the coke in the trunk of my car. I only had one set of keys and if anybody wanted any they had to locate me. Paul couldn't have any and he just didn't have any. . . . In nine months' time I gave him only a half a gram, never used myself, and saved money for our down payment. (Case #504)

Hillary enjoyed the cocaine high, but always had her priorities. She would use it only if she was not pregnant and did not have to pay for it. But when the cost of using came out of her pocket or her selling stash she would forgo her short-term pleasure for long-term goals—enough money to take care of her child and make a down payment on a house. Her home and family commitments constrained her use so she could remain a successful seller.

Because of the referral chains we tapped, we interviewed only a few gram dealers who worked the streets. However, one of our interviewers was a Latino "homeboy" who lived in San Francisco's Mission District, and he located five street dealers who operated out of two parks. Most of them were reluctant to talk about their cocaine sales and the interviewer did not press the issue. Most of these youths lived with their parents and conducted their sales activities in the streets. They often would attempt to sell to strangers despite the fact that narcotics agents were active in the area. In general, their lack of private space meant that they were less careful than their counterpart gram dealers who were older and mostly middle-class. They also tended to cut their cocaine more than other dealers because their own weekend binges reduced their profit margins.

PART-GRAM AND STREET CRACK DEALERS

We were unable to interview many half- and quarter-gram dealers. Most members of this group are street and bar dealers, adolescents, or new users of cocaine. We did not interview minors for the study and our respondents had to be heavy users of cocaine with at least six months of heavy use or one year of daily use. Persons who sell parts of grams usually do so in return for cocaine for personal use and are generally known as stash dealers. Profits at this level are usually quite small, $5 or $10 a sale, and it is usually not worth a person's time or effort to sell these amounts if he or she has any profit motive. Bar dealers usually operate out of selected bars primarily for on-premises consumption. According to our respondents, user lore has it that "bar grams" bought in such establishments are called "Fred Astaire and Ginger Rogers grams" because they are "stepped on" [cut] so often it is as if they had been "danced on." Sophisticated cocaine users avoid such purchases because they assume they will get very low-quality cocaine.

As we mentioned earlier, at the time of our study crack cocaine was not marketed to any significant extent in the San Francisco area; it was just beginning to be sold in New York City, Miami, and Los Angeles. It was available in some San Francisco neighborhoods during the latter part of our study, but we located only two people who had purchased crack from street dealers. One was a regular street buyer, but the second said that he bought from street dealers only when he did not have the money to purchase larger amounts of powder that he would process into crack himself. We did not interview any crack dealers for this study.

MOTIVATIONS FOR SELLING

These illustrative cases clearly suggest that our respondents' reasons for selling cocaine were neither simple nor solely mercenary. As we noted at the outset, some users sell primarily to pay for their own supplies and are usually gram dealers or half or quarter gram dealers. Some end up selling only for stash because they are sloppy or incompetent sellers—those who use too much of their product, cannot keep enough customers, do not know how to price their product properly, give away too many sample snorts, front cocaine to customers but fail to collect, or owe too much money to connections who have fronted them. Many others sell for stash simply because they do not want the hassles or risks entailed in selling larger amounts, or because they do not wish to be considered drug sellers. Stash dealers tend to see themselves as providing the ongoing favor of selling small supplies to close friends.

A number of our respondents who sold cocaine began doing so just for stash, but learned rather quickly that drug sales can be lucrative. Initially, they would buy for their own or their friends' supplies and sell at cost or at a nominal markup. If these buyers had a number of friends who regularly seek the drug, then they might slowly drift into profit-oriented selling after recognizing that they had resources other people wanted. Others undertook drug sales as a money-making venture from the beginning, as did Patty. Her motives were not complicated; she sold the drug for the modest profits she needed to support her family, although she did enjoy having some to use, too.

Other motives for selling cocaine have to do with sociability, prestige, and social standing. During her first selling episode Hillary found herself newly separated from her husband, with little money and a small child to support. Extra income aside, however, she had few friends and could not afford to go out; she stayed home a good deal and welcomed the visits of friends whom she might not have seen had they not stopped by her house to buy drugs. Other small-time sellers said much the same thing. Persons who were shy or lacked friends often found that they were sought out for their drug connections, and they enjoyed the sociability. To be sure, some sellers discovered that there are limits to such friendships. Those who sold drugs in part for the social contacts often began to feel that some "friends" only associated with them for their access to drugs.

Prestige and social status were also motives for selling. In general, cocaine is expensive, short-lived, and both legally and pharmacologically risky. Media reports of the ruin and redemption of Hollywood celebrities, rock stars, and wealthy Wall Streeters glamorized it. Erickson and her colleagues heard users speak of the "thrill of just knowing I was doing coke." For some users, they concluded, "Coke is status" (1987, 79). A 29-year-old white female freebaser told us much the same thing and helped explain the drug's appeal to people who have little status.

> Cocaine is really powerful. When I first started listening to people talk about cocaine, they would always call it the rich man's drug. You know, we're not rich, but when we have coke, we kind of feel, "Hey, we're rich!" . . . Maybe it's their egos, you know, they don't really have anything, and yet if they have coke people would say, "Yeah, they've got coke, they've got things." (Case #615)

If cocaine offered status to some users, this attraction was even stronger for many suppliers. This status and prestige seemed more important for men than for women. Some of our first interviews were with women sellers who were very organized and systematic. They had very specific, short-term monetary goals; regularly weighed and prepackaged their products; had strict rules about how and to whom they sold; and were discreet about the fact that they were dealers. Not even women who dealt on a large scale adopted the demeanor of persons for whom dealing was a way to garner prestige or status.

Men more frequently had grandiose goals and were less careful with their supplies. Far more than women sellers, men tended to play the high roller by laying out lines at parties and other social gatherings. Sometimes this was merely an aid to seduction, as for the marijuana seller quoted in Chapter 3. But more generally male sellers at social gatherings often displayed conspicuous affluence and cool daring by placing eighth or quarter ounces out on the coffee table for all to partake. If the party was large and not everyone knew each other, then male sellers sometimes took friends into bathrooms and other private places for small or large "toots."

During subsequent interviews we came to believe that these gender differences were not universal or rigid. We discovered that some male sellers had a more rational, less showy style; we also got accounts from female sellers who took friends into the bathroom for toots, albeit with less flare and more discretion. Men dealers tended to use dealing as a means of status more than women, but some of this had to do with personal styles. And there were exceptions like Janis, the ounce dealer described earlier: "Yeah, well I gave a lot away, I was Mrs. Santa Claus every place I went, every place I went. One time I took a half ounce to a party and set it on the table and told everybody to go ahead. Would you believe a 'baser' stole it?! . . . isn't that lame?"

There are at least two reasons why women sellers, even highly competent ones, tended to be "cool" and to avoid displaying dealer identities. First, women would be more vulnerable to rip-offs and violence than males if their dealing became widely known, so their low-key style would certainly be prudent. Second, women in general are far less apt to seek prestige or social standing by taking on outlaw styles. Historically, women have tended to be more law-abiding than men. In patriarchal cultures, it is not good gender form for females to play the big-time drug dealer role that some men play with regularity and relish. Perhaps the new freedoms brought by the women's movement that have opened up licit opportunities also have allowed women more illicit opportunities. If so, they may be more apt to play these rogue roles in the future. But there may be more to women's dealing than feminist ideals, for the feminization of poverty and the rise in the number of female-headed households like those of Patty and Hillary surely provide financial incentives for women to enter the cocaine-selling branch of the underground economy.[5]

By discussing prestige, profits, stash, and status, we do not wish to oversimplify a complex phenomenon. There were many motives for selling, and most of our respondents who became involved in some level of sales had more than one reason for doing so. In contrast to common stereotypes, few of the dealers we interviewed were in it solely for the riches or just to feed their own habits. In capitalist cultures, commerce—even criminalized commerce—can offer identities as well as incomes, sociability and status as well as stash. In Eastern Europe, a Russian or Pole who could get great vodka at a good price without standing in line all day would be a prized friend. So, too, in the drug-using circles of the United States, part of the allure of coke dealing had to do with being able to provide one's friends with a desired commodity.

OCCUPATIONAL HAZARDS

Cocaine sellers mentioned a variety of problems that result from dealing, few of which had to do directly with law-enforcement pressures. Many gram and ounce dealers found that the large numbers of people coming to their homes to buy small supplies disrupted their family and work routines. Many buyers behaved as if sellers should be available at any time of the day or night. Very often the visiting customer would want to stay and use with the seller, sometimes even expecting to be "turned on" to a few lines from the dealer's stash. Some customers were eager to use cocaine, so they broke open their purchase, chopped up some lines, and snorted then and there. Regardless of whose supplies were used, this sort of social snorting with customers led many sellers to escalate their own drug use. Even dealers who initially enjoyed the sociability of using with the customer often came to resent the expectation that their time, home, and consciousness were available with every purchase.

Customers also tended to call and visit at unusual times of the day or night, infringing upon the seller's privacy and leisure. Most sellers got around this problem by being available for purchases only at certain times; for example, between 6:00 and 8:00 P.M., or on certain days. Phone calls were often controlled by using answering machines to screen calls.

When many regular customers make many short stops over long time periods, neighbors may come to suspect what the continual traffic is about. A couple who sold pounds and kilograms from their home found a notice attached to a tree near their house one day: "Notice: All drivers of cars that are parked here for the purpose of buying drugs should know that we will be taking license plate numbers and reporting them to the police." The dealers moved out of the house the next day when they realized they had been discovered. They were much more careful about regulating traffic at their next house.

A second respondent who was an ounce dealer got a similar but less contentious response from a neighbor when a customer parked his car in front of the neighbor's house one time too often. The neighbor told the seller, "We know what you are doing, don't think we don't. Now, we don't care, but we can't have people always using our parking place. It has got to stop now." To make matters worse, the dealer knew that her neighbor's husband was a policeman in a nearby suburb. The dealer could not move because she owned the house, so she made sure her neighbor's parking place remained empty and cut back on sales activities.

Many sellers deal with the problems of traffic by not allowing customers to come to their homes, instead delivering drugs directly to the customers. Large sellers used this technique more than gram sellers because they made fewer sales and because the risks of arrest, should someone be watching their homes, were greater. One respondent told of a gram seller who also used this technique. He dubbed her "Jenny Appleseed" because she ran around town depositing packets of cocaine.

> She would come right to your door but usually an hour or two late. . . . She looked like a hippie woman and carried a backpack with a big hair spray or deodorant can in it. She unscrewed the

bottom of the can and kept her stash—an ounce or half ounce—in there. She had a suitcase in the back of her car with a scale in it, so if you wanted weight she would do that. (Case #439)

Certain kinds of customers can also cause problems for sellers. Many sellers consider freebasers or crack users and persons who are having difficulties with their drug use to be problematic. "Crackheads" and "basers" are often thought to act like "dope fiends"—more committed, compulsive users who "draw more heat" or attention from the police. Sellers who do not freebase or use crack themselves are particularly vociferous about freebasers and claim to "cut off" customers when they begin to smoke instead of snort.

These dealers also differed from popular stereotypes in their concerns about customers' problems with cocaine. When friends or people they liked began to have physical, financial, or emotional problems because of their cocaine use, many sellers expressed concern for the individual and sometimes even withheld supplies. One who sold grams to an old and cherished friend "half consciously missed appointments" with him—in effect, withheld the drug—when she realized that he was buying too frequently, using too much, and having trouble regulating his use. Another ounce dealer told us that he stopped selling and even using cocaine because he saw too many of his friends get in trouble with it. He did not want to be personally responsible for their difficulties.

One of the most obvious occupational hazards reported by sellers was the paranoia some users experience. Whenever sellers noted that customers were getting "too paranoid," they became concerned not only for the customer but for their own safety. Paranoid coke users were considered unpredictable and even potentially violent, so sellers became very cautious whenever they observed signs of such cocaine-related psychological problems.

"Rip-offs" (thefts) and violence were also regular concerns, although the sellers we spoke to never experienced anything like the gang warfare and Uzi submachine guns that figure

prominently in media and police reports. A few violent episodes did occur, particularly at higher levels of sales, but they
were not prevalent among our seller respondents. Sellers successfully minimize such risks most of the time by restricting
sales to close friends and associates. However, a seller who is
too ambitious or greedy might take on unknown customers
who may steal supplies, inform police, or even cause bodily
harm.

Our respondents reported a few such episodes that occurred as a result of incautiousness. One woman ounce dealer
reported that she had been held up at gunpoint three times
before she retired. She suspected that one of her regular customers arranged to have her ripped off. A kilo dealer was
ripped off by four men masquerading as police officers. They
held him, his wife, and two children at gunpoint while they
searched the house and took two pounds of cocaine and
$32,000. He never discovered who was behind the holdup.
Another rather ambitious kilo dealer who made deliveries to
rough, working-class, high–drug use neighborhoods in Oakland had an associate riding shotgun to protect him from
holdups.

"If You've Got It, You'll Use It"

The most frequently mentioned occupational hazard is also
relevant to the rest of this book: the sellers' escalation of their
own cocaine use. Cocaine sellers, especially those above the
stash level who are dealing for profit, have to maintain a
constant supply to keep their customers happy and their cash
flow healthy. This means that sellers are in a unique position
as users. Unlike other users, they have cocaine available to
them almost all the time, and at wholesale prices. Those who
cut their product could often snort for free. Given the reinforcing qualities of the high and the tendency to find more and
more uses for cocaine, this presents a clear risk of escalation
and abuse. Most sellers we interviewed mentioned this risk

and agreed that too much use was likely to be as bad for one's business as it is for one's body.

Some managed such risks successfully; for example, by prepackaging all their inventory so that they would have to open up a packaged gram for their own use. One dealer made it a rule never to use from his own supply. When he wanted some cocaine for personal use, he would go to another dealer and pay full retail price. Both these self-imposed strategies discouraged excessive consumption. Moreover, sellers who were in the business not because they wanted more and better drugs at a lower price for their own use, but primarily because they needed the money, were often able to limit their use to maintain profits. A few hardly used the drug at all.[6]

Most sellers we spoke with, however, agreed that having constant cheap supplies on hand maintained the danger that they would consume their profits and develop cocaine-related problems. Several people we interviewed did just that. Among sellers it was easier for a few snorts to become binges, and easy to slip into using more cocaine to recover from such binges. They seemed to know that this was a recipe for commercial and personal disaster if it happened too often. Customers who would expect a free sample snort or who would open up their purchase and use some in the dealer's home only added to the tendency for sellers to increase their use. For all these reasons, the career cycle from use to escalation to abuse to problems was accelerated for some sellers. In fact, as we will show in later chapters, some dealers simply had to stop selling altogether as part of the process of cessation; they were using more and more cocaine and having less and less fun, so they had to put it out of reach. Yet selling made it difficult to give up using, and the money made it difficult for some to give up selling. Patty, who dealt in grams largely because she needed extra income to support her children, observed that she "never got hooked on the coke," but she did "get hooked on the money."

What differentiated those sellers who were able to control their own use from others who were not? As we will show in the next chapter, it is exceptionally difficult to predict which users will maintain control and which will become compulsive. For sellers with abundant supplies, the temptation is omnipresent, yet the outcome was not always abuse. For Ralph, the runner who found himself fully immersed in the limousine life-style of high-level dealing, personal use "got out of hand." For Hillary and Patty, who dealt to supplement their incomes from straight jobs to support families, personal use remained moderate. Even for a couple, Steve and Edie, the same diversity in use emerged. He was a full-time dealer who ended up abusing; she maintained her straight job and had primary responsibility for her three children throughout her dealing career and never let her personal use get out of control. The hypothesis we reached is this: if in the course of selling, cocaine becomes the core preoccupation of both work and leisure, then escalation to abuse is likely, as are business problems; but if cocaine is only one element in a life that is balanced by conventional roles and pursuits, then controlled use and competent dealing are likely.

CHAPTER 6

THE CALL OF THE PIPE:
CRACK USE AND FREEBASING

I only freebased once, and it lasted a month and a half.
—*Case #121*

T*he origins of* crack use lie in freebasing, a mode of cocaine
ingestion that begins with the processing of cocaine hydrochloride (HCL) or powder to extract a purer, more solid form
of cocaine for smoking, which provides a powerful high. Some
researchers say the process spread from the coca-producing
regions of Peru and Bolivia. Since the mid-1970s South American drug researchers have reported people smoking a partially
refined coca paste called *basuco* or mixing this paste with
tobacco or marijuana in the form of cigarettes called *pitillos*
or *papilloes* (Siegel, 1982). This practice reportedly found its
way along smuggling routes to the Caribbean and eventually
into the United States via Florida (Inciardi, 1987).

Others say that U.S. cocaine dealers discovered the process
in the course of testing the purity of powder cocaine by "basing it down," or heating it in a solution of water, ammonia,
and ether to get cocaine base. If, after cuts and impurities had
been removed, the remainder, or the return, was 80 to 85
percent of the original weight, the product was considered
pure. The resulting base crystals could not be snorted or
injected, and dealers did not want to waste them. The long-

standing practice of dipping the ends of cigarettes in cocaine powder gave them the idea of smoking the leftovers from their purity tests (McDonnell, Irwin, and Rosenbaum, 1990). No doubt there are other pieces of this history, and competing accounts may not be mutually exclusive.

If the cocaine HCL is heated in a water solution with ammonia and ether, the results are crystalline flakes of cocaine base that are free of impurities and other residual salts and solids used in processing coca paste; hence the term "free-base" (Siegel, 1982). If cocaine powder is instead "cooked" in a bicarbonate of soda solution, the result is a solid chunk or "rock," which tends to make a crackling sound when burned; hence the term "crack" (Inciardi, 1987). Processing by the bicarbonate of soda method does not purify the drug the same way the ether method does; many impurities remain but the cocaine is still in a form that burns more easily than powder cocaine. In either case the resulting product is heated in a pipe until it vaporizes.[1] These vapors are then inhaled by the user.

The rather fine distinction between freebase and crack is often a confusing one. A long-term snorter and small-time dealer who once experimented with freebase told us that the difference between freebasing and crack use was like "the difference between preparing a gourmet meal and going out to McDonald's." Other respondents agreed. Freebasers usually took pains to prepare their own pure base from relatively large quantities of cocaine powder. It was prepared and used in private homes. The crack that is sold on the street, on the other hand, is typically precooked by dealers in mass quantities in a solution unknown to the user; often cut, prepackaged in smaller units; and frequently smoked in public places.

Freebasing has become almost identical to crack smoking, but this was not always so. In the mid- to late 1970s, when many of our subjects began to employ this mode of ingestion, ammonia and ether were used in the extraction process. Although the ether method yielded a pure base that was said to be a cleaner, somewhat stronger high than that now offered by crack, ether was both troublesome to use and dangerously flammable, as Americans learned when comedian Richard

Pryor experienced near-fatal burns while using the ether method.[2]

By the early 1980s many freebasers, including most of those in our sample, had switched from ether to the simpler, safer method of cooking that used only bicarbonate of soda and water. This baking soda method yields a less pure, yet still solid form of cocaine suitable for smoking, which is virtually the same as what we now know as crack.[3] With the baking soda method now nearly universal, the current differences between freebase and crack inhere only in who makes it and how it is sold. If made by a dealer rather than by the user, crack can contain more adulterants; and retail dealers tend to sell crack in small, inexpensive units often on street corners and out of crack houses. Thus, although most of our respondents who employed this mode of ingestion used the term "freebase," they now agree that what they are smoking is the same as crack. We will therefore use the terms interchangeably.

Although this form of ingestion is referred to as smoking, which it closely resembles, it is really the inhalation of the vapors ("the cloud") rather than any residual smoke that provides the intense "rush" reported by freebasers and crack smokers. The high from "basing" and crack smoking is said to be far more fast-acting and intense than the high from snorting because relatively pure cocaine vapors are absorbed directly into the bloodstream through the vascular bed of the lung rather than powder being absorbed slowly through the nasal membrane. Thus, higher concentrations of cocaine reach the brain all at once in a matter of seconds rather than a little at a time over a longer period.

A sizable albeit unknown proportion of America's cocaine users began freebasing in the late 1970s or early 1980s (Siegel, 1982). Yet the now ubiquitous term "crack" (or, in San Francisco and Los Angeles, "rock," "work," or "hubba") had not then entered the lexicon (Inciardi, 1987). Crack became recognized as a public problem only in spring 1986 when politicians and the mass media jumped on it as if it were an end-zone fumble.

Although then unknown outside of a few neighborhoods in a handful of major cities, crack caught popular attention for two reasons. First, although freebasing had been around for a number of years, by 1985 dealers had begun to sell smaller, cheaper units of this precooked cocaine base on ghetto street corners. They sold to the increasingly impoverished youth of the black and Latino underclass, many of whom soon became involved in these sales as a faster and arguably effective means of moving out of poverty toward the American dream. Thus crack was cast as a great threat in part because it became associated with a class that was already perceived as "dangerous" (Reinarman and Levine, 1989; see also Duster, 1970). In addition to this shift in the class and racial composition of cocaine smokers (e.g., Washton and Gold, 1987), a growing number of clinical reports claimed that, compared to cocaine powder for intranasal use, this form of cocaine was more "instantly addicting" and more devastating in its consequences.

We have devoted a separate chapter to crack users and freebasers for two reasons. First, we felt that our data on freebasing as an early form of crack use among a largely middle- and working-class, predominantly white population might provide an interesting comparison to accounts about crack use among impoverished minorities. Second, crack use and freebasing warrant special attention because our interviews suggest that this method of use tends to become compulsive more often and more rapidly than snorting, and because moderate use seems far more difficult to sustain. Indeed, our freebasers generally agree that while snorting cocaine often can be kept under control, rare is the baser or crackhead who is a controlled user.

THE FREEBASER SUBSAMPLE

The freebasers and crack users described below were identified and interviewed by the same snowball sampling procedures used to generate all the other interviews. Fifty-three of our respondents had regularly used this mode of ingestion. Most had snorted cocaine for years before beginning to "base," and some went back to snorting after they stopped basing. But to be categorized as a freebaser (or crack user),[4] respondents had to have been primarily "smokers" for some substantial portion of the peak period of their cocaine careers. Those who simply experimented with smoking without ever adopting it as their primary mode were not included in this subsample.

To our surprise, the freebasers were in many ways similar to the snorters. Few statistically significant differences were found between them on dozens of different variables. The mean age of both groups was 31. This is noteworthy in that our freebasers are considerably older and are therefore presumably more mature individuals and more experienced drug users than many of the teenagers now exposed to crack. The gender mix was also similar; in both groups, one in five were women. There were no statistically significant differences between smokers and snorters in terms of marital status. Freebasers used slightly higher amounts of cocaine on average, but again this difference was not statistically significant. No significant differences appeared between snorters and basers in terms of criminality. Although the mean number of lifetime convictions was slightly higher for freebasers and crack users, this mean was well below one for both groups. This too seems noteworthy in light of media reporters that crack causes users to commit crime.

Qualitative data from our life-history interviews suggest that basers and crack users tended to experience various cocaine-related problems more rapidly and more profoundly than snorters. However, the two groups reported no statistically significant differences in the number of cocaine-related problems with health, work, sex, or relationships. Basers and crack users reported no greater numbers of attempts to get help for their cocaine problems or to quit. Nor did they seem more immersed in cocaine-using circles than snorters; our

freebase/crack user subsample had no more sources for cocaine, nor more friends who used it.

While our freebasers and crack users were generally similar
to snorters, there were some significant differences. First, freebasers were more often African-American or Latino, perhaps
because crack first appeared in neighborhoods of these two
ethnic groups. In a context of high unemployment and low
opportunity, some residents of such neighborhoods quickly
became involved in crack sales as a profitable new branch of
the underground economy. Moreover, numerous small-time
crack sellers worked street corners and marketed smaller,
cheaper units of the drug, which helped to spread its use. The
somewhat higher proportion of racial minorities in this subsample may also be a peculiarity of our location procedures,
for more than half our African-American basers were interviewed by a veteran baser who moved in those social circles.

In terms of education, basers had somewhat fewer years
of formal education; for example, twice as many basers as
snorters had not finished high school (17 percent vs. 8 percent), and fewer basers had postgraduate or professional
training (11.3 percent vs. 18.4 percent). Similarly, there were
fewer basers than snorters in the high-income, professional-
managerial occupations, and proportionately more basers in
the low-income, low-skill occupations. Of course, these racial, educational, and occupational differences are bound up
with each other, but it seems safe to say that the freebasers and
crack users had somewhat different racial and social class
backgrounds than the rest of our respondents.

Becoming a Baser

Non—drug users probably find it curious that ostensibly "normal" people would even try freebasing or crack. In light of all
the media horror stories, why would sane human beings subject themselves to the increasingly well-known risks? First, we
should note that most of the freebasers in our sample began

using this mode of ingestion before word of the dangers of crack had spread through the user folklore and before all the media attention. Second, and perhaps more important, almost all of our freebasers had been snorting powdered cocaine for some time before they began smoking it in freebase or crack form. Thus, the step to this new mode of ingestion was a small one down a well-worn path rather than a giant one down a road never before taken.

The accounts of how individuals first came to try freebasing varied, but were typically quite mundane: "I was there and they [friends] were cookin' it" was what one respondent said (Case #642). One young woman who eventually spent all her resources freebasing developed serious problems before quitting with the help of treatment. She explained the start of her cocaine smoking in simple subcultural and generational terms: "I'm a product of the late sixties and drugs were an identity and it was part of who we were. So that made me open to it. There was nothing wrong with drugs in my mind" (Case #121). Indeed, she had already been snorting powder cocaine and using other illicit drugs for some years without problems, so to try freebasing for the first time was not a big deal for her. Like many of the others, she described her decision to try freebasing as a nondecision.

Another young man cited several different factors to explain his entry into freebasing: peer associations, a sort of desensitizing momentum in which freebasing becomes less strange with each use, and a touch of what might be called the "forbidden fruit" phenomenon.

INTERVIEWER: If you were going to explain how you got into this, how would you explain it?

RESPONDENT: Just through rationalization and association with others who already convinced themselves that cocaine use is acceptable and that they are able to deal with it and that they are under control. Initially the crowd wasn't bad and the people weren't bad, [although] the longer you stay in it the dirtier it gets. . . . Once you do it once it's easy to do it a second time, and it gets easier to do a third time and then you have a guy doing a bag of it there. . . .

I have always liked the excitement and have always liked to ride the edge a little bit, and it was like . . . we did it because they told us not to. (Case #433)

Another male respondent had used illicit drugs for about a dozen years before he first freebased, including occasional injection of cocaine and methamphetamines. He was dealing and snorting small amounts of cocaine when he met people who showed him how to freebase. He had already used cocaine in a risky, rapid-delivery way, and then simply learned a new technique. A woman told us she first freebased because she was "trying to lose weight" and a girlfriend told her that smoking cocaine would help. She did lose twenty-five pounds in four months, but found she was "smoking it more and more" (Case #633). Yet another female respondent explained, with a "this-is-only-common-sense" shrug, "I heard all about it and I wanted to try it. [I wasn't] really looking for it, but it was just part of the environment; everybody else was doin' it" (Case #636).

Despite the variation in these accounts, we do not think any elaborate explanation of how one specifically becomes a freebaser is necessary. Several of our respondents briefly experimented with crack or freebasing but either knew of or sensed the risks, sometimes categorizing it with intravenous injection as a drug experience to avoid. These people never adopted smoking as their primary mode of cocaine ingestion. Those who did spoke of their first freebasing or crack experiences quite briefly and in rather matter-of-fact language. As with snorters, virtually all learned to do it from friends on ordinary social occasions. It seems relatively easy to drift into this mode of use if one is already initiated into cocaine use. All that is necessary to explain most freebasers' entry into this method is a relatively common desire to achieve what might be called more bang for the buck—given that they were already going after the bang anyway. For example, one of our respondents said that he first freebased when a cousin told him he was "wasting coke" by merely snorting it (Case #627). In short, if it is fair to say that people ingest illicit substances because they enjoy the highs, then their interest in more, different, faster, or "better" highs is not mysterious.

However, one aspect of the process of initiation to freebasing does require comment, and that is "learning the high." Since Becker's classic study, "Becoming a Marijuana User" (1953), researchers have demonstrated that the felt effects or highs offered by various drugs are only partly the products of pharmacology interacting with physiology. In fact, Weil (1972) has argued that, with many drugs, the results of ingestion are ambiguous physiological cues that must be actively interpreted by the user. Much of what a user feels is the product of his or her psychological makeup and expectations (set), and the situational and cultural context (setting) in which the drug use occurs.[5] That is, highs are usually not merely physiological reflexes induced by the pharmacological properties of drugs but are in significant part learned by users in an interpretive process involving both their character and the cultural context.

We expected our respondents to describe such a learning process, and, indeed, in Chapter 2 we reported that many snorters did not get high at first and had to learn to appreciate the subtlety of cocaine. Most freebasers, too, reported that the first time they based or smoked crack they did not feel much of anything (though no one claimed the high was subtle). An experienced and articulate baser told us:

> It took me a while to figure. I was getting extra instruction and it took me, you know, probably a couple of hours to get like the real good hit. . . . I got some tastes of it, but . . . I probably didn't get real good at it 'til maybe five, six sessions. (Case #616)

At first we thought that such reports implied the need for "learning the high" and that users had to learn to experience the extreme central nervous system excitation as a euphoric "rush" (Siegel, 1982). However, after reviewing our respondents' accounts of their initiation we have become convinced that for freebasing and crack use, "learning the high" is less a process of interpreting drug effects than a process of learning the *technique* necessary for getting a "real good hit." By "technique," we mean quite specific knowledge and equipment. Although these techniques vary from user to user, there seemed to be considerable consensus on the basics.

- One must have a "good fire," meaning steady heat at the correct temperature for "making milk" (the water turns white when the cocaine and bicarbonate mix begins to "cook"), so that the base will form into a solid ball—"a good return, a good, hard rock" (Case #616).
- One should not put too large a chunk of the ball into the pipe, for this can be wasteful and impede proper burning: "The trick with base is, if you get it too hot or put too much on, it runs off the screen and down the outside of the pipe. You're just losin' it" (Case #616).
- To get the base to stay inside the pipe so it can be burned, and to be able to draw on the pipe properly, the chunk of base or crack is placed on a screen or screens in the outer flange of the pipe so that when the base begins to melt it will be trapped rather than lost: "The more screens the better" (Case #635).
- Then, when the smoking begins, the "right burn" is essential: "You have to get it [the chunk of base] liquid to get it cookin', you know, to get it burnin' right. But the liquid is hard to control. Burnin' it is really an art, it really is" (Case #616). Depending on setting and user circumstances, propane torches, cigarette lighters, or "literally ten thousand matches" (Case #640) are used to get the "right burn . . . just where it starts to smoke" (Case #635).
- A fine-tuned carburetion is required on the part of the smoker in order not to "miss": "Somehow you either breathe wrong or it doesn't burn as fast. . . . You don't get much smoke or you cough or you can't pull it all in, you run out of air. It's gotta be synced just right, because if you suck in too much you wind up suckin' in kind of hot air. . . . You've gotta keep the flame right and steady . . . and [inhale] at the right speed, too. Pull a little

too fast, they'll fuck it up; they pull a little too slow, they'll miss it" (Case #616). Moreover, the vapors must be inhaled rather than swallowed: "[At first] it made me sick to my stomach. They told me the reason . . . was because I was swallowing the smoke when I inhaled it. I had to learn not to swallow. . . . I got sick for about the first two months. . . . You're supposed to hold it in for a couple of seconds and then blow it out your nose and your mouth, but very slowly" (Case #633).

- This smoking process often involves close coordination between the person operating the flame and the person holding the pipe: "It takes a sort of, you develop almost like an understanding; there's a rapport between the person burning and the person hitting" (Case #616).

Across different user groups there are bound to be variations in such techniques, as well as in style, tools, and personal preferences. There is no central clearinghouse for such illicit information, and few of the details about freebasing procedures have been published in the mass media. Thus, freebasers and crack users are left to their own folk-experimental devices for testing tools or techniques. And, user innovations can get downright creative if the desire to freebase is strong and resources are meager: "Now the really hard-core people, they don't want to do nothin' except get the rock and smoke it. They don't even use pipes anymore. They use antennas off a car—a car antenna with a screen or a piece of Brillo in the end. Seriously!" (Case #E–013). Our point in recounting some of these basic techniques is that with base, learning the high seems to be predominantly learning the technical requisites of getting a good hit. Once users do, they need not do a lot of learning or interpreting to realize that they are high.

THE RUSH, THE HIGH, . . . AND THEN THE LOW

What happens when crack users get that "good hit"? Treatment clinicians routinely claim, and the media routinely echo them, that crack is instantly addicting, and that once users get that first good hit they will stop at nothing to get another and another until their very lives are destroyed. Most of our crack cases suggest that this view is overly simple. Many of our freebasers and crack users experimented with this mode of ingestion for months without getting into a pattern that could be called seriously abusive or compulsive. A few even continued to freebase or smoke crack on an occasional basis without letting the drug overtake their lives. Others quickly recognized the powerful lure of this mode of ingestion and simply walked away from it, without experiencing physical withdrawal.

That said, however, we must report that a clear majority of our freebasers offered compelling testimony on the extraordinary hold this form of cocaine use can have over those who indulge in it more than a few times. For many, relationships were ruined, families neglected, jobs lost, savings accounts emptied, and health imperiled because they found freebasing simply overpowering. For the young members of the underclass who use crack without benefit of jobs and savings accounts, the consequences often have been still more serious.

To fathom the allure of this mode of cocaine use, we began by trying to understand phenomenologically the rush or high it offers. Although the descriptions of the freebase or crack high varied, the terms used were virtually all positive. One young man who had been on a year-long binge before quitting spoke for most others when he exclaimed, "I've never felt nothin' like that! . . . There's not one person I know who doesn't think freebasing is the ultimate high" (Case #621). Other comments ranged from descriptions of the euphoric boost of self-confidence one gets from strong central nervous system stimulants ("the feeling that you're on top of things" [Case #622]) to superlative statements about how basing makes one feel "hyper and smarter, faster and better, you know, sort of like the Six-Million–Dollar Man" (Case #636).

Another respondent observed that freebasing "puts you right up there," though he quickly added, "but not for long." When asked, "What's 'there' like for you?" he answered, "You don't care about *nothin'* else" (Case #635). This response was echoed by a number of others, including one who noted that after a couple of hits on the pipe "the rest of the world is gone" (Case #616). Thus, in addition to general euphoria and improved self-confidence, respondents often described a carefree, nirvanalike state: "It just puts you in a frame of mind that separates you from everybody else. It puts your head on a different level. It's a thousand things. It's a way of coping and it's a way of escape" (Case #635).

Perhaps the most important theme in their descriptions of the freebase or crack high was the "intensity" of the euphoria. Most of our respondents used the word "intense" at one point or another to distinguish this high from most others. They often likened the intense pleasure to sexual orgasm, albeit throughout one's whole being rather than merely in the genital area: e.g., "an orgasmic killer rush . . . really sexual . . . like your whole body is just your cock" (Case #616). Most claimed that basing was the most intense high one could experience.

> The intensity of it was just so enormous, and I couldn't believe the rush. It was similar if not better than the rush we received from shooting it but you didn't have to put the holes in your arms. . . . The sensation starts in your head and goes down through your body. . . . It's very similar to an orgasm, the intensity of it. (Case #613)

We do not want to create the impression that our respondents simply raved about this mode of cocaine use. As we will show, they were more negative than positive about crack use and freebasing. In fact, most seemed all too aware that, ironically, the effects they described in such glowing terms were precisely what made the practice so dangerous. They seemed to be saying that basing is so "good" it is bad.

> It's ruined my relationship with [my girlfriend], put a total strain on my social life, . . . lowered my grades [from an A to a B average], . . . [and] when I'm not high I'm a much better employee. . . . I know all that and yet I get high. I don't understand myself. That tells me how good the drug is. (Case #621)

Part of this paradox is the fleeting character of the rush. All the euphoria, escape, and empowerment described by free-basers was very short-lived. Reports ranged from a rush that lasts "maybe like for thirty seconds" (Case #427) to a bit longer for the high and its afterglow ("about fifteen minutes or a half hour, which is why you use so much" [Case #636]). But all agreed that the high, although more intensely pleasurable than other highs, also faded more rapidly. One elaborated, "If we got about $200 worth, okay, I'd be high for about an hour after it's gone. Maybe an hour, but not long. It's just that it doesn't last long, it doesn't last long" (Case #601). And, because it was experienced as so intensely pleasurable, the desire to repeat this rapidly receding rush was extremely strong.

We heard numerous reports of "chasing that first rush," a chase that was invariably described as futile, a tease: "You're lookin' for something that never gets there, just looking for a high that never comes back" (Case #635). Our respondents agreed that one simply never gets quite as high from the second or the twenty-second hit in a session as one did from the first (see Siegel, 1982). However, knowing that this "first hit" rush was ever-illusive or miragelike deterred almost no one from trying to recapture it.

> Basers always try to reach that first hit intensity and they never do. That's why they're always lighting it again and again. The first two or three hits are so intense, your body is so high [you feel] you're not gonna need another hit. But that intense hit was so good you're always striving to reach it again. And that's the key to it, it's possessive. (Case #621)

> It was great. I just stepped to the ceiling for like five minutes and immediately wanted more. . . . The first hit that I ever did in my life was the best hit that I ever did in my life, and from that point on every time you do it you try and get that first high. (Case #640)

Many also reported diminishing returns: "The more you do the less you get high per hit and the more you want for the next hit to come that much faster" (Case #640).

Yet the intense, orgasmic high, the desire to repeat that fleeting first rush, and the experience of diminishing returns are not the only reasons freebasers and crack smokers so often end up on binges. They also described a phenomenon known as "the lows," "the down," or "the heebie-jeebies"— the downward "crash" that quickly leaves users feeling lower than they were before they began; the only antidote was seen to be yet another hit. One user described this "down" feeling as a "blaze depression" (Case #621), by which he meant depression accompanied by "burning anxiety" about when he was going to get another hit. Some felt this low more acutely than others. Another baser, for example, spoke of the "jones"[6] and the "extreme nervousness" he felt "between hits" as well as a longer-term "desperation" when supplies ran out.

> As long as I know there's product there, I just get kind of jittery and kind of "waiting for the pipe." . . . But the heebie-jeebies that come when there isn't any more and you can't get it, then it's a real serious thing. I mean, for me and for most of the people I know, you know, it's hell. . . . [The word] "need" understates it. It's like desperation. It's like you've lost your best friend. There's this big vacuum. It's like, "What am I gonna do?!" I've curled up in bed in the fetal position and just groaned and moaned and [felt] just, just horrible, horrified. (Case #616)

One crack user described this cycle of extreme highs followed quickly by extreme lows as "waves": "You have your waves. . . . You're ridin' high in April and shot down in May, kind of, and you're still chasing that rush" (Case #E–013). Perhaps even more appropriate was the roller coaster metaphor used by a freebaser.

> I started getting to the point where I would just get really high and base like from five o'clock in the afternoon to about midnight and then get depressed. It's like a roller coaster, you get up there and you come down and then you have to take another hit to get back up there. Then when you run out it gets so depressing and strange. (Case #109)

Almost all of our respondents' descriptions of this roller coaster ride contained three interacting elements which help explain the power of the pipe. First, the freebaser or crack smoker is rapidly brought way "up" to that "orgasmic rush." Second, this euphoria begins to ebb almost immediately. Third, one proceeds downward almost as quickly as one has just been brought up—and "down" not only to where one was before the rush but below it. This feared feeling seems still lower precisely because one has just been higher than ever before. Thus, the intense high, coupled with its seemingly brutal brevity and with the lower low that immediately follows, add up to a powerful three-way reinforcement for repeated use. For it is only by rapidly repeating the high that one staves off the painful "low." Thus, in phenomenological terms, the psychopharmacology of crack smoking or freebasing tends to lead to binges of compulsive use to maximize the ecstatic highs and minimize, or at least ward off, the excruciating lows that always follow.[7]

OBSESSION AND COMPULSION

Webster's dictionary defines obsession as "a persistent disturbing preoccupation with an often unreasonable idea or feeling," or "a compelling motivation." The same dictionary defines compulsion as "an irresistible impulse to perform an irrational act." The roller coaster–like reinforcements of the highs and lows led most of our freebasers toward use patterns that can only be described as obsessive and compulsive. Several respondents used precisely these words to describe their own freebasing or crack use. For at least a part of their freebasing careers, most of our freebasers found that when they had a supply of cocaine or crack, they simply could not stop smoking it until it was gone and they could not get any more. This helped us understand why freebasing sessions tend to last for many hours, often until dawn, and sometimes for two or three days, and why several hundred or even a thousand dollars might be spent on cocaine in a single episode. This compulsive quality was taken for granted by our respondents; they described it routinely but never remarked upon it.

Interestingly, there was no clear line between our respondents' descriptions of the rush or high and their tales of obsession. In fact, in the open-ended portions of our interviews, they spoke far more often and with greater amazement about "obsession" and "possession" than they did about the high or rush. From their accounts, obsession seemed an intrinsic feature of freebasing and crack use. As two basers put it:

> I can't think of any other way to describe it other than a total obsession. I did absolutely nothing but sit cross-legged on the floor, cooking it, cleaning the pipe, and smoking it, you know, constantly doing that. The only time I would get up would be to go bang on some dealer's door. (Case #121)
>
> I would say that snorting is more controllable and basing seems to be an obsession. Once you start you don't want to stop. . . . Snorting you can take a hit and not think about it until like a day or so or maybe even a month. But with base, it's there and when it's gone . . . I've never felt so angry about something being gone. That's crazy, it really is. It's sick. (Case #642)

Most of our crack users described feelings of obsession or compulsion in some form. For example, several respondents characterized basing as "better than sex" (Case #621) and then struggled to describe an ineffable pleasure that they found more commanding than even their basic human drive for sexual gratification. One middle-class, middle-aged white male freebaser put the point this way: "Basing is the reward, I mean sex is almost [superfluous]. The reward is right there. . . . It's the pipe. . . . The hit is the thing in the end" (Case #616). Another white male observed, "It's remarkable how quickly the change takes place after that first hit. It's like 'Never mind you' or 'never mind your desire for sex, let's just get the pipe out'" (Case #433).

A white 35-year-old legal secretary spoke of "a real physical change" she experienced while freebasing. In the beginning of her use she could "do it and then stop," but, as it did for most of the others, this soon changed: "My body no longer had the ability to just comfortably stop . . . at any point, no matter how much or how little [was smoked]. . . . There was a physical craving that overcame me when I was basing that I couldn't control" (Case #432).

A different dimension of this obsession emerged when users spoke of their activities during a freebasing session. One respondent captured the point succinctly when we asked what he liked to do when freebasing. "Just base some more," was all he said (Case #635). Other things, including friends, social activities, and, for many, even sex, all seemed to pale in importance next to the pipe, the sole *objet du desir*.

In the early stages of a freebaser's or crack user's career, sessions tended to be social. Friends would plan elaborate evenings together that were focused on freebasing but included music, conversation, or sex. For some, basing was at first a ritual that often led to "amazing camaraderie" and "opening up" (Case #616). Yet, very soon in the course of both a session and a career, these social activities tended to fall by the wayside. Unlike other forms of drug use such as drinking, smoking marijuana, or even snorting cocaine, freebasers did not get high and then go out to dinner or to a concert or a party. Many said they simply could not "deal with it," "it" meaning anything that required them to function or cope in their overamped state, or that came between them and the next hit. One white male veteran described the experience this way:

RESPONDENT: You don't want to deal with it in any kind of way. If you have to go out to the store, you can, but it's kind of gruesome.

INTERVIEWER: You'd rather not?

RESPONDENT: Yeah, you'd rather just stay at home.

INTERVIEWER: In other words, you want to try and keep a pleasant, congenial atmosphere?

RESPONDENT: Yeah, and you certainly don't want to deal with anything besides the pipe. . . . [Y]ou don't want to deal with anyone, so it becomes completely introverted. So you really feel kind of isolated, kind of weird, you know, 'cause I can't relate to anyone else once I get really high. (Case #616)

This quality of the high is why, as one respondent told us, basing is "an indoor sport," why one tends to "forget about everybody," and to end up "in some room or some corner somewhere just hittin' the pipe" (Case #635). Others, using slightly different terms, spoke of the same sort of isolation. One 22-year-old Latino described his tendency to withdraw.

See, throughout the years I went from bein' sociable and partying with coke [to being] withdrawn, and as I did more quantities I got more withdrawn. The more I got into it the more people saw less of me. . . . I was disconnecting my phone and shit, and not answering my door because I'm all tweaked on blow and freebasing and shit. . . . I would feel totally fuckin' weird. I can't look people in the eye and I can't . . . I don't want to see anybody. (Case #606)

Unlike other drugs such as marijuana, which is ritually passed around, and unlike even powdered cocaine, which is regularly snorted with friends, an unsocial, or even antisocial, ethic seems to take hold of crackheads and basers. This mode of ingestion is, as one respondent told us, "a completely selfish disease."

You take one hit and you don't stop thinking about taking another hit until it's all gone. Four and five and six hours will pass and nothing will take your mind off of it unless someone is gonna give you more. It's like you can't even think about anything else. It's hard even to try to think about other things. You find yourself staring at the ground a lot. . . . You stare at the floor and look for extra pieces of coke that might have fallen onto the floor. You pick through the carpet and stuff like that. (Case #640)

Half a dozen respondents recounted this carpet anecdote. One even had a name for it—the carpet crusade—which implied that such obsessive searching on hands and knees was routine among basers and crack users. While under the influence, many apparently cannot believe their supply is gone and that they cannot, therefore, have another hit. Of course, no one ever mentioned *finding* any pieces on the carpet.

The same obsession that led so many users to crawl around on the floor looking for nonexistent crumbs also led many to suspect their own friends and spouses of taking more than their share. In fact, several respondents admitted to engaging in just such selfish behavior. Apparently the pleasure of the rush and the desire to repeat it are so strong that a narcissistic greed often supplants the ethic of sharing or "turning on" others that has long held sway in illicit drug subcultures. During the course of a run, long-time friends and even spouses and lovers frequently ended up "arguing over what's on the plate" (Case #642). Others were turned off to freebasing precisely because of this greed among users. Thus, isolation often supplanted sociability because, when alone, one does not have to deal with anyone else or share the precious supply. One respondent noted that basers often tried to "find an empty hole somewhere" in which to freebase, and that he had once even rented a hotel room in order to be alone with his pipe.

RESPONDENT: It's a selfish drug and no one is interested in getting the other guy high. When you smoke pot, or at least when I smoke pot, we'll be smoking the pot and somebody will come in who hasn't had any pot. . . . "Here, you need to get high." With freebase you are sitting there and you're not interested. . . . For one thing you don't think the hit that the guy gives you is big enough. Or you don't think that the hit you got was as big as the guy who took a hit before you. There's always something you don't like about the fact you're not getting enough or whatever. . . . You're always working for your own shit all the time and no one gives a Goddamn about anybody else.

INTERVIEWER: Does it get worse and worse?

RESPONDENT: It tends to. . . . Your outside attention dwindles. . . . The first couple of times it's still kind of social and people are still able to hold a conversation. That goes on for about fifteen or twenty minutes. But the longer the night goes the more people are definitely into the coke and don't talk or think about anything else. . . . Snorting it is usually a social situation and the coke usually sits on a mirror and everybody does a line, and then they're all talking about it and it's like a half an hour before another line gets done. I don't think it's nearly as intense. . . . [Freebase is] an addictive drug and psychologically you do feel that you need it and you can feel it in your palms of your hands that you want that. But when you're snorting it you can also drink and think about other things and talk and drive and smoke pot and party. Whereas with freebase you don't think about anything else, which is why people who do it in social situations, I think, end up doing it by themselves. . . . You don't go to freebase parties. It's more like, "I've got a gram of coke, where can I go? What closet can I sit in?" (Case #640)

Under the spell of the pipe, freebasers and crack users often behaved in otherwise unthinkable ways. They often lied to, neglected, and even stole from spouses and close friends who were dearly loved during nonfreebase time in order to continue basing. One 32-year-old Latina, for example, noted that desire for crack can overpower feelings for family: "We cut-throat each other a lot, me and my brother. . . . I see it now because he used to steal from me and I used to steal from him" (Case #118).

Another measure of obsession might be the amount of money that a freebaser is willing to sacrifice to continue a freebasing session. By sacrifice, we mean more than the $50 to $500 our respondents spent in a single session—expenditures that even they would have rejected as absurdly extravagant for anything else. One college student freebaser told us of watching a friend enthusiastically offer to trade his Rolex watch, worth several thousand dollars, for a few grams of crack. Another baser eventually quit in part because he saw firsthand the drug's power over people's purses.

I'd go to a couple of dealers' houses and I would notice seeing these guys behind freebasing selling like their brand new Mercedes for like two or three thousand dollars. They would lose their house and everything! That was the main reason why I quit because I realized that it could break you financially more than anything else and that scared me. I said, "I don't need that." (Case #622)

Spending hundreds of dollars in a few hours, pawning valuables for a few cents on the dollar, arguing with family and friends over who has had more of a tiny remaining chunk, and crawling around the carpet searching for nonexistent crumbs of crack—surely these forms of obsession tell us something basic about the problems with this mode of cocaine ingestion. But perhaps the clearest indicator of the obsessive or compulsive character of this form of drug use is the extent to which people continue to use in the face of overwhelming evidence of harm. Our respondents described taking hit after hit until they felt their lungs would collapse or until heart palpitations forced them to stop. One long-term baser told of a helping a friend who was "freaked" by heart pains during a session. He felt shocked when "about an hour later the sucker was back on the pipe. I couldn't believe it" (Case #616).

Evidence of physical harm and of the disintegration of their daily lives eventually prompted many to quit.[8] But we heard many life histories in which people who knew they were risking their health, and even perhaps their lives, continued to freebase anyway. Here are excerpts from a long, graphic account offered by an upper-middle-class black male college student:

So we're like into our seventh gram and all of a sudden George is about to hit the pipe . . . and he has a coke seizure. . . . [He] just starts twitching and his hand is shaking. Vinnie . . . is trying to hold his head up and stuff and George is biting down on his tongue and he's just slammin' his head against the refrigerator or something, and some blood is spitting out of his mouth and stuff. Vinnie's holding him down and right then his eyes are up inside of his head, and Vinnie calls the paramedics and the house is full of smoke and I'm rushing to get the pipe and vials, rocks, and run them to the garbage. . . . But I get all this stuff out of the house and George is still, and all of a sudden he just goes to sleep. . . . You have to understand, me and Vinnie have just smoked six grams, too, and he had a seizure, but we're so high the situation is like totally, like . . . "he's dead" is all I can say. "We killed him, our buddy." We really believe the guy is dead. You know, I've known him since I was in first grade. My parents . . . you know, life is over for me. . . .

The blood is all over in a pile. Vinnie wipes it all up. The paramedics want to take him to the hospital. George goes, "No, I'm okay, I'm okay." So Vinnie decides to take George home about ten in the morning. I've just been getting high since twelve midnight, it's like nine-thirty now. I put on my uniform and go to work. . . . I'm so tired but I'm working anyway. I'm trippin' over how I've seen George hitting his head upside the refrigerator and blood spitting out of his mouth. I'm goin', "Heavy!" Okay, George is through with coke. I am through with coke. About ten that night, George goes, "Hey, do you think you can get a gram?" "Hey, George, you didn't see yourself. You were in a seizure, blood spitting out of your mouth." "Yeah, but let's get a gram tonight."

Oh, no, I've seen it. People talk about coke seizures, your heart and stuff. I've seen it, I've seen one of my best friends have a coke seizure and to tell you how good the drug is, he's basing today. . . . If ever you were gonna do coke, if you would've seen the seizure, there [would be] no more coke for nobody, you know. This guy, it tells me what basing is: he's still doin' it today. . . . He was ready to go back that night! (Case #621)

A subtext that had to do with powerlessness ran through most of these tales of obsession. Most of our respondents often went days or even weeks at a time without freebasing. However, during a single session, most found that they simply did not have the power to stop or to resist an offer. One of our most experienced respondents, a middle-class, middle-aged white man who for years had been a controlled user of many illicit drugs, was amazed at his inability to say no to the pipe.

It's some kind of body thing. I remember once, lighting up with my friend and starting maybe at ten in the morning and he had a thing he had to kind of keep up with so we cut at seven in the evening. And I went through a kind of withdrawal jones thing and drank a bunch and then took a Valium, and it comes in waves. And after about two or three hours, you know, I was almost out. But I still found that by nine or ten o'clock I could get some and he would come back. . . . [H]e didn't get back until about midnight. By then I was almost asleep and sick of everything, you know, sick of drinking, I felt like shit. I already had a half a hangover. My body and my mind and everything was kind of saying, you know, I mean, I just wanted to go to sleep. It's like . . . a real fun day that turns into the usual kind of minor nightmare at 7 P.M.

By twelve every rational thing in my mind said, "All you have to do is go to sleep." You know, every single piece of rationality. And then I got the phone call [that] said, "Well, do you want to do it?" And my body's saying no and my mind's saying no, but he comes over and we started all over again. I didn't need it, I didn't want it, you know what I mean. It's . . . like some kind of molecular thing is in my *cells* that would go for it, you know. I felt like a fucking robot. (Case #616)

TROUBLE AND TAILSPINS—CONSEQUENCES AND CAREERS

Where does compulsive crack use and freebasing lead the user? Although tales of obsession may appear to indicate "trouble," in the early parts of their freebase or crack careers, the users themselves did not define their experiences this way. Many were still basing or smoking crack at the time of our interviews, although some of them at much reduced levels. They had learned that they were taking special risks with this rapid-delivery mode of cocaine ingestion. But, for surprisingly long periods of time, most seemed to act as if such intense highs were worth the risks or as if the risks could be managed so they could enjoy those highs a while longer.

Yet, at some point, many began to recognize an accumulation of negative consequences which they did define as "trouble." Others described a downward spiral in their lives caused by their obsession with basing or crack; one user called these "tailspins" (Case #627). These troubles and tailspins led some to exert enough control to cut down on their freebasing and others to quit entirely. We will save for Chapter 8 the details of the problems our crack users and freebasers recounted. We can summarize them by saying that virtually all of the ill effects experienced by many of the heavy cocaine snorters—problems with mental and physical health, families, finances, and functioning in daily life—were amplified and accelerated for crack users and freebasers.[9] This suggests again the importance of the mode of ingestion, for the potential for abuse or problems does not inhere merely in the pharmacological properties of a drug, but in the way in which it is used (see Weil, 1972).

Perhaps the best way to see where freebasing and crack use can lead is to look at how these types of problems cohere in a concrete case over time. As we have suggested, the life histories of our respondents contain both shared themes and considerable variation. Most reported at least some serious problems which they attributed to freebasing or crack use, although these were often dealt with differently. Here are two case summaries.

Jessie is a 28-year-old black man who came from an upper-middle-class family. He began freebasing at the end of the night shift at the data processing center where he worked when a group of senior coworkers asked him to join them: "At first it's like you hit the pipe and then go home. But then it got to be we were doing this every night, and I started doing it on our lunch hour."

In the early phases of his use, Jessie got his supplies free because he "hung" with a dealer. Even when he began to buy cocaine regularly he could afford it on his salary. For several months, basing was only a "recreational sport" to him. He liked both the rush and the fact that freebasing did not bother his nose: "When snorting coke it feels like your nose is gonna fall off your face. But smoking it is easier and the high is a lot quicker and a lot more powerful." Although he didn't free-base at work, in the early stages he felt as though he was more productive at work after having hit the pipe. "I worked quicker," he said, but this later changed.

His use gradually escalated to basing nearly every day. At his peak, Jessie used six grams per week for about a month, although he had previously used between one and three grams a week for several months. Unlike most of the other freebasers and crack users we interviewed, he did not continue to chase the first rush or to use well beyond the point when he was no longer getting high: "I get to a point where I just can't get high anymore so I leave it alone then. It usually takes about a gram and I smoke that gram by myself. I can't get any higher than that, so I just lay down and go to sleep."

Then, still relatively early in his career, he decided to stop. Basing was taking a toll he no longer wanted to pay. It was not just the money or the fatigue or the "ten or fifteen pounds" he'd lost, and he reported no health problems. But the cumulative social-psychological strain did induce him to quit.

> It went on for months on almost an everyday basis. If it wasn't getting high with these guys it was with my old buddies, so I was actually getting high all the time. I could even sit at home and actually taste it. Then you start making excuses why you should. It just progressed and then I just stopped paying bills and the shit started going down the tubes. I got really scared and really uptight about that. Between the drug and the pressures of not taking care of your responsibilities and getting caught in the middle of that, my brain was about to just bomb. I just had to stop. I remember the night I stopped and I went over there and I had done a gram. When I get high I start thinking and I decided I couldn't do it anymore. That night I made up my mind to not do it and I didn't. The next day I said to them, "Don't come out with it," and they respected that. (Case #419)

Craving experiences made his first month off the pipe difficult: "You can sit there and you can taste it or you could be sitting there and all of a sudden just smell it. Then you start thinkin' about it. I just had to keep telling myself 'No, you can't do this.'" He felt slightly depressed for a short time, although he said that this was "not because I didn't like myself but . . . because my bills weren't getting paid." His friends continued to hang out with him but respected his wishes about staying away from cocaine. Jessie told us that his craving "just faded away" after a few weeks.

Jack had a much more difficult time before he ultimately quit. He is a white male merchant marine turned electrician, 36 years old, married with a son. Jack had been a regular marijuana smoker and had experimented with various other drugs as a teenager. Later he even tried a few intravenous injections of cocaine. He enjoyed that high but never made shooting a regular practice because he found it "kinda scary" and because the needle marks were an embarrassment. He took care to hide them from his wife and work mates.

Jack had snorted moderate amounts of cocaine in a controlled fashion for almost five years before he tried freebasing. Snorting, he said, "didn't make me want to do more." This was not so of freebasing. He was introduced to the pipe by a coworker for whom he was serving as a go-between with a dealer friend. Freebasing, Jack said, "was the closest thing to shooting I could get to without sticking a needle in my arm." The first time he based he stayed for three or four hours: "It was one of the highest highs I'd ever been through. From then on it just started going downhill."

After this first freebasing experience, Jack never snorted cocaine again. He concealed his escalating use, and his relationship with his wife and son suffered.

RESPONDENT: My wife actually just thought I was still snorting. I wasn't freebasing at the house and it was always like going over to somebody's house and doing it. Or when she would go out I would do it. It was getting so bad that she just finally didn't want me around no more. We split up and I figured that I would get out and get my life together and really show her, you know. It didn't work that way, though. I moved out and I got me a small apartment in Oakland, and I was seeing my son and I had him about half the time. When she had to go somewhere in the evenings she would bring him by there. I was hitting the pipe so much, it's hard to say, but he was getting in the way, you know. When she brought him over and if I had the stuff all ready to do and he was there, I couldn't do it in front of him. I didn't want expose him to that so I would have to wait until she came back to pick him up.

INTERVIEWER: So you stayed down while you were with him and you didn't get high?

RESPONDENT: Unless he came over to spend the night with me. After he went to bed I'd get high, stay up all night. . . . One night I was hitting the pipe in the living room and he came walking out of the bedroom and I kind of hid it real fast. He goes, "I got a stomachache, Dad." Then I would put him back to bed, you know, and rub his back and rub his head or something and give him some water and then he would go back to sleep . . . and I would go back to the pipe. Then one night I didn't have any more coke so I called my dealer and said, "Hey, can I come over and get some?" and he said, "Sure, come on over." I was really thinking about leaving him in the apartment by himself! I couldn't do that. I went downstairs; there was an old man who lived downstairs, and I asked him, "Hey Joe, I'm not feeling too well and I have to go to the drugstore. Will you come up and just sit in my apartment because my kid is here?" He said sure, so he came and sat in my apartment while I went to my dealer's house. I was back in fifteen minutes, but still . . . (Case #109)

There was amazement in Jack's voice as he told of being so tempted by freebasing that he would even consider leaving the child he loved so much to make a run to the dealer. Although he ultimately found a baby-sitter for the brief time it took to buy more, he did not like what the incident told him about his desire to freebase.

Jack moved again into a small apartment with another baser whom he hardly knew in order to save money on rent so that he'd have "more money to base." He liked the freebase high in part because "it enhanced my sexual thing," but the woman who meant the most to him, his wife, was increasingly distant. "She never let me get close enough to her, you know, or even near her." He based so much he lost forty pounds, and his friends scolded him for hurting his wife. As a result he "started feeling real depressed." One particularly desperate night he asked a friend with whom he had snorted occasionally to call Jack's wife and get her to let Jack visit. He planned to persuade her to freebase with him and then to have sex. His friend objected. Jack said, "That got me real upset and I started thinking that I was really ruining my life." He persisted, to no avail.

> RESPONDENT: I called her up and I told her that I had something I wanted to tell her. She took Eric to the neighbors and I went over there, and when I walked in the vein in my neck was just . . . and also the vein in my head right here was bulging. My heart was just going a thousand miles an hour. Getting back to the sexual thing, what I had planned, I was gonna get her high and get her on the same level as me and have sex right there in the house, you know. I confronted her with it and I said, "Kim, I want you to try this, please, just try it and you'll like it." That's weird trying to turn her on.
>
> INTERVIEWER: Were you missing her?
>
> RESPONDENT: Oh yeah, I was missing her. She just totally turned off to it. She said, "Look Jack, I really care about you and love you so let's break your pipe and flush this stuff down the toilet and start clean right here. You can move back in and things will work out, but it's up to you." You know what I did? I picked up my little bag and got in my car and left and went back to my apartment and ended up freebasing it all myself and went back and got more! It was crazy. . . . I was basing and that's all I cared about.

Jack continued freebasing heavily for another six months before he took steps to stop. He swore to his wife that he "wasn't getting high anymore," and she let him move back in. But he admitted to us that when she went out of town he would freebase ("from like five in the afternoon to about midnight, and then get real depressed"). He promised that he would go into a treatment program, but he continued to put this off. One Thursday evening he told his wife he was going to a union meeting.

> There was a union meeting that night and I was gonna go to it. I really thought myself that I was gonna go. She goes, "Are you sure you are going to that union meeting?" She asked what time I was gonna be home and I told her around ten or ten-thirty. It was about six-thirty. . . . I got on the freeway and I started driving to the union meeting, but for some reason I got off and I ended up at this other friend of mine's house and we started getting high. We got high and that was a Thursday night and the next day was a Friday, which is a payday. I called in to work and I knew the secretary real well and said . . . she knew I had a problem . . . and told her that I couldn't come in to work. She told me that I had to talk to the supervisor so I talked to him and I made up a big excuse. It was payday and I owed all these bills and owed the dealer money. I had to get my check somehow. I came into work and she met me . . . in front of the building and gave me my check. I went and cashed it and paid off my dealer and plus I got some more. I was telling myself that this was it, the last time. Okay, so I was supposed to go the union meeting on Thursday night and I told Kim I would be home at ten-thirty, and now here it is Friday morning and I still hadn't called. She knew what was going on.

Having blown his last chance to preserve his family, Jack finally gained admission to a then-new treatment program. His health insurance covered the costs and his union held his job for him. When he drove up to the rural retreat where the program was located, he noticed fellow basers and crack users in their cars smoking up "their last bit right at the gate before they went in." He successfully completed the treatment and continued in outpatient therapy for several months, holding down his job all the while. Jack said there were moments when he was tempted to go back on the pipe, but a dealer's assistant, oddly enough, exerted a kind of informal social control that kept him away.

> There would be times when I would call the dealer's number. Once his girlfriend answered and she had known I went through a program and she goes, "He's not here and I'm not gonna give you anything." She would sell for him when he wasn't there. She just hung up and I was really grateful later because that could have been a start of a whole new thing.

Jack felt some craving for crack in the first months after quitting. He told us that just driving "around the area of my old apartments would get me thinking about it" and produce "this little queasy feeling in my stomach." But he practiced the relaxation techniques he learned in treatment, and the cravings gradually disappeared. While he said the program had helped him, he hastened to add, "No programs will help you, though, until you're ready to get some help."

Within a year, Jack lost all desire for freebasing. Prior to our interview he had attended a New Year's Eve party where cocaine was being shared. We asked, "Did that bother you?" Jack replied, "Not at all. I have no intention or desire for it at all." Although he found treatment useful, what ultimately moved him to pull out of freebasing and to stay out was his fear of losing what he valued most.

> Well, I saved the house that we owned, and if eventually we had split up that would have been gone too. The biggest thing I think I achieved is my son. . . . Every time I got high on coke that's one thing I would think about—"I'm losing my kid." It was the only thing that meant anything to me.

Both Jessie and Jack eventually mustered enough control to pull out of freebasing, Jessie relatively easily, Jack after considerable trouble. But both men, and the majority of the other basers and crack users we interviewed, regardless of class, race, or gender, told tales of obsession. Some of these tales were tragic and some more mundane. One of our crack-using respondents contemplated suicide (Case #627); another actually attempted it (Case #606). A few reported heart palpitations. Most mentioned strained relationships (as one put it, "Basing *was* my relationship" [Case #121]). And virtually all dumped dollars galore into their pipes.

While we have little doubt about the extraordinary abuse potential of this mode of cocaine ingestion, we were also left with some perplexing questions. One concerns the extent to which freebasing or crack use is so uncontrollable that users are driven to desperate deeds. Most told of being unable to control their use for at least some portion of their heavy-use periods. Two sold their cars, and more than a few wiped out their savings accounts in addition to their disposable incomes. But many managed to smoke cocaine for years and yet hold down jobs, or made it a point to pay all their bills before spending a cent on drugs. Many managed for months to restrict their use to weekends. Several walked away from crack use precisely because they feared its powerful call.[10] Perhaps most telling, the majority described their obsession as *episodic* rather than chronic. Almost none sat smoking all day, day after day; most used in a clearly compulsive manner *during a session,* but did not remold their lives into one long session.

Is freebasing, then, impossible to control? Many of our subjects intimated as much. One baser described some informal rules he had employed to limit his use. Asked if he stuck with those rules, "No, never," was all he said (Case #616). Another explained the essential problem with basing this way:

It's like motorcycle riders, and there are two kinds: those who have had accidents and those that haven't had them yet. . . . People who start doing it on Saturday or Friday and then sneak a little bit on Monday or Tuesday, and then it pretty quick comes to be Friday, and after a while it gets to be every day. Then it becomes not just every day but earlier in the day. It just keeps building and I think it's just a very seductive type of drug . . . for most people. It's only a matter of time if they continue to toy around with it. It's like explosives—you can only play with it for so long [before you] get hurt. (Case #433)

Exceptions notwithstanding, both these respondents and most others agreed that, because basing offers such an intensely pleasurable high and is so powerfully reinforcing, real control is exceedingly difficult to maintain. Many of our subjects were seasoned users of illicit drugs who had never before fallen into abuse; some had managed to snort cocaine for years in a moderate, controlled fashion. Yet many of these same people found themselves in a clearly compulsive use pattern with freebasing or crack. One of our findings, then, is that most of the fifty-three freebasers and crack users we studied were unable, at least in the course of an episode, to maintain control over their use.

CRACK AND CRIME IN CONTEXT

During the years we were doing the research for this book the news media ran thousands of frightening stories that claimed that crack use spurred all manner of violence, robbery, theft, and prostitution. They implied that the peculiarly potent psychopharmacology of this form of cocaine use is the direct cause of the crime and other problems plaguing our inner cities. This is the raison d'être invoked by government officials for the war on drugs.

We must admit at the outset that there is surely a kernel of truth in all this. Our data suggest, however, that crack's criminogenic image is too simplistic. First, when media reports are read carefully it becomes clear that most of what are called "crack-related homicides" occur among crack dealers rather than users.[11] Given both the enormous profits to be made when a desired product is illegal and dealers' lack of recourse to legal forms of dispute resolution, there should be little wonder that suppliers who are in fierce competition would resort to their own, often brutal forms of social control (Black, 1983). Moreover, the war on drugs is only the latest term for decades-old public policies that are specifically designed to deter drug dealing by making it as dangerous and hair-raising as possible. Thus, we should not be surprised when the illicit drug industry attracts and retains especially callous, even vicious, individuals who shoot at each other. Of course, innocent bystanders in several cities have been killed or wounded by stray bullets fired by such individuals. These tragedies should not be minimized, but neither should they obscure the fact that shootings between dealers tell us little about the relationship between crack use and violent crime (Goldstein et al., 1989; Williams, 1989).

Such visible homicides notwithstanding, our data on the compulsive use patterns and the sometimes desperate behaviors reported by most of our subjects support the notion that crack has something to do with crime. As we have shown, the call of the pipe was indeed powerful enough to lead people to do many things that they might not have done otherwise. Beyond that, however, our data suggest that the putative causal connection between crack and crime has at least as much to do with the social context of crack use as with its effects on users.

While we did not study the impact of crack on the community, we do not doubt that many poor, inner-city neighborhoods have been disrupted by the violence associated with crack sales and by the effects of crack on individual families. However, such neighborhoods and families already had been disrupted for years before crack came along. After decades of racism and poverty, the 1970s brought capital flight and economic restructuring. The shift from manufacturing toward a service economy eliminated thousands of blue-collar jobs that once provided minorities with decent lives (Wilson, 1987). On top of such structural shifts came ten years of funding cuts in virtually every government program that even marginally improved the life chances of poor people. Although the effects of freebasing and crack use were serious, even for more affluent users, surely no drug can be made to stand as the sole source of suffering among America's urban poor. It would be far more accurate to say that this new drug problem exacerbated existing hardships and accelerated ongoing devastation.

Most of the crack users and freebasers in our study behaved in ways they were not proud of, but, tellingly, very few engaged in the sort of street crime, violence, or prostitution that media reports imply are inevitable consequences of this form of cocaine use. One obvious reason for this is that a large proportion of our sample are educated and employed, or had other middle-class resources. This logic suggests a telling hypothesis: if freebasers and crack users who have resources rarely get violent or become street criminals, then the crack-crime connection may be as much a function of finances as of pharmacology.

We suggest that, while the call of the pipe was strong enough to influence people to engage in misdeeds, it was not so strong as to push them beyond all constraints. Among the most criminal of our freebasers and crack users were a lawyer who embezzled and a payroll clerk who filed a false insurance claim in order to get money, which they spent on cocaine. They committed crimes they knew how to do; they did not become burglars. They engaged in forms of criminal behavior that, in the context of their lives, seemed conceivable and available; their crack use did not make them muggers.

For criminologists, the notion that specific criminal behaviors are learned, as are all other behaviors, is old news (Sutherland and Cressey, 1978). Moreover, we know from prior research on heroin and alcohol that the ingestion of drugs simply does not yield specific behavioral consequences. Yes, many impoverished street junkies steal and rob to support their habits. But affluent addicts or those who happen to be doctors, nurses, or pharmacists with alternative supplies, do not. Yes, a majority of violent crimes involve alcohol, but a very small proportion of drinking incidents involve crime or violence. The criminal behaviors so often attributed to one drug or another are not in any direct, mechanistic sense "caused" by the pharmacology of those substances. As criminologists have shown again and again, crime and violence are learned responses to situational exigencies, and they are more likely to be learned under certain conditions by certain groups of people.

Once our freebasers and crack users began to experience fiscal exhaustion on top of physical exhaustion, many simply stopped using. When we asked why, their typical responses were simple: "I just couldn't afford it anymore" (Case #641). For most of our respondents, the idea of solving their money problems and getting more drugs through street crime simply did not occur to them. For most working- and middle-class people, serious crime is simply not part of their culture or behavioral repertoire.

A 22-year-old upper-middle-class black college student unintentionally made a related point while telling us how powerful freebasing is.

> If you don't have the money to afford it, it can easily make someone go out and rob a bank. . . . The coke is so strong, it's tellin' you, "Rob a bank." Someone that didn't have the money to afford it, someone that doesn't think sensible, no education and stuff, would easily just go out and shoot someone up just to get the coke. (Case #621)

Did he rob a bank when he ran out of crack and money? No. He seemed to say that crack indeed does cause crime, but both his own lack of criminal behavior and his statement force a qualification. Crack clearly can "cause" crime—if one has no alternative means of getting it, if crime is already "thinkable," if there are no other constraints preventing it.

The surprising, albeit subtle force of such constraints was illustrated by another upper-middle-class respondent in explaining why he gave up basing: "I could no longer afford the habit . . . and I'm too chicken to steal" (Case #419). For us, there is important insight as well as appropriate modesty in this remark, for it shows that the extraordinary power of the pipe is mediated by the social circumstances of the user (Zinberg, 1984). While freebasing seemed to push people to break norms and even laws on occasion, it always did so within bounds that were set by socialization, by subculture, and by the self. Crack surely may "cause" crime and other unwanted behaviors, but its power to do so does not operate in a vacuum. To judge from our respondents, this mode of cocaine ingestion is most likely to cause crime among those who have no other means of supporting their use, few normative bonds to conventional society, and little to lose by throwing off constraints.

We believe this finding helps explain why the consequences of this form of drug use appear to be more serious in impoverished urban communities than among our more working- and middle-class users. We cannot overgeneralize here because we cannot "prove" anything with fifty-three subjects. But if our respondents are any guide, then we have hit upon a hypothesis worthy of further investigation: Crack users who are not already involved in criminal activities, who have legal means of getting money for their drugs, and who have ties to conventional life, will be far less likely to engage in violent or criminal behavior than members of the underclass. If this concept is borne out by other researchers with larger samples, then the crack-crime connection will have to be understood as context-specific, that is, as a function of social inequality as well as psychopharmacology.

CHAPTER 7

CONTROLLED USERS

M*any of our* respondents used cocaine for years in a controlled manner. We define controlled use as regularly ingestion of cocaine without escalation to abuse or addiction, and without disruption of daily social functioning. We have described many other respondents who did not fit this definition. Unfortunately, most of what is known about cocaine users is based on this latter type of user.

With few exceptions, most of the writing and research on drug users up to the 1970s expressed both stated and unstated presumptions that people could not use illicit drugs in controlled ways. There are at least two sources of this presumption. First, the middle-class moralism of the nineteenth-century temperance movement has remained a unique and forceful facet of our culture throughout Prohibition and since its repeal (Gusfield, 1963; Levine, 1984, and forthcoming). Compared to other industrialized democracies, a higher proportion of Americans fear altered states of consciousness, attribute diabolical powers to consciousness-altering substances, and believe in the disease concept of alcoholism and addiction, which was invented in the United States.

Second, since the turn of the century, stereotypes about the malevolent behavior of some heroin addicts have been continually reinforced by the media's penchant for dramatic ruin-and-redemption stories, by politicians who find in drug abusers a handy scapegoat for many social problems, and by treatment experts who see only the most extreme, negative cases. Under such influences government agencies and researchers almost automatically equated drug use with abuse. Users' reports of the pleasure, insight, comfort, or relief that they derived from drugs were routinely discounted as prodrug propaganda. Any notion that people could use illicit drugs in a controlled manner or integrate drug use into otherwise functional lives remained heretical.

Such extreme positions about drug use and users coexist with common knowledge that contradicts them. In 1989 U.S. Surgeon General C. Everett Koop reported that nicotine is "as addicting as heroin," and indeed it often is. Yet cigarette smokers have long displayed an array of use patterns. Most of us know the common two-pack-a-day smoker who always seems to have a cigarette in hand, and many of us, including two of the authors, personally know how difficult it is to stop smoking. But most people also know at least some smokers who smoke only after dinner, or who routinely limit the places where they smoke or the number of cigarettes they consume in a day. Casual smokers are more common, although still far from a majority, in European and Latin American cultures.

Drinkers demonstrate similar controlled use patterns in far higher proportions than smokers. The hopeless alcoholic who drinks all day, every day is but one pattern. By far the majority of drinkers drink in controlled ways—with meals, outside of working hours, in limited amounts, or only on ceremonial occasions and seldom at inappropriate times.

This knowledge about varying drug use patterns is not, however, often generalized to illicit drugs. For years both experts and lay people believed that all illicit drug users were by definition drug abusers, that nearly all use led users to be overwhelmed by their drug use to the point of "addiction."

These beliefs began to lose their hegemonic status in the 1970s. The dominant paradigm was shaken when new research on heroin addiction uncovered some surprises. Lee Robins (1979) and her colleagues discovered, contrary to all

expectations, that most Vietnam veterans who became habit-
uated to heroin in Southeast Asia were able to quit when they
returned to the United States. Outside of the horrendous war
setting, the pharmacological power of heroin simply did not
by itself lead to an inevitable or permanent addiction (for
similar findings on inner-city heroin users in the United States,
see Hanson et al., 1985).

These findings were followed by those of Norman Zinberg,
a professor of psychiatry at Harvard Medical School. During
the 1970s he undertook a series of related studies of people
who used heroin and other drugs in controlled, nonaddictive
ways. At first most other experts and funding agencies insisted
that heroin was invariably addicting and that such occasional
heroin users simply did not exist. But Zinberg was able to
demonstrate that they did exist, and in numbers larger than
anyone had believed. He set out to learn what kinds of controls they employed so that they were able to avoid the addictive patterns that had been thought inevitable (Zinberg,
Harding, Stelmack, and Mablestone, 1978; Zinberg, Harding
and Winkeller, 1977; Zinberg and Harding, 1982; Zinberg,
1984). In general, Zinberg and his colleagues found that *informal sanctions and controls*—users' rules about appropriate
times and places to use drugs, user folklore, protective rituals,
and group pressures—effectively influenced many people to
control their drug use and prevent problems over long periods.

Judith Blackwell (1983) of Brock University and formerly
with the Addiction Research Foundation in Toronto undertook a similar intensive study of fifty-one heroin users in
London. Plotting the use patterns and outcomes of each user
at two points, this study found that twenty-two (44 percent)
employed a wide variety of self-regulation strategies. Another
eleven (22 percent) used heroin for a time, but showed no
commitment to the drug or the life-style and simply drifted
away from heroin. Like Zinberg, Blackwell found that some
people can use even heroin in controlled ways and that "addiction" is not an inevitable outcome of regular use.

Patricia Erickson, another scientist at the Addiction Research Foundation in Toronto, recently reached similar conclusions about cocaine use (Erickson and Alexander, 1989; Erickson et al., 1987; Cheung, Erickson, and Landau, 1991). After reviewing an array of animal studies, clinical studies, population surveys, and community studies, Erickson and her colleagues concluded that the potential for controlled cocaine use has been understated in the scientific literature. She summarizes studies of cocaine users in the community, outside of treatment and prison (e.g., Cohen, 1987; Erickson et al., 1987; Siegel, 1985; Murphy, Reinarman, and Waldorf, 1989), and concludes: "Most social-recreational [cocaine] users can maintain a fairly low use pattern over lengthy periods without escalation to addiction. Users appear to recognize the need to limit their use of cocaine, and most seem to be able to accomplish this without professional intervention" (Erickson and Alexander, 1989).

In this study, we had no difficulty locating controlled cocaine users—even though to qualify for inclusion, all had to have used heavily at some point. We estimate that approximately 50 percent of our respondents who were using cocaine at the time of our interview did so moderately and in ways that minimized negative effects and maximized positive effects. Some of these men and women had previously used the drug heavily during occasional binges or periods of daily use, but had since reasserted and maintained control. Even many of our respondents who had quit using had always been controlled users. Furthermore, in follow-up interviews with twenty-one users we originally interviewed in 1975, we were able to chronicle the long careers of seven persons who were continuously controlled users for at least fourteen years and seven more who at one point used heavily but who had abandoned heavy use for more moderate controlled patterns (Murphy, Reinarman, and Waldorf, 1989).

In this chapter we return to two case histories of white, middle-class users from which we quoted earlier: Nancy, the 36-year-old stockbroker who remained a controlled user for years despite a heavy use period; and Stephen, the 35-year-old psychologist at The Company who also controlled his use for years, but who eventually lost control and quit for a time. At this writing both use cocaine only ceremonially. The fact that they started from similar circumstances and yet had different experiences provides a useful comparison. We also chose these two because, unlike many other controlled users whose pattern remained experimental or occasional and who never went on binges, Nancy and Stephen both used cocaine regularly and sometimes heavily.

Maintaining Controlled Use

Nancy is a very dynamic, well-organized woman who seems to have it all—a challenging career, a good marriage to an equally dynamic mate, healthy children, a nice home, money in the bank, and a secure future. She began to use cocaine in 1974 when a woman friend gave her a gram as a wedding present, which she tried some days later on her honeymoon. Between 1974 and 1980 she used intermittently at parties or when her husband purchased some from time to time. On one such occasion she injected the drug with a small group of friends but did not "get high because they did not hit the vein."

Her cocaine use began to escalate when a close friend and colleague, Eva, began to sell cocaine to a small network of friends. The general pattern of her use was as follows: She arrived at work at eight o'clock and did her most demanding creative work before noon. She then went to a gym for her regular workout and had lunch at one. Upon returning to the office she worked for another hour or so and then she and Eva would "do a line." At that point she put aside her creative work and dealt with the general administrative aspects of her job. At four or four-thirty she often had another line, and another at six just before she left work.

Upon arriving home she generally had a drink and then prepared the evening meal for her husband and their children.

Sometimes just before eating she would go to the bathroom and take a fourth line. Returning to the table she would find that she no longer was hungry, but the decreased appetite helped keep her weight down and maintain her slim figure. After dinner she and her husband would clean up the dishes, put the kids to bed, rest or read for a while, and then go to bed about 10:30 or 11:00 P.M. She was unusually asleep by midnight.

RESPONDENT: It must have been like a year and a half that we used to do it all the time.

INTERVIEWER: That's every afternoon, about three or four lines every day?

RESPONDENT: And then on weekends once in a while before going out and partying. Then I did a whole bar number in '81 or '82 when I did coke a lot every time I would go into a bar, which was almost every night.

INTERVIEWER: So describe the scene.

RESPONDENT: I was having kind of a relationship with a guy who was an engineer. I met him through an old friend and he had this whole crowd of people who did all sorts of things. . . . I suppose they were all middle- or upper-middle-class and they were all single and they do that bar thing every night.

INTERVIEWER: It was somewhere they stopped in after work?

RESPONDENT: All the time. Everyone stopped in after work and stayed hours and hours. I really had fun because I had never been part of a scene like that when I could walk into either one of those two bars and know people, sit down, and be comfortable.

INTERVIEWER: So, pleasant?

RESPONDENT: It was real fun and I had a good time for a while.

INTERVIEWER: So would you go into the john and do a couple of lines?

RESPONDENT: Oh, constantly. . . . We would have this little vial, you know, and we would hand it back and forth—real discreetly, but it wasn't discreet at all. I mean, everybody knew what everybody was doing. You go into the bathroom and you're giggling in there and all that stuff. So that went on for almost a year and I was pretty well into using at work, at the bar, and on the weekends.

During the summer of 1981 Nancy went away with her family to Oregon for two months and did not use any coke at all for the full two months. Upon her return she resumed the earlier pattern, using in the afternoon and at the bar, and she maintained that routine into 1982.

INTERVIEWER: Didn't you get pregnant in there?

RESPONDENT: Well, part of the getting pregnant part was that the whole bar scene began to really sour and I didn't like it anymore.

INTERVIEWER: Did the people change or did you just get tired of it?

RESPONDENT: Oh, just a couple of disappointments. . . . I was just disgusted. I just kind of looked at my life and decided, I think I'll go home. For me one of the ways of doing that is going home and having a baby. It was intentional, I intended to do that, and that's what I did. I do remember that it took about four months to get pregnant and I wasn't doing much coke at all. But I remember the day I was going to find out if I was pregnant. Right before I called I said, "Just one more line," because once I got the results . . .

INTERVIEWER: So you made a conscious decision to stop?

RESPONDENT: Yeah, so we did a line and that was the end of that.

INTERVIEWER: So for nine months you didn't use.

RESPONDENT: Yeah, actually probably for a little bit more.

INTERVIEWER: How did you handle quitting?

RESPONDENT: No problem at all. . . . I don't know about all this talk about addiction. I don't know where that came from because everybody I know just walked away from it.

INTERVIEWER: You were using it every day?

RESPONDENT: Yeah, I was using it every day for a long time.

INTERVIEWER: When you stopped doing it, and you stopped a number of times, what did you feel?

RESPONDENT: Nothing really. I just stopped. There was only one time that I can remember that I ever felt anything. One week my husband had taken . . . the two kids . . . up to Arrowhead for a week for Easter vacation. I was heavy into that bar scene then and I spent a week of just doing coke all the time. I would finally get to sleep whenever that was and I would wake up in time to shower, and by then it would be the cocktail hour and by that time it was time to go start drinking again and snorting.

INTERVIEWER: So you weren't working then?

RESPONDENT: I think I was making some minor attempt to come in here because I know Eva and I were doing that together. We had a hell of a week, we were going out drinking later together too. And then Peter came back and I just knew so vividly . . . there was no food in the house, nothing. The refrigerator was bone empty, so I was getting ready to go to the market. I'm just remembering the feeling I had. . . . I threw myself on the bed and I announced to him that life was very boring and going to the market was extremely boring. That's the only word I could think of was boring. He says to me, "You and your friend have been doing a lot of coke this week, haven't you?" And of course I said, "Well, what does that have to do with anything?"

INTERVIEWER: But you put it away [quit] too.

RESPONDENT: Oh, I can put it away.

INTERVIEWER: So you use in certain situations, and in certain situations you don't use. Whenever you stopped you didn't have any problems?

RESPONDENT: No.

INTERVIEWER: No twinges, no depression or . . . ?

RESPONDENT: No.

INTERVIEWER: Cravings?

RESPONDENT: Um . . . I don't think so.

INTERVIEWER: Did your nose open up?

RESPONDENT: Open up?

INTERVIEWER: Yeah, you know, talking to people and suddenly you say, "Yeah, let's go get some"?

RESPONDENT: No, but I wish I would have brought some with me today so I can have some with my cocktail tonight, because I'm thinking about it right now. (Case #559)

Nancy resumed regular use of cocaine at very moderate levels two months after her third child was born and used for two more years. Again she abstained in the summer months on her family vacation. At one point she used cocaine on and off to lose weight and found it very effective. Her strategy was to snort a little line just before meals. During one such attempt she lost ten pounds in a single week.

At the beginning of 1985 her colleague, Eva, decided to retire from her sideline as a part-time dealer, and Nancy characteristically put cocaine behind her and never looked back. Twelve months after our interview we telephoned Nancy to ask how she was doing and what her present pattern of use was.

RESPONDENT: I bought a gram last June for some special occasion. So now it's January.

INTERVIEWER: Seven months ago?

RESPONDENT: I think I have a half a gram left.

INTERVIEWER: God, you're a serious abuser!

RESPONDENT: Yeah, and I keep saying, "Gee, there's a lot in here." I use it so rarely that it's hardly worth talking about. Like if I'm gonna go out really drinking and partying it up, which I do so rarely anymore, then I take one or two trips to the bathroom. (Case #559)

It should be noted that Peter, her husband, never knew all the details of her two long runs with coke. He knew that she was using but not how much and how often. Years ago Peter used cocaine and other drugs heavily for an extended period, but he is now generally moderate in his drug use, preferring a little wine or marijuana and very occasionally using MDMA (Ecstasy) or cocaine. Had he known how much she was using he probably would have intervened. We suspect that Nancy was careful not to let her cocaine use become so obvious that he would notice it. Furthermore, she believes now in retrospect that both of her long runs were secret acts of rebellion against her husband.

Nancy had a period of binge use when she was going to bars, but ultimately, and without real effort, she always managed to subordinate her cocaine use to her career and family. Of course, fulfilling careers and rich family lives are not so easy to come by for everyone who uses cocaine, and particularly not for the inner-city poor now exposed to crack. We think such anchors are important for keeping one's life balanced and for not allowing cocaine use to overshadow other aspects of existence. However, some people slip into uncontrolled or problematic use after years of controlled use, despite their interesting careers and other meaningful life investments.

LOSING CONTROL OF COCAINE USE

Stephen, one of the workers at The Company whom we discussed briefly in Chapter 4, is just such a person. We return to his case now because he illustrates how someone who thought he could remain a controlled user can ultimately lose control. For several years Stephen could indulge but not overindulge; he had managed, seemingly without effort, to keep his life together while regularly snorting cocaine. Indeed, he had used cocaine in a controlled and even highly productive fashion for a long time. Yet, in the end, he had to admit to himself that he had not been able to keep his use in check.

Stephen was a graduate student at a northern California

university when we first interviewed him in 1974. In general he led an ordered and controlled life. He earned high grades, established good relationships with faculty members, and was an exemplary student. While living with a friend who dated a cocaine smuggler and had regular cocaine contacts, he used cocaine in a limited way for approximately two years. He seldom could afford to buy the drug on his student stipends.

Upon moving to Los Angeles to work on his Ph.D., Stephen had even less money and used cocaine very infrequently there—perhaps once or twice a year when it was offered at a party. Upon finishing his degree he returned to the bay area and went to work for The Company. With his salary, he had enough money to buy cocaine.

Stephen knew three small-time dealers, so cocaine was suddenly easily available as well as affordable. He gradually moved from occasional purchases to keeping a steady supply on hand in his desk drawer. Initially, he bought and used cocaine just to socialize, but over time he used it more to help him work, primarily to finish a book he was writing. For more than a year he was convinced that cocaine helped him to focus and gave him more energy to work regularly on his manuscript. He would arrive home about 6:00 P.M., snort a line or two, and put in two or three hours on his book every evening. He consumed perhaps one gram per week for more than a year.

This boost in productivity began to wane in his second year of regular use. He began to lose focus and, instead of feeling energized, he often felt depressed. Friends were no longer as much fun and, when he was "coked up and writing," he even resented their phone calls. The work was going much too slowly, and he frequently became bogged down, focusing so intensely on a single page or paragraph that he wasn't making any real progress.

At the same time that cocaine was providing him decreasing energy and concentration, Stephen used increasingly more cocaine and had progressively less control over his usage. He now brought cocaine to the office and snorted out of his desk drawer during the day. At this point he used two to three grams a week.

In a few months, recognizing that he could no longer call himself a controlled user, Stephen was prompted to some soul searching. He began to regain control of his use. As a means of "avoiding denial and self-delusion," he wrote notes to himself recording his "junkie behavior" and recording the money he was spending on cocaine. He took some pride in using this diarylike process to force himself to acknowledge exactly what he was doing. He read some of his entries for us at the interview.

> You've actually done what junkies do: you're going out at ten o'clock at night and you're meeting somebody at a gas station to exchange money for a drug—an amount of money that if you weren't a cocaine user would seem absolutely absurd and used to seem absurd to you. And now you think nothing of it!
>
> Your binge before the 1984 convention was more proof of serious degeneration. You are less, rather than more, productive.
>
> You've been literally powerless before it, handing over hundreds of dollars in the course of a single week. Now, as you are and must be struggling against it, you are empowering yourself, a greater form of power, a glimpse of a joyous form of power with which you will develop the means of self-actualization
>
> You just did a half gram of potent stuff in twelve hours. Tell everybody you can about this, for if drug use is learned in a culture, then so, too, must that culture help you [cut down or control your use]. If you announce to people who matter to you that you have quit, then they'll help you stay quit. You'd be embarrassed to admit you were using again.

Stephen's internal dialogues were equally scathing and self-critical. Through such assertions of control for several months, he was able to stop escalating his use. He had not, however, decided to quit. An article in *Playboy* magazine about the risks of cocaine gave him "a giant 'aha!'" Avoiding "the antidrug hysteria of moralistic assholes who don't know anything about drugs," the article made the case that cocaine is hard to control because it bypasses "the rational part of the brain." This made tremendous sense to Stephen, who had been puzzled by "the fact that part of me kept saying 'don't do another line,' while another part of me just kept on chopping and snorting."

In response to his growing understanding of the loss of control, he did three things to regain it. He persuaded one of his dealer friends "who was getting in trouble" to stop selling and using. He went home to New Jersey for Christmas and did not use while he was there. Upon returning, rather than buying cocaine he bought a personal computer to use in the second revision of his manuscript. His new fascination with word processing, combined with the progress he began to make on his book, was an adequate substitute for cocaine.

Stephen stopped using cocaine entirely at that point and, aside from "feeling a little low on energy" for a few weeks, he experienced no withdrawal symptoms. He now has a healthy respect for cocaine's "seductiveness" and has made it a rule never to have a supply of the drug around. In the three years since he regained control, Stephen has never bought cocaine and has used small amounts on only half a dozen special occasions.

> INTERVIEWER: As I see it, you had a six- or eight-month dialogue when you were trying to control [your use], but then there was a final decision to stop.

> RESPONDENT: Right . . . a decision not to buy and not to have it around. Several times I took the damn mirror [on which he used to chop up cocaine] out of my drawer at home and cleaned if off with Windex and hung it back on the wall instead of using it [to chop cocaine]. And a few times I took it back down off the wall and put it in my drawer again and used some more, but eventually I just hung it up. (Case #439)

CHARACTERISTICS OF CONTROLLED USERS

After reviewing these and other cases, we have drawn a few tentative conclusions[1] about how controlled users managed to avoid abuse and negative effects. First, this group is made up of people who did not report or display any obvious evidence of serious, underlying psychological problems. As a rule they were not particularly neurotic and did not use cocaine to manage stress or other life problems.

Second, controlled users nearly always had lives (careers, interests, families, etc.) that gave them basic economic security, life options, a sense of community, and personal satisfaction. They had few reasons, therefore, to develop deeply drug-centered lives, and, conversely, many reasons not to subordinate their life activities to their drug use. They typically met—indeed, enjoyed meeting—their responsibilities and generally relegated their cocaine use to a lesser role whenever it threatened to conflict with the demands of family or friends, career or community. In short, they had priorities in their lives, and cocaine use simply was not compelling enough, despite its admitted allure, to dwarf all other things. Controlled users like Stephen in his early years and Nancy throughout her using career generally "took care of business" first. For most of them, cocaine use was not business but pleasure, and just as they did not let other leisure activities dominate their work and family spheres, they did not allow their drug use to spill over into other spheres. Even when they also used cocaine to work, they tended to use it in this way only so long as it helped them "take care of business."

Lastly, controlled users tended to develop routines, rules, and rituals that helped them limit their drug consumption. For example, Nancy nearly always stopped her cocaine use at dinnertime so as to get to sleep by midnight. She never used in the morning or let it interfere with her work. She had specific plans for her life and career, and whenever cocaine threatened to interfere with those plans she regulated her use accordingly. For Nancy and many others, pharmacology is not destiny.

Although such informal rules and routines were important for most of our controlled users, they have not stopped cocaine abuse for many others. Stephen often said, "Never a line after nine"; paid all his bills before spending money on cocaine; he always ate "three squares" and got a good night's rest. Yet, although these rules worked well for the first few years of his cocaine use, they did not keep him from several months of problematic use.

What distinguishes Stephen from Nancy? Both are middle-class professionals with fulfilling careers. Neither reported nor displayed psychological problems. Both snorted cocaine and steered clear of riskier methods like injection or smoking. If they both employed rules to keep their cocaine use within bounds, why did she stick to hers while in the end he stretched and broke his? Perhaps Stephen was a bit more driven—trying to get his career into high gear by taking on several jobs and finishing a book all at once—so that his increasing reliance on extra stimulation from cocaine as an aid to productivity put him at additional risk. Perhaps, too, being single and unattached, a continent away from his family, and without children to be responsible for, Stephen had fewer checks on his cocaine use than Nancy had. Surely, the effect of having more reasons for using and fewer reasons to avoid using helps explain why he eventually lost control while she did not. Yet, after scouring our other interview transcripts, we could not put our fingers on any one magical "factor X" that explained why some people got into trouble and others did not. Clearly the pharmacological powers of cocaine on human physiology matter, even though they are mediated by sociological variables having to do with how a user's life is organized. Rules, rituals, and other informal social controls also matter, but these always interact with pharmacology, life organization, and other factors.

Obviously, informal social controls are not foolproof techniques for maintaining controlled use. Our interviews suggest that they played an important part in keeping cocaine use from getting out of hand for many respondents. But under existing circumstances there are limits to how far such user practices can go to prevent abuse and addiction. First, neither the principle that people should limit their use nor the practices by which some have learned to do so have had a long gestation period in the United States. When a drug is criminalized, as cocaine has been since 1914, its use tends to be marginalized or pushed out of conventional society into deviant subcultures. In such circles few drug users place a premium on moderation; on the contrary, many look for ways to get more bang for their buck. Communication about ill effects and other risks tends to remain subterranean and therefore difficult to accomplish.

Drinking norms in family settings minimize the harm of alcohol consumption better than do the norms in boomtown saloons. But by creating the preconditions for deviant subcultures of illicit drug use (the equivalent, in effect, of boomtown saloons for alcohol), our society has minimized the normative influences of family, friends, and moderate users. When cocaine becomes increasingly available and a more dangerous mode of ingestion is introduced in this kind of cultural setting, the development of user-generated controls is further impeded.[2] Under such conditions, users can only slowly pass along knowledge of cocaine's dangers and of how to avoid or minimize them. And when users are, as one respondent put it, "enemies of the state," they typically perceive official warnings as the suspect propaganda of drug warriors and conservative moral crusaders rather than as potentially helpful public health information. Thus, instead of working together to minimize problems, formal and informal controls often work against each other (Zinberg, 1984).

Nonetheless, the surprisingly high proportion of our users whose patterns were rational and moderate has led us generally to agree with Erickson's and Alexander's (1989) conclusion that controlled cocaine use is possible (see also Cohen, 1989). Generalizations from animal and clinical studies of cocaine's potential for addiction are often extrapolated well beyond the bounds of observed user behavior.[3] Certainly there are people who become dependent upon cocaine and who, as a consequence, sometimes behave in ways that they themselves define as deplorable. Our case study of Stephen suggests that even some people who use in a controlled fashion for long periods can eventually lose control. But it also should be noted that Stephen and many others did not have to go to treatment to regain control or overcome this dependence. He eventually made up his mind to quit and did so, without any withdrawal or even marked difficulty. Since quitting, he has used on a few ceremonial occasions without ever craving more. Stephen's case illustrates a theme we saw among others who experienced periods of abuse or addiction: while it is not difficult to lose control, it is not impossible to find it again either.

Many treatment professionals, members of Twelve-Step recovery groups, and former addicts wince at the concept of controlled use and recoil at the suggestion that, once lost, control can be regained. Among those who subscribe to the disease concept of addiction, there is an ideological, almost theological, presumption against such ideas. As a practical or clinical matter, it makes sense for them not to dwell on such risky possibilities.

From our vantage point, the existence of controlled users—in fact, the very idea that cocaine use can be controlled at least by some people under some conditions—is a double-edged sword. On one hand, there is danger in seeing people use cocaine without experiencing problems, for it allows others to believe that they, too, can try it or continue to use it without risk. For some, as we will document in the next chapter, use clearly leads to problems. On the other hand, there is hope in the evidence that controlled use is possible, for it establishes the reality that one need not and thus should not abuse (Nancy). The existence of controlled users also suggests that even if one does go overboard, one can reassert control (Stephen).

While control over cocaine use is not easy for everyone and is no doubt difficult for most, the possibility cannot and should not be denied. Our respondents were among the heaviest users in the nation and, if many of them are controlled users, then surely most of the other twenty-five million Americans who have tried cocaine are too. If we cannot make such uncomfortable facts go away, perhaps we can learn from them how to reduce the harm that cocaine and other drugs can do.

PART II

HAVING TROUBLE WITH COCAINE

CHAPTER 8

COCAINE-RELATED PROBLEMS

Having described controlled, nonproblematic cocaine use, let us now look at the ways in which cocaine use can be dysfunctional and harmful. Both our own preliminary research and the existing literature suggest that long-term daily use or regular heavy binges often lead to difficulties with health, relationships, finances, work, or sex. We asked our respondents about their cocaine-related troubles in each of these domains. In this chapter we will present our findings on the prevalence of these problems.

We begin with health problems. We divided these into two distinct areas, physical and mental, although in the users' experience the two were often bound up with each other. We asked each respondent some two dozen questions about the specific effects of cocaine on their physical health, ranging from mere nervousness to convulsions and seizures. We also asked about four types of mental health problems commonly reported in the literature: frequent insomnia, paranoia, hallucinations, and "cocaine bugs." To cast the widest possible net, we gave each respondent the opportunity to talk more generally about both physical and mental health problems in open-ended questions. To our surprise there were only a few statistically significant differences between users and quitters, usually in the total number of problems reported within a given domain.

Physical Health Problems

The most serious cocaine-related physical health problem reported was seizures and convulsions. During the second week of the interviewing one of our more knowledgeable and experienced researchers interviewed a 20-year-old student who had experienced a grand mal seizure after using a combination of cocaine and caffeine pills. The interviewer wrote the following description of the three-and-a-half-year career of this respondent.

> Claude began using cocaine casually when he was 16 years old. He was introduced to the drug by his stepbrother, but did not get high the first time. . . . Some weeks later he . . . "located the high in my head." He continued moderate use, usually at parties with friends or a girlfriend, until after graduation.
>
> After high school he entered college at the University of Southern California and began to sell cocaine periodically to friends. His source for the drug was his stepbrother, from whom he usually bought a half ounce. He took his own supply out and cut the remains with one or two ounces of milk sugar. This left him with what he considered to be "pure" coke which he then shared with friends. In general, he found that cocaine enhanced his friendships and that the scene he was in was "lots of fun."
>
> Over the next four or five months his use escalated to approximately two grams per week. This escalation continued to three grams per week and then to an eighth of an ounce shortly thereafter. Despite this increased use Claude was still able to support his cocaine use by drug sales—cocaine, some marijuana and psychedelic mushrooms. His stepbrother was not handling his own coke use very well; he lost his job because of his cocaine use and began to deal full-time. He then raised the price of the ounces he sold to Claude.
>
> At this point Claude's parents began to suspect the stepbrother of drug use and asked Claude about it. This in turn caused Claude to worry that his parents would discover his own use. Several times when he was high on cocaine he ruminated on how "horrible" it would be if his parents, and especially his mother, found out about his drug use.

These thoughts about his parents prompted him to resolve to stop using over Christmas vacation when he would be at home with them. In anticipation of this plan he reduced his use to about a half gram per week one month prior to the holiday vacation. He . . . intended to resume his use when he returned to campus after Christmas vacation. During the visit he stopped completely and experienced no withdrawal symptoms. He stayed home for a week and then decided to go on a skiing trip to Mammoth Mountain with some friends.

At Mammoth he went on a round of parties, did a lot of drinking, snorted a few lines of coke, and generally slept very little. For the drive back to Los Angeles he took an unknown number of No-Doz caffeine tablets to stay awake. They stopped at a friend's house in Ventura, ate a little, and then he and the friend snorted approximately three-quarters of a gram of cocaine between them. The next thing he remembers was that he was lying on his back with paramedics asking him, "How many fingers do you see?" He had experienced a grand mal seizure—so serious that he gave himself a black eye during the convulsion.

The paramedics took him to a hospital where he underwent a number of tests both during the hospital stay and after. Claude had never experienced any previous seizures so was not considered epileptic. . . . Eventually his sister revealed both his and his stepbrother's drug use to their parents. This revelation caused him to feel extreme embarrassment because he really cared about his mother's love and her opinion of him. This period was brutally hard for him, but eventually with the support of his parents he worked through it.

At the interview Claude had not used cocaine for eighteen months and was adamant that he can never use cocaine again. All of his friends still use cocaine and that is alright with him, but he feels that if he ever did as much as one line he would have another seizure. This belief was bolstered when a friend experienced a second seizure. In general, Claude feels that cocaine is not worth the risk, although if he knew for sure that he would not have another seizure he would snort more coke in a minute—"I love that stuff, it just doesn't love me." He remains shaken by the experience and believes that he suffered permanent brain damage as a result. "I will never be the same," he exclaimed. (Case #301)

Claude was one of six men and women who reported that they had suffered some form of convulsion or seizure as a consequence of cocaine use. This was the least prevalent problem, reported by less than 3 percent of our total sample of heavy users. Five of these six had stopped using cocaine completely by the time we interviewed them.

Angina or "heart attacks" were reported by another seven people (3.1 percent), three of whom were quitters. One was Cecil, described in Chapter 3, who had used cocaine for fourteen years, at some points very heavily. After he experienced an angina attack he consulted his physician who advised him that his condition probably occurred because of a specific "cut" or adulterant and not because of the cocaine itself, which he had used without incident for so long. He continues to use cocaine but at a reduced amount, largely because he no longer sells it and thus cannot afford to buy a large quantity.

Minor nasal irritations were the most prevalent problem reported by our respondents, aside from nervousness. We asked about five different nasal problems—dryness, running nose, bleeding, infections, and burnt septum (see Table 8.1). Nearly three of four reported occasional nasal bleeding, while one in five reported more serious problems like burned or perforated septums and nasal infections. Current users reported more nasal problems than quitters: a mean of 2.80 nasal problems compared to 2.49 for quitters.

Mental Health Problems

To explore mental health problems associated with cocaine we asked about four common complaints: frequent insomnia, hallucinations, paranoia, and seeing "cocaine bugs." Respondents who had experienced any of these conditions were asked for more details about their experiences. The most frequently mentioned mental health problem was paranoia; two-thirds of our respondents reported feeling paranoid at some point in their cocaine-using careers. Current users reported this more

TABLE 8.1
Lifetime Prevalence of Cocaine-Related Physical Health Problems
of Users and Quitters: Percentage Answering Yes

Have you ever experienced these cocaine-related health problems?	Users (N = 122)	Quitters (N = 106)	TOTAL (N = 228)	Rank Order
NASAL PROBLEMS				
Nasal dryness	(92) 75.4%	(64) 60.3%	(156) 68.4%	6
Running nose	(111) 91.0	(85) 80.2	(196) 86.0	2
Nasal bleeding	(97) 79.5	(68) 64.2	(165) 72.4	5
Nasal infections	(18) 14.8	(24) 22.6	(42) 18.4	18
Burnt septum	(24) 19.7	(23) 21.7	(47) 20.6	17
OTHER PROBLEMS				
Nervousness	(109) 89.3	(92) 86.8	(201) 88.2	1
Trembling hands	(97) 79.5	(73) 68.9	(170) 74.6	4
Grinding teeth	(89) 73.0	(85) 80.2	(174) 76.3	3
Frequent colds	(34) 27.9	(33) 31.1	(67) 29.4	14
Frequent sore throat	(31) 25.4	(37) 34.9	(68) 29.8	13
Feeling faint	(45) 36.9	(45) 42.5	(90) 39.5	12
Feeling dizzy	(52) 42.6	(45) 42.5	(97) 42.5	9
Cold hands and feet	(78) 63.9	(63) 59.4	(141) 61.8	7
Cold sweats	(54) 44.3	(52) 49.0	(106) 46.5	8
Diarrhea	(59) 48.4	(36) 34.0	(95) 41.7	11
Cysts or boils	(10) 8.2	(6) 5.7	(16) 7.0	20
Skin problems	(41) 33.6	(24) 22.6	(65) 28.5	15
Frequent urination	(48) 39.3	(48) 45.3	(96) 42.1	10
Urinary problems	(23) 18.9	(15) 14.1	(38) 16.7	19
Heart palpitations	(3) 2.5	(4) 3.8	(7) 3.1	21
Angina or heart attacks	(4) 3.3	(3) 2.8	(7) 3.1	21
Convulsions or seizures	(1) 0.8	(5) 4.7	(6) 2.6	22
Other	(19) 15.6	(32) 30.2	(51) 22.4	16

Note: Percentages were rounded in most instances.

frequently than quitters, but the difference was not significant (see Table 8.2).

The most frequently mentioned form of paranoia was fear of police or of discovery by others who would not approve of cocaine use. Nearly half of those who experienced paranoia

TABLE 8.2
Cocaine-Related Mental Health Problems
by Users and Quitters: Percentage Answering Yes

Have you ever had these cocaine-related problems?	Users (N = 122)	Quitters (N = 106)	TOTAL (N = 228)
Frequent insomnia	(65) 53.3%	(63) 59.4%	(128) 56.1%
Hallucinations	(24) 19.7	(39) 36.8	(63) 27.6
Paranoia	(77) 63.1	(75) 70.8	(152) 66.7
Seeing cocaine bugs	(10) 8.2	(13) 12.3	(23) 10.1

said they had fears of the police and one-quarter reported fears of discovery. Anxieties about police did not seem out of the ordinary as cocaine possession and sales are illegal. But beyond rational fears of arrest, many people suggested that cocaine exaggerated whatever other anxieties people already felt—about a dark street, say, or a problematic relationship. Several respondents also told tales of "jumping" at sights and sounds that might have gone unnoticed when they were not under the influence of cocaine. We suspect that the hyperexcitation of the central nervous system, on top of worries about police or discovery, made users overly sensitive to a whole array of stimuli in their environments.

Frequent insomnia was reported by more than half our respondents, with no significant differences between users and quitters. This finding is not surprising since cocaine is a central nervous system stimulant that is valued by users precisely for its energizing effects (e.g., "It keeps the party goin' a while longer"). Only exceptional heavy users did not have difficulty getting to sleep after ingesting cocaine at least at some point in their careers. Controlled users often declined use after a certain point in the evening so that they would be able to "come down" in time to go to sleep at a reasonable hour. Heavy bingers often failed to do this, instead snorting and then partying until the wee hours when their supplies were gone.

Slightly more than one-quarter of our respondents reported experiencing some form of hallucination. Quitters were almost twice as likely to report hallucinations as current users—36.8 percent as compared to 19.7 percent, a statistically significant difference. Hallucinations usually took the form of imagining for a moment that inanimate objects were moving or seeing human figures that were not there.

The last mental health problem we asked about specifically is known in user folklore and the research literature as "cocaine bugs." One in ten of our subjects reported having this experience at least once. Cocaine bugs might be understood as a subset of hallucination, albeit sometimes experienced tactilely as well as visually. The user ingests so much cocaine and is so stimulated that ordinary skin sensations such as hair movement or goose bumps feel like tiny bugs on or under the skin. Here is one account of the phenomena.

> Janice was a pound dealer of cocaine who lived in a North Bay town. She regularly snorted large amounts of cocaine, on some occasions as much as seven grams in a single day. She reported that after such heavy use she regularly saw bugs or insects crawling on her skin which she would pick off and put into a glass of water beside her bed. Invariably she would wake up in the morning to find a glass with numerous pieces of skin off her arms and legs. (Case #518)

Descriptions such as "feeling itchy" or "feeling things crawling on the skin" were mentioned by nearly half of the one in ten of our subjects who experienced cocaine bugs. Nearly one-third of those who experienced such "bugs" called it "seeing things" on the skin.

In general, the people who reported these four types of mental health problems were not inordinately frightened or traumatized by the experiences. In fact, they were blasé in their descriptions; in most instances they knew that these conditions were induced by their cocaine use and would soon pass.

PROBLEMS WITH INTERPERSONAL RELATIONSHIPS

Our case study of Jessie, the freebaser discussed in Chapter 6, suggests that cocaine abuse can take a huge toll on personal relationships. Jessie's obsession with the pipe nearly ruined his marriage to a devoted wife and alienated more than a few of his close friends, even many of those who used cocaine with him. Unfortunately, his story was not unique. However, early in our research we spoke with users who had said positive things about cocaine's effects on their relationships. We knew that drug use among friends or between spouses or lovers need not entail negative effects or cause problems. Indeed, as we showed in Chapter 3, cocaine often led friends to new heights of camaraderie and spouses or lovers to be more expressive of feelings and less inhibited both socially and sexually. Therefore, we could not assume that cocaine's effects on social relationships would always be negative. Rather we had to design our questionnaires on the premise that there could be a complex array of responses—no effects, positive effects, negative effects, or both positive and negative effects—depending on amount used, set and setting, career stage, and other factors.

Among our sample of heavy users, cocaine seemed to have the least impact on family-of-origin and work relationships, which is not to imply that it did not cause problems in such relationships (see Table 8.3). Half of all respondents told us that cocaine had no effect on their relationships with their families. More than two of five respondents said that cocaine use had no effect on their relations with coworkers. In comparison, only about one in five reported no effect on relationships with spouses, lovers, or friends.

When cocaine did have effects on family-of-origin relationships, they were apt to be negative; nearly two in five of our respondents reported such negative impacts. Less than one in ten reported mixed effects, both positive and negative, on relations with family members; and less than one in twenty said cocaine had any positive effects on family.

TABLE 8.3
Self-Reports on the Effects of Cocaine Use on Social Relationships
of Users and Quitters

Did cocaine ever affect your relationship with:	If yes: Was the effect positive, negative, or both?			
	No Effect	Positive	Negative	Both
YOUR SPOUSE OR LOVER?				
Users (N = 122)	(26) 21.3%	(10) 8.2%	(46) 37.7%	(40) 32.8%
Quitters (N = 104)	(18) 17.3	(3) 2.9	(50) 48.1	(33) 31.7
Total (N = 226)	(44) 19.5	(13) 5.7	(96) 42.5	(73) 32.3
YOUR FAMILY?				
Users (N = 122)	(73) 59.8	(5) 4.1	(35) 28.7	(9) 7.4
Quitters (N = 103)	(40) 38.8	(2) 1.9	(54) 52.4	(7) 6.8
Total (N = 225)	(113) 50.2	(7) 3.1	(89) 39.5	(16) 7.1
YOUR FRIENDS?				
Users (N = 122)	(25) 20.5	(21) 17.2	(33) 27.0	(43) 35.2
Quitters (N = 104)	(20) 19.2	(15) 14.4	(40) 38.5	(29) 27.9
Total (N = 226)	(45) 19.9	(36) 15.9	(73) 32.3	(72) 31.9
THE PEOPLE YOU WORK WITH?				
Users (N = 120)	(57) 47.5	(18) 15.0	(29) 24.2	(16) 13.3
Quitters (N = 103)	(37) 35.9	(8) 7.8	(39) 37.9	(19) 18.4
Total (N = 223)	(94) 42.2	(26) 11.7	(68) 30.5	(35) 15.7

Note: N's vary slightly because of instances where no answer was given. Percentages may not total exactly 100 because of rounding.

Cocaine-related problems with a spouses, lovers, or friends were more apparent. One in five respondents reported that cocaine had no effect upon spousal relationships. When respondents reported effects in spousal relationships they were largely negative (42.5 percent). Only about one in twenty reported that cocaine had positive effects on their spousal relationships. Effects on friends were somewhat less often negative (32 percent).

One clear pattern in Table 8.3 is the difference between quitters and users. Our quitters more often reported negative effects of cocaine use on all categories of relationships than did current users. On spousal or lover relationships, quitters less often reported no effects or positive effects, and mentioned negative effects significantly more often than users. With regard to their families, quitters less often reported no effects; about half the quitters but only a little more than one in four users reported negative impacts on their families. Quitters also more often reported negative effects of cocaine use on relationships with friends and coworkers. This pattern of responses suggests that quitters generally had experienced more consequences from their cocaine use in all their relationships than users did. No doubt this effect is among the reasons they quit. For the current users, conversely, the lower levels of negative consequences as well as the higher levels of "no effect" and positive consequences suggests that they had fewer incentives for quitting.

FINANCIAL PROBLEMS

One regular feature of antidrug stories in the media and treatment program advertisements is the portrayal of people who have squandered huge sums or gone heavily into debt to buy cocaine. One recent San Francisco TV documentary presented a program client training her horse at her family's ranch. She claimed to have blown a quarter of a million dollars on cocaine before entering private treatment and discovering the joys of "recovery." Very few of our respondents were that affluent or spent such sums on cocaine. But our interviews left us with little doubt that there is some truth in such stories.

One respondent, when asked how much money he had spent snorting cocaine, replied, "Well, put it this way: Over the last three, four years, I snorted a new Volvo up my nose." Many others, although they did not sell their belongings or go into debt, still spent much of their disposable income on cocaine. At the time of our study a single gram of cocaine sold for $100 to $130 (retail) in the San Francisco Bay area, depending upon quality. These prices dropped in the late 1980s and rose again in 1990, but clearly cocaine use has remained expensive. This was especially true for freebasers or crack users who often went through a gram in less than an hour. As comedian Robin Williams once quipped, "Why do they call it *free*base? It's not free, you can lose your home on that stuff. They ought to call it homebase." Some users tried to offset the costs by dealing. As we saw in Chapter 5, two in five of our respondents (40.0 percent) sold cocaine at least for stash. But this cost-cutting strategy made supplies more readily available and thus tended to increase use.

To explore the financial problems that often occur with cocaine use we asked three questions. The first was general and open-ended: "Did you have any cocaine-related money problems while you were (are) using coke?" If respondents replied yes, we asked them to give us details. We asked everyone a third, seven-item question about specific things they might have lost or sold in order to purchase cocaine; these ranged from savings to a car or a business.

In response to the first question, about half said they had experienced money problems as a consequence of their cocaine use (see Table 8.4). Not unexpectedly, a higher proportion of smokers and shooters (63.3 percent) than snorters (49.4 percent) said they had experienced money problems. Responses to the open-ended question that followed fell into four basic categories. Nearly half ran out of money or had no money; more than one-fifth went into debt; and more than one in ten sold valuable items or could not pay for essentials.

Answers to the question on specific items lost or sold as a result of cocaine use give a more detailed picture of financial problems. More than two in five reported that they had lost savings or other money assets, and nearly one-fifth sold large items such as boats, television sets, or stereo equipment. The only differences between users and quitters on these items were on savings and money assets—over half the quitters said they had used them up on cocaine, while about one in three users made such reports. Counting the items lost or sold as a result of cocaine use, we found that the overall mean was 1.3, with quitters averaging more than users.

These data on financial problems point to two contradic-

TABLE 8.4
Cocaine-Related Financial Problems of Users and Quitters

I. *Did you have any cocaine-related money problems while you were (are) using coke?*	*Users* (N = 122)	*Quitters* (N = 106)	*TOTAL* (N = 228)
No	(53) 43.4%	(54) 50.9%	(107) 46.9%
Yes	(69) 56.6	(52) 49.1	(121) 53.1
II. *If yes: Tell me about them.*	(N = 69)	(N = 52)	(N = 121)
Ran out of money	(38) 55.1	(17) 32.7	(55) 45.4
Went into debt	(10) 14.5	(16) 30.8	(26) 21.5
Sold valuable items	(9) 13.0	(7) 13.5	(16) 13.2
Could not pay for essentials	(9) 13.0	(7) 13.5	(16) 13.2
Lost mortgage/house	(1) 1.4	(2) 3.8	(3) 2.5
Other	(12) 17.4	(14) 26.9	(26) 21.5
III. *Which of the following did you lose or have to sell because of your cocaine use?*	(N = 122)	(N = 106)	(N = 228)
Savings or other money assets	(43) 35.2	(58) 54.7	(101) 44.3
House	(4) 3.3	(4) 3.8	(8) 3.5
Car	(10) 8.2	(10) 9.4	(20) 8.8
Large material items	(23) 18.8	(20) 18.9	(43) 18.9
Furniture	(9) 7.4	(8) 7.5	(17) 7.4
Business	(6) 4.9	(9) 8.5	(15) 6.6
Other	(10) 8.2	(9) 8.5	(19) 8.3

Note: Percentages do not total 100 because of multiple responses.

tory conclusions. First, despite their heavy use, most of our respondents did not go as far toward fiscal collapse as the figures given in media accounts or treatment advertisements. Second, however, a significant minority of our users reported spending large enough sums on cocaine to experience serious financial strain. While most seemed to stop when cocaine use got "too expensive," there were exceptions:

- An attorney became a secret, compulsive freebaser. At his peak period he used more than fifty grams a week for eight weeks, and embezzled money from his clients for a year and a half. He was never caught, but after he went to treatment he revealed the crime to his partner and arranged to make restitution. (Case #106)
- A young woman inherited $25,000 at 16 years of age and began a long run of heavy use as a freebaser (fourteen grams a week for three months). At age 22 she was in an automobile accident in which two people were killed; she suffered a severe brain injury, was in a coma for ten days, and was partially paralyzed for six months. An insurance company paid her $15,000 for her injuries and she spent most of that amount on cocaine also. At the interview she was 23 years old and still using regularly but not in such heavy amounts. (Case #624)
- A yacht sales manager went on a four-year uninterrupted run, using ten grams of cocaine a week. He estimates that he spent $200,000 during that period. He simply stopped when he realized that his use was having a profound effect on his wife and children. At the interview he had not used in eighteen months and was confident that he could maintain his resolve. (Case #404)

Workplace Problems

There has been little systematic research on the incidence of cocaine use in the workplace or its impact on work performance. Much has been written about the topic, both in the popular media and in journals aimed at employee assistance–program (EAP) clinicians. Yet most of the information in the media is either anecdotal or speculative, and EAP journals typically cover people who present themselves for treatment in specific companies (mostly for alcohol and mental health problems). Representatives of industry, EAP professionals, and treatment practitioners have sounded alarms about the devastating impact of cocaine. But there is little systematic data with which to evaluate the many claims that an epidemic of cocaine abuse in U.S. workplaces is causing a decline in productivity or increases in absenteeism and health costs.[1]

We gathered some limited data about cocaine and work, but our information is neither extensive or definitive. The workplace was but one of several domains in which we thought cocaine users might have problems and we did not attempt to explore it comprehensively. Any thorough study must consider the ways in which cocaine use interacts with a variety of other factors known to affect productivity and costs (e.g., capital investment [or the lack thereof] in productivity-enhancing plants and equipment, labor-management relations, the nature of the labor process, individual performance levels, working conditions, job satisfaction, and other drug use, especially alcohol [Reinarman, Waldorf, and Murphy, 1988]).

Ideally, a more in-depth approach also would include questions on the ways in which cocaine enhances or increases work performance as well as how it detracts from it. Indeed, in our focused interviews many respondents reported that cocaine use allowed them to tolerate tasks they otherwise regarded as too repetitive, alienating, or boring. Many reported that cocaine made them more productive or assisted them in meeting deadlines or working long hours. For example, one 24-year-old white woman worked two jobs, as a window display artist and as a waitress and found that cocaine helped her be more productive in both.

Wendy was a rare case of someone who used cocaine mostly for work. Her two jobs meant a seventy-to-eighty–hour work week. As a store window artist, she found cocaine boosted both her energy and her creativity. "I did some really cool and outrageous displays, and I might not have gone as far with [them] if I hadn't been on coke." With "tedious work" like her restaurant job, cocaine "made me work a lot faster." She eventually quit this job and [stopped using] cocaine for a time in part because she "realized how much money I had spent on it." Months later she ended up living with a dealer and using again. After suffering the "hassles" of dealing and seeing some friends get into trouble, Wendy eventually stopped using. She was going back to college and had things she was "striving for." Unlike her previous jobs, she found that cocaine did not help her with her studies: "It inhibited me completely and [I] just couldn't study at all while I was doing it. . . . I couldn't focus on anything." (Case #569)

In our structured questionnaire, we focused only on the potential negative consequences of cocaine use vis-à-vis work. We asked our respondents four questions that were designed to explore some of the basic cocaine-related problems that users might experience at work: "Did you ever: (a) take days off from your job (or school) as result of cocaine use? (b) have a strained relationship with your boss (or teachers) because of coke use? (c) lose a job (or quit school) as a result of coke use? (d) feel you were not working well because of your coke use?"

The most frequently reported workplace problems were absenteeism, (a), and erosion of productivity, (d). About two in three of our respondents had been absent from work at least once and felt that at least on some occasions they had not worked well because of cocaine use (see Table 8.5). One in three said they had experienced strain in relationships with a boss or teachers at least in part because of cocaine use. Quitters reported such strained relations more than users, but the difference was not statistically significant. Finally, one in five of our heavy users reported that they had lost a job or quit school as a result of cocaine use.

Clearly these data suggest significant workplace problems related to heavy cocaine use. As with heavy drinkers who have frequent hangovers, a majority of our respondents missed days of work or did not work at their full capacity on at least some occasions because of their cocaine use. This was true for both users and quitters, males and females, smokers and snorters, and for all ethnic groups. Our in-depth interviews suggest that such negative impacts vary among individuals, types of job, stage of using career, etc. For many of our respondents, cocaine use was an aid to productivity in the beginning of their

TABLE 8.5
Workplace Problems of Users and Quitters: Percentage Answering Yes

Which of the following did you ever do because of cocaine use?	Users (N = 122)	Quitters (N = 106)	TOTAL (N = 228)
Take days off	(78) 63.9%	(76) 71.7%	(154) 67.5%
Have strained relationships with your boss or teachers	(36) 29.5	(43) 40.6	(79) 34.6
Lose a job or quit school	(21) 17.2	(27) 25.5	(48) 21.1
Feel you were not working well	(81) 66.4	(69) 65.1	(150) 65.8

Note: None of the differences is statistically significant.

use or when they were nippers or controlled users. However, if their use escalated or they began extended binges, they tended to have more cocaine-related problems at work.

Interestingly, these workplace problems also mitigated *against* forms of cocaine use that might affect work. Many respondents maintained rules, the specific purpose of which was to control use so that it would not impinge on work or career. Others told us that the potential of cocaine use to affect their jobs negatively had led them to cut down or avoid using at work. For example, Roger, a white, 36-year-old comptroller for a national corporation, used to snort cocaine at work, but then stopped the practice precisely because he did not want it to affect his work or his relations with colleagues, including workers he supervised.

> It was almost like gamesmanship, and I would sneak off [to snort] because you could keep yourself amused. . . . But it could make me edgy. And because I was dealing with the public that was a problem. That's the same reason I quit drinking at lunches. . . . I reached a point I couldn't do those things. . . . I got promoted to the biggest operation we ever had . . . at which point I got very serious and I guess all my energy was put into work, totally. . . .
> It's a fine line between subordinates and friends. You got to

be friends before you're willing to take chances with the image because, right or wrong, they [subordinates] are different. There is some level of image that's necessary to be able to function. I'm not a manager who's big on form, but the reality still remains that if all the people know I do drugs, there are a whole lot of prospective problems that come out of it. If you are supposed to lead and be respected . . . you are dealing with a whole lot of people's perception—"The boss is a junkie"—and who knows what else would come out of that. . . .

I had work and a career that I had to maintain just for personal self-respect. . . . M—— and I used to go off at lunch and drink beers and smoke a joint over tabletop hockey and come back too silly to cope. I just had to stop because I couldn't do the job in the afternoon, or at least not the way I thought I had to. . . . I started feeling that I was embarrassing myself at work and I was not willing to do that. So you start cleaning up your act because you want to the world to perceive you like *you* want to be perceived. (Case #910)

Roger's description of his own moral calculus struck us as telling. His investment in his career and his sense of identity and self-respect ultimately determined his pattern of drug use, not the reverse. Others, of course, for one reason or another were not always able to stick to such a calculus. We hypothesize, however, that the allures of cocaine are mediated by the allures of work with which they invariably interact. Thus, we suspect that the more important and meaningful a job is to an individual, the more likely she or he will be able to regulate drug use so that it does not adversely affect work.

We would be naïve not to add that we are speaking of probabilities here rather than certainties, because there is no shortage of heavy users who have ruined or jeopardized interesting, high-status careers on cocaine. Nonetheless, the idea that investment in a job and a work-based identity can moderate one's drug use helps explain why the consequences of cocaine use appear more devastating among the unemployed of the inner cities than among our working- and middle-class respondents (e.g., Bourgois, 1989).

Sexual Problems

The last problem domain we explored was sex. As with cocaine-related work problems, much has been written about this topic but little systematic empirical research has been done on it with users in the community. Most of the studies that exist are either anecdotal accounts of a few cases or are based on samples from treatment programs (e.g., Siegel, 1982; Smith, Wesson, and Apter-Marsh, 1984; Gay and Sheppard, 1973; Gay et al., 1982; Washton and Gold, 1984). Because our subjects were drawn from natural settings in the community, their reports may help flesh out our knowledge about cocaine's effects on sex.

Our exploration of this topic was biased toward the negative. We were not attempting a definitive or balanced account that would include questions about cocaine's reputation as an aphrodisiac or enhancer of sexual relations. We were primarily interested in problems that might lead users to stop using. We asked six questions on sexual problems. The first was neutral and open-ended: "What kind of effect did cocaine have on your sex life?"

The pattern of responses was complex. One in six of our subjects reported that cocaine had no effects on their sex lives. About one in three mentioned only positive effects, and the same proportion mentioned only negative effects. The remaining one-sixth gave mixed reports. The most frequent type of response was a general one about cocaine's positive effects on sexuality; one-fifth of our respondents gave such accounts. Smaller numbers spoke in more specific terms about increased endurance ("longer hang time" was the phrase used by several of the men), heightened sensation or awareness ("makes you tingle all over"), or lowered inhibitions ("it relaxed me, let me get a little crazy"). This open-ended question also elicited accounts of negative sexual effects. One in six gave responses that were generally negative. One-fifth reported that cocaine caused them to feel specifically insensitive, asexual, or "too jittery for sex."

We followed this general question with three structured items about sexual troubles commonly reported by cocaine users: feeling too sensitive to have sex, feeling insensitive, and trouble having an orgasm. In addition, all males were asked about erection problems. Although one in five respondents reported none of these problems, four in five did experience at least one such cocaine-related sexual difficulty on at least some occasions. Those who did most frequently cited trouble getting or maintaining erections, feeling insensitive, and trouble having orgasms (see Table 8.6–I).

Three out of five males said they had at some time experienced erection problems because of their cocaine use. A 26-year-old Asian man told us, for example, that after snorting, "I can be horny as hell, but erections are sometimes difficult" (Case #560). Others made the same point in just these terms. A white male snorter, also in his late twenties, observed, "Sometimes it was terrible and I couldn't get it up. You want it and you're horny as hell, but it ain't workin' " (Case #557). A 39-year-old black male freebaser put it most succinctly: "My mind was hard, but everything else was soft" (Case #627). These accounts were corroborated by several of the women. One 35-year-old black woman who freebased with her husband reported that "it aroused his sexual feelings . . . but it didn't arouse his penis" (Case #107).

In the open-ended section of our interviews we confirmed that cocaine tends to have a biphasic, dose-related effect on male sexuality. As Shakespeare's porter explained to Macbeth about alcohol, it "provokes the desire, but takes away the performance." The quotations above suggest that cocaine's effects on sexuality are strikingly similar, particularly for men. Early in a user's career or at low doses most of our male respondents had no trouble getting an erection and in fact often became more easily aroused. But after prolonged use or large doses many reported difficulties attaining or maintaining an erection, and for some, including many shooters and smokers, the turn-on of the drug often supplanted that of sex.

After erection problems, the next most frequently men-

TABLE 8.6
Sexual Problems of Users and Quitters: Percentage Answering Yes

I. Did you ever have any of the following problems because of cocaine?	Users (N = 122)	Quitters (N = 106)	TOTAL (N = 228)
Feeling too sensitive to have sex	(33) 27.0%	(36) 34.0%	(69) 30.3%
Feeling insensitive	(69) 56.6	(68) 64.2	(137) 60.1
Trouble having orgasm	(69) 56.6	(66) 62.3	(135) 59.2
(Males only)	(N = 80)	(N = 59)	(N = 139)
Trouble getting an erection	(48) 60.0	(37) 62.7	(85) 61.2

II. Which one occurred most frequently?			(N = 183)*
Feeling too sensitive to have sex			(23) 12.6%
Feeling insensitive			(66) 36.1
Trouble having orgasms			(72) 39.3
(Males only) Trouble getting an erection			(41) 48.2%†

Note: None of the differences is statistically significant.
*45 Respondents did not have any problems "frequently," so the total N is less than in part I.
†Percentage of the 85 males who reported erection problems.

tioned sexual problems were feeling insensitive and trouble having orgasms, mentioned by about three respondents in five. The problem of insensitivity was captured by a 37-year-old white female snorter: "I felt like a mannequin, no feelings at all" (Case #319). Conversely, a 49-year-old white woman snorter reported "more intensity . . . and more energy" for sex, but "no satisfaction" (Case #310). Another middle-aged white female snorter said that both she and her partner had difficulty achieving orgasm: "Our sex life became really fucked because on coke he never came and it was hard for me to come. So it was this endless and frustrating sexual encounter" (Case #411). Last, nearly one in three reported that they had felt too sensitive (e.g., "overamped") to have sex. As a 33-year-old white woman snorter reported, "Coke tenses you up, it doesn't relax you, so it's really counterproductive to sex, I think" (Case #441). A Latino male in his mid-twenties similarly noted that after a lot of cocaine, the feeling both he and his partner had was "get away from me" (Case #506).

We also asked which of the four specific problems occurred most frequently (see Table 8.6–II). Again our respondents cited erection problems most often; nearly half of the males who said they had ever experienced cocaine-related sexual problems said that erection problems were the most frequently recurring. Trouble having orgasms and feeling insensitive were the next most frequently recurring problems (see also Macdonald et al., 1988). There were no significant differences in the prevalence of these problems between users and quitters.

Significant differences became apparent when we considered length of cocaine-using career. The longer heavy use continues, the more likely respondents of both genders were to report feeling too insensitive to have sex because of cocaine (see Table 8.7). Seven in ten of our long-term heavy users who reported sexual difficulties reported feeling insensitive in at least some sexual encounters, while less than half of the shorter-term heavy users made such reports. Similarly, male long-term users also reported more erection problems than male short-term users.

These data, along with our more open-ended discussions with respondents, brought us to the same conclusion as clinicians and most users themselves: the longer one uses large amounts of cocaine, the more likely one is to experience sexual as well as other problems. Most of our respondents initially found cocaine to be an aphrodisiac and generally experienced positive effects during the early stages of their use, or when they had reduced their use to lower doses and lower frequency. However, as doses increased and as regular use continued over longer periods, a large proportion of males began to have erection problems and a somewhat smaller but still substantial proportion of women came to feel insensitive or had difficulty achieving orgasm. Other than this, there were few gender differences in rates of cocaine-related sexual problems. Although as many as one in four experienced none of

TABLE 8.7
Sexual Problems by Length of Heavy Cocaine Use

	Length of Heavy Use		
	6.9 Months or Less	7–10.9 Months	11 Months or More
I. *Did you ever feel too insensitive to have sex because of cocaine?*	(N = 72)	(N = 43)	(N = 113)
Percentage answering yes	(33) 45.8%	(25) 58.1%	(79) 69.9%
		[Chi Square = 10.715, 1 df; significance: p = <.0047]	
II. *(Males only): Did you ever have trouble getting an erection because of cocaine?*	(N = 46)	(N = 28)	(N = 74)
Percentage answering yes	(20) 43.5%	(16) 57.1%	(49) 66.2%
		[Chi Square = 6.000, 1 df; significance: p = <.0498]	

these troubles, the majority of our respondents reported experiencing at least one of them on at least some occasions.[2]

Given the prevalence of such cocaine-related sexual problems among our users, it is worth asking why so many persisted in their cocaine use. Surely even occasional sexual dysfunction would provide a significant spur to cessation. To judge from their accounts, most of our users seemed to answer that on most occasions, cocaine continued to have positive sexual effects overall—loosening inhibitions and allowing more innovation, erotic sensation, and, importantly for men prone to premature ejaculation, sexual endurance.

WHO HAD THE MOST PROBLEMS?

In an effort to unravel the obvious complexities of our data on cocaine-related problems, we undertook an analysis of variance to determine which among the basic subgroups reported the most problems. We compared users with quitters, treated quitters with untreated quitters, men with women, whites with minorities, and snorters with smokers and shooters. To our surprise the only statistically significant differences occurred between users and quitters, and among quitters, between the treated and the untreated.

Users Compared with Quitters

We began our study with the hypothesis that those who experienced the most problems would be more likely to quit than those who continued to use. We therefore expected our quitters to report more problems than our users. In most problem domains, however, the data did not support this notion, at least with respect to the total number of problems. Among the seven different problem domains, we found significant differences between users and quitters in only two: mental health problems and relationship problems. In the case of mental health, quitters reported a higher mean number of problems than did users (1.79 to 1.44). For relationship problems, similarly, quitters reported an average of 3.23 problems and users reported only 2.29 (see Table 8.8). The fact that quitters reported significantly more mental health problems and relationship problems than users is unsurprising. In our in-depth life history interviews we heard many accounts of how prolonged heavy cocaine use made people "stressed out" and strained their relationships. We also got the impression that cocaine-related problems in the other realms, say, at work or with money, either were expressed in or added to cocaine's toll on intimate relationships and psychological well-being.

As for why significant differences between users and quitters did not appear in the other problem domains, several reasons come to mind. Time could be a factor, for many quitters had given up cocaine a number of years prior to our interview, and some may have simply forgotten how heavy cocaine use had affected their lives. Others may have had selective recall about the problems they did experience—per-

TABLE 8.8
Mean Number of Yes Answers, Combined Problem Variables of Users and Quitters

Problem Areas (Combined Variables)	Subsamples		Analysis of Variance	
	Users (N = 122)	Quitters (N = 106)	F Test	Significance
Health problems (19 variables)	5.96	5.58	1.653	n.s.
Nasal problems (5 variables)	2.80	2.49	3.848	n.s.
Mental problems (4 variables)	1.44	1.79	5.456	.020
Relationship problems (4 variables)	2.29	3.23	4.665	.032
Financial problems (8 variables)	0.86	1.11	1.844	n.s.
Workplace problems (4 variables)	1.77	2.02	2.377	n.s.
Sexual problems (3 variables)	1.40	1.60	2.194	n.s.

Note: n.s. = not statistically significant.

haps remembering more of the positive aspects of their drug use or not wanting to remember the negative aspects. And, as clinicians often note, some current users may be "in denial" about the extent to which their drug use is causing problems. In research about illicit activities among hard-to-reach groups, self-reports are the only method for gathering information, and they are vulnerable to all the vicissitudes of subjectivity.

It may also be the case, however, that users in fact had about as many problems as quitters but merely interpreted them as less important or had a higher tolerance for them. For example, the vast majority of all our snorters experienced nasal irritations, but some felt these were frightening omens while others found them a mere annoyance. Recall, too, that George, the freebaser described in Chapter 6, wanted to go "back on the pipe" only hours after having a severe seizure, while others quit immediately after the first sign of health trouble. Obviously, we cannot say that a specific number or type of problems will prompt a user to quit; some quit without experiencing any problems while others persisted long after any sane person should have stopped. We will analyze motivations for quitting more fully in the next chapter. What we can say here is that the relationship between cocaine-related problems and decisions to use or quit is mediated by a range of subjective factors. We could see these ethnographically and in our in-depth interviews, but we could rarely build precise measures of them into our questionnaire. Whether problems lead to cessation depends on how much pleasure a user feels is at stake, and on how much trouble he or she can manage, put up with, or rationalize away, given other elements in his or her life.

Treated Quitters Compared with Untreated Quitters

Among the quitters we found that those who had sought and received treatment reported more problems than those who had not. This pattern held for five of the seven problem domains (see Table 8.9). Thus, treated quitters reported significantly more nasal, other physical health, mental health, financial, and work problems than untreated quitters.

These differences may be explained in at least two ways. First and foremost, treated quitters may, as our data suggest, have experienced more problems in more domains than the untreated and thus were prompted to get help. This is a commonsensical explanation that fits well with our data. A second explanation is also possible, however, and it is not incompatible with the first. Going to treatment typically involves several rather radical learning experiences, one of which is retrospectively reinterpreting one's drug-using career. Treatment programs immerse clients in a new world with a unique discourse—the conceptual vocabulary of "addictive disease." To succeed in almost any treatment program, drug users-cum-

TABLE 8.9
Mean Number of Yes Answers, Combined Problem Variables
of Treated and Untreated Quitters

Problem Areas (Combined Variables)	Subsamples		Analysis of Variance	
	Treated (N = 30)	Untreated (N = 76)	F-Test	Significances
Health problems (19 variables)	6.87	5.07	13.775	.004
Nasal problems (5 variables)	3.03	2.28	7.623	.007
Mental problems (4 variables)	2.30	1.59	8.325	.005
Financial problems (8 variables)	1.77	0.85	8.652	−.004
Work problems (4 variables)	2.83	1.71	20.466	.0000
Sexual problems (3 variables)	1.87	1.50	2.723	n.s.
Relationship problems (4 variables)	3.00	3.31	0.113	n.s.

Note: n.s. = not statistically significant.

treatment clients must use this new vocabulary to recognize, describe, and express feelings about their problems with drugs. This kind of learning and reinterpretation occurs in Twelve-Step programs, hospital-based programs, and individual and group therapies.

Many of our treated respondents found this learning experience helpful, and, whether or not it "worked," it did tend to make them at least more aware of and articulate about cocaine-related problems. Further, in treatment discourse, drugs are conceived of as central causal forces. Thus, treated quitters may also learn to attribute more of their life troubles to their cocaine use, regardless of whether the drug caused, only exacerbated, or was only incidentally related to those problems. The converse may also be true; untreated quitters may attribute fewer of their problems to cocaine than may have been the case. Thus, under the influence of treatment programs, treated quitters may overestimate the causal influence of cocaine on their life problems, just as in the absence of such influence untreated quitters may underestimate the problems they had with the drug. In each instance, there is no easy way to assess empirically the truth of such causal attributions. But in attempting to make sense of our data we must note that the difference between the number of problems reported by treated and untreated quitters may be real, or an artifact of selective perception, or a bit of both. That is, treated quitters may actually have experienced more problems, *and* they may have learned how to talk about them better than those who have not received treatment.

While a minority of our long-term heavy users never experienced cocaine-related problems, a clear majority experienced some problems at some point in their careers. Among the most frequently mentioned were nasal irritations, insomnia, paranoia, strained spousal relationships, depleted savings, hangover days at work, and periodic sexual difficulties. As we noted, quitters reported somewhat more problems with relationships and mental health than users, and treated quitters mentioned more problems in most areas than untreated quitters.

Some of these problems were experienced as serious, but most were not. Most of our subjects appeared to find most of these problems manageable most of the time. Again and again in our in-depth interviews we heard cocaine-related troubles discussed in matter-of-fact tones. We pressed them with dozens of questions about problems, but rarely heard amazement or alarm in their admissions, even in retrospect. For every seizure story we heard perhaps a hundred hangover stories. They seemed to get pleasure from cocaine, and they seemed to understand that the hassles and risks simply went with the territory. "You buy the ticket, you take the ride," as one put it. We say this not to minimize the problems we have spent a chapter documenting, but rather to render understandable our respondents' continued use in the face of them.

At some point, however, many of them came to find themselves in more trouble, in more ways, and in less time than they had anticipated. Certainly the quitters described in the next chapter, and even many current users, would agree that cocaine is not a drug that can be used heavily for long by many without risking problems.

PART III

QUITTING COCAINE

CHAPTER 9

QUITTING COCAINE: MOTIVES, STRATEGIES, AND ACTIONS

C*laude, the 20-year-old* student who experienced a grand
mal seizure and promptly quit using cocaine, was unusual; in
most cases the motivations for stopping are more complicated. In this chapter we will illustrate this complexity by
juxtaposing case summaries with quantitative data on the
motives for quitting reported by the 106 quitters we interviewed. Then we will explore their strategies and the specific
steps they took to quit.

CASE SUMMARIES

Edie (Case #436)

Edie, the dealer we described in Chapter 5, began using
cocaine when she was 30 years old in 1967. At that time she
was working as a waitress in a rock nightclub in San Francisco
that she called a "salt and pepper bar," meaning that patrons
were both black and white. She initially used cocaine at a
party after work and continued occasional use for two years at
similar social occasions. She used approximately once a week
during that period and seldom bought the drug herself. When
she changed jobs her pattern of use changed. "I moved downtown to a Montgomery Street Bar—more money, but no

cocaine." Rather than once a week she used once a month. She typically snorted the drug, but on five or six occasions over the next ten years she injected with friends.

The next change in her use occurred when she and her husband Steve began to sell cocaine. They had sold marijuana at various levels for a number of years, and when an old marijuana customer developed a connection for good-quality cocaine, they began to sell cocaine in small amounts to their marijuana customers. The margin of profit on marijuana was declining, so they gradually stopped selling marijuana in favor of cocaine.

When they started selling cocaine both Edie and her husband began to use it more often. She used moderately for three years, but gradually escalated her use to one gram a week for two years. As a nipper, she used small amounts nearly every day, but never went on heavy binges. She was working regularly and raising three children. Her husband became an extremely heavy binge user and resisted all her efforts to keep his use at a manageable level. Unlike Edie, Steve had never held a "straight" job, had always sold drugs, and consequently assumed the values of a "hustler." She began to feel that he was "shorting" her on profits.

With her husband's heavy binge use their sex life began to deteriorate; he became impotent without losing his desire and she became disinterested. At the same time his behavior grew more bizarre and his relations with her children became strained. She began to feel that he was "going to pieces" and there was nothing she could do about it. He thwarted her efforts to contain his cocaine use, often making secret arrangements to get cocaine from customers when she tried to limit his supply.

At that point they discovered that some of their old marijuana suppliers were being "rolled up" by federal drug agents, so they moved to another county and cut back their sales activities. Edie did not like the new house or the town and felt isolated from her friends in the city. At one point she left Steve for three months and took her children to a seaside town. She tried to stop using cocaine, but could not because she was still selling. After Edie moved back in with him, Steve's bizarre behavior subsided, but only temporarily. He continued to binge on cocaine and soon became paranoid (often hiding from imaginary threats) and difficult to live with. After some months of feeling that he was "beyond help," she left him and moved to another city.

Nine months later Steve approached Edie with a lucrative sales proposition, proceeds from which they were to share equally. She did most of the work and bore most of the risk, but when it came time to divide the proceeds he again shorted her. She decided to stop seeing him, stop selling, and stop using. And she did.

In a recent follow-up, Edie told us that she had used only four lines of cocaine in the past three years. She bought it twice but gave the drug away because she no longer enjoyed it. She was living with a new lover who did not use cocaine and she was happy at her new job.

It seems safe to say that Edie had many motives for quitting her involvement with cocaine. She had no serious health problems, but she did not like what the drug had done to her sex life. Her legitimate work was never affected because she always "took care of business." Nor did she have financial problems (in fact, they made "good money" dealing). She did, however, feel ripped off by Steve in regard to their sales profits. Perhaps most important, the key relationships in her life suffered because of cocaine. She did not like Steve's heavy binges, bizarre behavior, and paranoia, or especially the strained relationships between him and her children. Moreover, when they had to move for fear of arrest she not only felt a general loss of community but was isolated from the very friends who might have compensated for the strain in those important relationships. The theme here, it seems to us, is that the fabric of human relations that gave meaning to Edie's everyday life had worn thin because of cocaine. When that occurred, she simply gave up the drug.

Henry (Case #402)

Relationships were also an important factor in Henry's decision to quit using cocaine. He is an outgoing, charming, 31-year-old attorney who was a childhood friend of one of the project staff. She had seen him regularly while he used and sold cocaine.

Henry began using cocaine in high school and used for nearly ten years. He used heavily for a year, a gram per day for three weeks at his peak. He began to sell cocaine shortly after he began to use, "I couldn't afford to purchase it, so it was a matter of if I wanted to imbibe I had to sell." And sell he did for seven years, starting small, buying parts of ounces and selling grams, and then buying multiple ounces and selling or fronting quarter ounces. During most of this period, he attended a major university, played sports regularly, and worked at a variety of "straight" jobs.

Toward the end of his cocaine-using career he began to have severe sinus problems as a direct result of snorting cocaine. "I couldn't breathe for two days afterward," he once told us. His mother knew that he was selling cocaine and disapproved. At one point she asked him to move out of her house because she did not want him to think that she condoned his actions. He moved out, but did not stop selling until two years later. Henry's father, who was dying of cancer, knew of his sales business and while he did not outwardly disapprove, "He asked me if I would be good enough to stop selling for my mother's sake."

Henry planned to go to law school and believed that continued sales might risk a "felony bust" and jeopardize his future career. Furthermore, he knew he would not buy just for his own use, so if he stopped selling he would also stop using. Without fanfare and on the first attempt he stopped selling and stopped using. He experienced no withdrawal symptoms and found nothing especially difficult about quitting. For two years he did not use a single line of cocaine, but more recently has used occasionally when it was offered. Since he stopped selling and using he has completed law school, passed the bar exam the first time, and opened a new private law practice.

Like Edie, Henry had many motives for quitting cocaine. His sinuses remained stuffed up long after the euphoria had evaporated. This unpleasant aftereffect grew more annoying as the years went by. The people who mattered most to him—his mother and his dying father—wanted him to stop selling. Henry also worried that the career in law he had long envisioned might be put at risk. As cocaine conflicted with people and plans in which he was invested, Henry just stopped.

In other interviews we uncovered various combinations of such motives. For some people, the loss of large sums of money was a spur to cessation. One woman described a litany of cocaine-related woes centering on "how much money I had spent on it," and on the destructiveness of those around her—people becoming "addicted, selfish, and weird," and "junkies . . . doin' a lot of heroin to come off the coke." Another told us she was simply tired of "getting very paranoid" whenever she "did more than three lines." While the configuration of motives was unique in each case, there were common complaints with a similar subtext: quitters seemed to be saying that when the cocaine that had once enhanced and enriched their lives began to make those lives more difficult, they were moved to stop.

QUANTITATIVE FINDINGS

In the quantitative section of our interviews we presented respondents a list of thirteen possible motives or reasons for quitting. The most frequently mentioned was health problems; nearly half cited this reason as instrumental in their decision to quit (see Table 9.1). The next most frequently cited were financial problems, mentioned by two in five, and problems at work and pressure from a spouse or lover cited by one in three.

To our surprise, criminal justice sanctions did not rank

TABLE 9.1
Self-Reports of Reasons to Quit Using Cocaine, by Treated and Untreated: Percentage Answering Yes

	Total Quitters (N = 106)	Rank Order	Treated (N = 30)	Untreated (N = 76)	Chi Square	Significance
Reason to quit			Subsamples			
Health problems	(50) 47.2%	1	(15) 50.0%	(35) 46.1%	0.92	n.s.
Financial problems	(43) 40.6	2	(19) 63.3	(24) 31.6	7.45	.006
Work problems	(38) 35.8	3	(20) 66.7	(18) 23.7	14.73	.0001
Pressure from spouse and/or lover	(35) 33.0	4	(16) 53.3	(19) 25.0	6.35	.01
Decision to stop selling	(31) 29.2	5				
Fear of arrest for possession or sales	(30) 28.3	6				
Pressure from friends	(29) 27.3	7				
Pressure from family	(28) 26.4	8				
Decline in quality of cocaine	(18) 17.0	9				
Difficulties obtaining cocaine	(13) 12.3	10				
Pressures from fellow users	(12) 11.3	11				
Other	(8) 7.5	12				
Arrest for possession	(6) 5.7	13				
Arrest for drug sales	(1) 0.9	14				

Note: After the fourth most frequent reason to quit, the number of responses was too small for meaningful comparisons between treated and untreated groups or for tests of statistical significance. Percentages do not totally exactly 100 because of multiple responses. Degrees of freedom = 1; n.s. = not significant.

high among our respondents' reasons to quit. Only seven persons cited actual arrests, although about one in four mentioned fear of arrest for possession or sales as one reason for their decision. These data suggest that direct criminal justice pressure through actual arrests was not a major reason for quitting, although indirect pressure felt as fear of arrest was a factor for some. Like Erickson and Murray (1989), our respondents reported that concerns about personal health, for example, were more compelling.

We analyzed the four most frequently cited reasons to quit by sex, ethnicity, method of use, and treatment status to see if different types of users tended to have different motives for quitting. Only treatment history proved to be significant.

Respondents who had been to treatment cited financial problems, work problems, and pressures from spouse or lover more than those who had not been treated. Nearly two-thirds of the treated cases cited financial problems while only a third of the treated cases did. Similarly, two-thirds of the treated group cited problems at work while only a quarter of the untreated cases did, and half the treated cited social pressures from a spouse or lover while only a quarter of the untreated gave this reason. There were no such significant differences with regard to health problems; roughly half of both groups cited health problems as a reason to quit. Together with our findings on problems cited in Chapter 8, these data suggest that for untreated users, cocaine does not appear to have affected finances, work, and spousal relations as much as it did for the treated respondents.

We asked all quitters an additional open-ended summary question on the most important reason or reasons to quit. From their responses we discovered that many respondents quit for reasons not specified in our structured list of possible motives. In response to the open-ended question, three-fifths mentioned some form of psychological problem or stressful state caused by cocaine as the most important reason to quit (see Table 9.2). The second most important reason to quit was financial problems, cited by nearly a quarter. The third most

TABLE 9.2
Self-Reports of Most Important Reasons
to Quit Using Cocaine (open-ended question)

What was the most important reason or reasons to quit?	Total Quitters (N = 106)	
Psychological problems or stressful states	(65)	61.3%
Financial problems	(24)	22.6%
Severe or recurrent health problems or concerns	(20)	18.9%
Changes in effects of the drug	(14)	13.2%
Fears of dying or suicide	(5)	4.7%
Fears of arrest or rip-off	(4)	3.8%
Stopped selling cocaine	(4)	3.8%
Pregnancy	(2)	1.9%
Decline in quality of the drug	(1)	.9%
Other	(60)	56.6%
No answers	(2)	1.9%

Note: Percentages do not total 100 because of multiple responses.

cited type of reason was recurrent health problems or concerns, mentioned by about one in five.[1]

While our case studies suggest that each quitter has a unique configuration of motives for giving up cocaine, the aggregate data show that psychological and physical health problems, financial strain, and pressure from significant others were especially important. Well-being, love, and money are, after all, central to human existence, so it is not surprising that when cocaine harms people in one or more of these basic realms they will be motivated to quit using it.

STRATEGIES FOR QUITTING

As might be expected there was great diversity in the actions our subjects took to quit using cocaine. At one extreme, individuals made several attempts to stop and took numerous actions before they actually succeeded. Some experienced profound anguish and despair over the powers the drug had over them and found it extremely difficult to maintain any resolve to stop using. For example, a 33-year-old freebaser whom we have called Harry went to great lengths.

Harry (Case #106)

Harry began using cocaine when he was 26 and moved to San Francisco from the Midwest. As we mentioned earlier, he worked as a stockbroker, went to law school in the evenings, and enjoyed many social activities among a group of smart-set bisexuals. For two years he used approximately two grams of cocaine a month and generally enjoyed the heightened awareness he experienced on cocaine. His use increased to two grams a week when he began to study for the bar examination, and he maintains to this day that he could not have passed the exam without cocaine: "it confirmed all of my beliefs that cocaine was a wonderful drug because I didn't think that I had the capacity of passing."

Upon passing the exam he set up a very lucrative practice with the contacts he had developed as a stockbroker and socialite. At the same time he began to experience severe headaches, sore throats, and general nasal problems, which he attributed to snorting the drug. To alleviate these problems he decided to freebase. Initially, freebasing provided some relief from the physical ailments he experienced snorting, but then he became a compulsive freebaser. At one point he even rented a separate apartment near his law office just for freebasing, away from the home he shared with his wife and children. Very quickly his use escalated to nearly an ounce (28 grams) a week, a pattern he maintained for six months. At his peak he claimed to have used two ounces a week for about a month, which is an extremely large amount. Harry did not sell cocaine, so purchasing such large amounts became expensive. He handled the expense by embezzling funds from some of his clients.

In this peak period he made a rather halfhearted decision

to get away from the drug and cut down. He was prompted by a bad car accident; he fell asleep at the wheel on the way to a trial and demolished his car and another along the side of the road. "I didn't consider myself an addict [and believed] I could break the sequence, stay clean for a while, and be able to use again when I wanted to."

After the accident Harry went to Cokenders, a short-term (one-week) residential treatment program, and participated actively. But upon returning to San Francisco he relapsed to his old pattern of one ounce a week. He was not under any pressure to go to Cokenders because he had successfully kept the police away from the accident scene, and his insurance covered the costs of replacing both cars. He continued to use for another month, then went to an outpatient program for a single session without any break in his pattern of use. A week after that attempt he decided to get away from San Francisco and his connection in the hope that he could clean up and stop for a time. He chose La Costa, a health resort, as the site for his vacation from coke and stayed there for ten days during which time he did not use. While in La Costa he conceived a scheme to make certain he would not use upon returning home. The scheme was to have a companion stay with him day and night to discourage him from using. He found a person who would serve in that role, but after maintaining the plan for three days he evaded the companion, bought an ounce, and returned to his freebasing apartment.

At that point his relationship with his parents and his wife began to seriously deteriorate. They knew of his heavy cocaine use but did not know how to help him. His relatives were despondent about it, and his wife was considering divorce. He felt his family pulling away from him because of his inability to stop freebasing compulsively.

After another two-month run of freebasing he tried again to clean up. This time he went to a friend's house and "crashed." In his earlier attempts to quit he would go to sleep for two or three days and upon awakening feel somewhat revived. This time he slept for only a day and awoke feeling just as bad. To ease his mounting anxiety he took fifty Valium tablets over a twenty-four-hour period. When his friend discovered his overdosed condition, he telephoned Harry's wife who put him in a psychiatric hospital for seventy-two hours. Describing the hospitalization he said, "I was incoherent, I don't remember any of that. All I remember is waking up in a hospital cocaine program." Harry remained in this second treatment program for twenty-eight days and began to attend Cocaine Anonymous meetings. Upon release from the hospital he continued daily C.A. meetings.

In general, he attributes his "recovery" to the treatment program and to C.A. Since stopping, Harry says, he has become "a more insightful, spiritual, calm person, but it hasn't been easy." His wife divorced him, and he did not return to his practice, but he did make restitution for his embezzlement. He now believes that he became a lawyer only to satisfy his mother's aspirations for him, although he slowly patched up his relationships with both his parents. At our interview, Harry was working as a counselor in a drug and alcohol program and attending psychology classes in preparation for a Ph.D. He hopes to become a therapist.

Patty (Case #437)

At the other extreme was Patty, the 36-year-old economist and part-time gram dealer we described in Chapter 5. She had a remarkable ability to work hard, keep up an active social life, and do a good job raising her children alone under difficult conditions. She has high reserves of energy and is active in a wide range of community activities.

Patty first used cocaine when she was 20 years old, but did not use regularly until she was 28. At one point she used cocaine almost daily for five years with three short breaks (three months at the longest). During her heaviest period she used four grams a week for one month, but generally remained a nipper, using small amounts daily. Her regular use occurred when she was selling cocaine.

She began selling cocaine while she was pregnant with her first child when a friend offered to front her two ounces. After the birth her husband took over the sales business while she went to work as an economist in a large bank. Slowly they saved money and bought a modest house with large monthly payments. At this time she used only sporadically and never while pregnant.

Over time her relationship with her husband began to deteriorate largely because of his abuse of both cocaine and heroin. They separated, and in order to pay the mortgage payments and her husband's debts to the connection and credit card accounts she decided to continue selling. The connection, a close friend, fronted her. She repaid the $2,000 her husband owed him within two or three months. She sold cocaine in varying amounts for five years. Initially, she was selling two to three ounces a week and over a period of eight months she paid off $12,000 in debts. Her finances were becoming more stable, but she suffered emotionally because of the separation: "That was the craziest time of my life and I was pretty spun out on getting a divorce . . . and then I realized that I was going to be a single parent and that he wasn't gonna come back. So I cooled it, drinking, doing drugs and shit, and cut back on the dealing."

At that point Patty stopped using for three months. Subsequently, she continued to sell at reduced levels except for two periods when she was not working regularly and needed more income. She always maintained the belief that her sales activities were temporary. In late 1984 she decided to stop selling after a series of incidents that made her feel vulnerable to arrest.

> Yeah, the girls were getting older and starting to have friends over, and it started getting embarrassing because people are coming to pick up something and the other kids are there and my kids are embarrassed. I'm also a P.T.A. president, right, and that is going to look fuckin' great when I get busted. You could read the newspaper . . .

Also in September of '84 my connection gets ripped off by thieves acting as if they are police. They get him for half a pound and $38,000. . . . Then two months later two cops come around to the connection's wife's office and question her about thieves acting as police. They say, "We have caught one of the guys who have represented themselves as police and had been ripping off dope dealers, and we know your husband is a dope dealer." She gives it all up and says, "You're right, he is a dope dealer, and you are right, this all did happen." They told her they didn't care about the dealing; they just wanted to "catch the dudes masquerading as police."

Then there is a final incident. What I used to do when my connection went on vacation, I would take over and distribute the drugs for him. I would drive over to Fremont and he would pay me real good money to do that. So what happened was somebody else delivered the drugs for him during that time (I was out of town for the weekend) and he got busted, and it could have been me. So luckily I had enough sense to quit selling.

When Patty stopped selling she stopped using:

INTERVIEWER: So when you stopped using did you feel anything?

RESPONDENT: No, not at all. I really didn't miss it and started feeling better. . . . I slept better. Yeah, and I felt great when I stopped using and I was much more positive. I think the coke, before I quit, was making me feel depressed, but I was attributing it to other things—not having a relationship and being bored at work.

INTERVIEWER: So did you ever feel addicted?

RESPONDENT: The only thing I was addicted to was the money. We went through some tight times when I quit but we learned how to live on less money.

INTERVIEWER: How do you compare stopping cocaine to stopping cigarette smoking?

RESPONDENT: Stopping smoking . . . my hands shook, I had terrible headaches, and I was mega-irritable. I drank brandy every night to get to sleep. I went through hard times for ten days after quitting smoking, but didn't experience much quitting the coke. Oh, for a time my nose opened up when I went out partying and drinking, but I learned how to handle that. You know, I never really decided to quit using, I just quit selling. Once I stopped selling I didn't have the money to buy it anymore. I would have literally had to say, "Sorry, girls, you don't eat this week" to buy some. I would have exactly $80 for two weeks of food.

INTERVIEWER: So your budget was tight?

RESPONDENT: Yeah, and the three times I did use it [in eighteen months] somebody gave it to me. A couple of times I've been offered and I said no. Last time I took a small line and felt overdosed; I didn't like it at all.

Surprisingly, Patty was not unusual in her ability simply to walk away from the drug. Roughly half of our seventy-six untreated quitters had no difficulty quitting. What Patty did to quit was relatively simple: she stopped selling, stopped seeing users (most of whom were her customers) for a time, and was careful at parties to hold out against the yen to use cocaine as she so often had in such situations.

QUANTITATIVE FINDINGS

In the structured section of our interviews we asked a number of questions that explored previous attempts to stop using and the social processes entailed in quitting. Based on existing literature and our own preliminary research, these processes were organized into six categories: geographic moves, changing social circles, getting into new health routines, developing new interests, seeking formal help, and seeking informal help.

Slightly more than half the quitters had made no previous attempts to quit using cocaine; that is, they successfully stopped using on the first try, although this was not always easy. There were large differences between the treated and the

TABLE 9.3
Prior Attempts to Quit by Treated and Untreated

Have you ever before tried to quit using cocaine?	Treated (N = 30)	Untreated (N = 76)	TOTAL (N = 106)
Yes	(24) 80.0%	(25) 32.9%	(49) 46.2%
No	(6) 20.0	(51) 67.1	(57) 53.8

Note: Chi Square = 17.352, 1 df; significance: p = <.000.

untreated on this score. Four out of five of the treated cases had tried to stop before their last, successful effort, while only one out of three of the untreated quitters had tried before (see Table 9.3). Of the forty-nine people who reported earlier attempts to quit, most said they made only one previous attempt. One treated quitter, however, had tried to stop so many times that he had lost count, but he felt forty was a good low estimate. These data suggest that some users, particularly those who ended up going to treatment, found it very difficult to stop using cocaine (cf. Adler and Adler, 1983).

Geographic Cures

For some years there has been an ongoing debate about the effectiveness of "geographic cures" for heroin addicts; that is, moving away from locales where one had previously obtained and used the drug. Most studies of heroin addicts in treatment indicate that geographic cures are not particularly effective. Simply moving to a new city or neighborhood does not necessarily help the treated addict to stay off opiates. Among untreated former heroin addicts, however, Scharse (1966), Waldorf (1983), and Biernacki (1986) found that geographic moves can help. Shaffer and Jones (1989) found that in general "energetic attempts to avoid the drug" were a key part of "active quitting" for cocaine users who successfully quit without treatment.

TABLE 9.4
Social Processes of Quitting—Geographic Moves:
Percentage Answering Yes

Did you make any geographic moves at this time? Did you:	Total Quitters (N = 106)	Movers (N = 47)
Move to another city or state?	(31) 29.2%	66.0%
Move to another neighborhood?	(22) 20.8	46.8
Take a long vacation?	(19) 17.9	40.4
Get out of town to avoid using?	(25) 23.6	53.2

Subsample	Mean Number of Yes Answers	Percentage Answering No to All 4 Questions
Treated (N = 30)	1.27	(14) 46.7%
Untreated (N = 76)	0.78	(45) 59.2

Note: F Test: 3.657; p = .059.

We explored such geographic cures by asking a four-part question: "Did you make any geographic moves at this time [while attempting to quit]? [If yes], did you: move to another city (or state), move to another neighborhood, take a long vacation, [or] get out of town to avoid using?" To our surprise, more than two out of five of all quitters reported making some geographic move as part of their successful attempt to quit. Of the forty-seven quitters who reported geographic moves, two-thirds said they moved to another city or state, at least in part to help them stay away from cocaine (see Table 9.4–I). The next most frequently mentioned moves were to temporarily get out of town to avoid using, followed by moving to another neighborhood and taking long vacations. This suggests that at least these people felt the lure of cocaine to be sufficiently strong that they had to give themselves a change of venue in order to keep from using again. On the other hand, it also suggests that the lure is not so strong that they would still find a way to use even after moving. Treated quitters generally were more likely to use such geographic cures (see Table 9.4–II).

Changing Social Circles

The most frequently used strategies for quitting cocaine were what we call social avoidance strategies. Such actions are obviously cousin to geographic cures in that they simply make cocaine use more difficult by removing the user from locations in which use is possible. Just as former alcoholics try to stay out of bars and compulsive gamblers avoid race tracks (and one of the authors does not keep chocolate in the house), so do people who feel they cannot control their cocaine use stay away from circles where they could use cocaine. This is part of user folklore. Again and again in our in-depth interviews we heard, "If it's there, you'll use it."[2] Nearly two-thirds of all quitters answered yes when we asked if they had stopped going to specific places where cocaine was being used or had made conscious efforts to avoid seeing coke-using friends (see Table 9.5). Both actions seem to be common strategies for changing social circles to avoid people or situations that might be tempting. The fact that they were used by most of our

TABLE 9.5
Social Processes of Quitting—Social Avoidance Strategies:
Percentage of Total Quitters Answering Yes

Let's explore some other ways people stop. Did you:		Total Quitters (N = 106)
Make conscious efforts to avoid coke-using friends?		(66) 62.3%
Stop going to specific places where coke was being used, i.e., parties, bars, etc.?		(69) 65.1
Seek new, non–drug-using friends?		(44) 41.5

Subsample	Mean Number of Yes Answers	Percentage Answering No to All 4 Questions
Treated (N = 30)	2.57	(0)
Untreated (N = 76)	1.34	(26) 34.2%

Note: F Test: 29.304; p = .000.

successful quitters, many of whose prior attempts had failed, suggests that, however commonsensical and obvious such strategies seem, they may be quite effective.

Two-fifths of all quitters said they also sought new, non–cocaine-using friends as a means of staying clean. Moreover, a number of the remaining quitters might have answered yes to this question were it not for our wording. Our in-depth interviews revealed that most had maintained existing friendships with people who did not use cocaine and so did not need to seek such friends anew.

Again, the treated quitters reported using significantly more of these strategies than did the untreated. On average, treated quitters reported using 2.57 of these three social avoidance strategies, compared to a mean of 1.34 for the untreated. Similarly, all treated quitters used at least one such strategy, while one in three of our untreated quitters used none (see Table 9.5–II).

Improving Physical Health

As we noted earlier, health concerns were among the most important motivations for quitting cocaine, as one might expect given the numerous and occasionally severe physical health problems reported. But for many quitters, improving their health was more than a motive; it was an integral part of the cessation process. In addition to better health, self-development, and improved self-esteem, exercise regimens offered the advantage of a rewarding activity with which to replace what was being given up (see Shaffer and Jones, 1989, 158). More than three in four quitters said they became more concerned with their physical health while quitting, and acted upon these concerns. Two-thirds improved their eating habits and half undertook new programs of physical conditioning (see Table 9.6). Again, treated quitters were significantly more likely than the untreated to report using such health strategies. However, unlike other cessation strategies we asked about, more than four in five untreated quitters took at least some action on the health front.

TABLE 9.6
Social Processes to Quit—Health Efforts:
Percentage of Total Quitters Answering Yes

Let's explore some other ways people stop. Did you:		Total Quitters (N = 106)
Get more concerned with physical health?		(82) 77.4%
Change your eating habits?		(71) 67.0
Start a new program of physical conditioning?		(53) 50.0
Start taking vitamins?		(40) 37.7

Subsample	Mean Number of Yes Answers	Percentage Answering No to All 4 Questions
Treated (N = 30)	3.13	(0)
Untreated (N = 76)	2.00	(11) 14.5%

Note: F Test: 18.970; p = .0000.

DEVELOPING NEW INTERESTS

For some heavy drug users, particularly heroin addicts, drug seeking and drug taking become the central organizing activities that structure daily life, much the same as some occupations (e.g., clergy, politicians, police) and statuses (parenthood) do. When drug use "inundates" (Rosenbaum, 1981) life in this way, it is usually difficult for users to find new activities as fulfilling as the high they are trying to give up. One way our quitters overcame this seeming void was to look for new interests to fill the hole once occupied by cocaine.

The qualitative data from our in-depth interviews suggest that the majority of both users and quitters were not inundated by cocaine and did not allow drug seeking and taking to structure their lives unduly. Nonetheless, many did feel inundated by cocaine, and more than half our quitters (55.7 percent) sought new interests, while nearly two in five (38.7 percent) participated in sports to help them avoid using cocaine again. At least in part to help them stay clean, one of our

quitters got involved in politics, another took up woodwork-
ing and basketball, several went back to school or changed
occupations, and at least one got married and had a family. As
with most of the other cessation strategies, treated quitters
were significantly more likely to use new interests than the
untreated. Whereas all the treated quitters either sought such
new interests or got involved in sports or both, nearly half
(47.7 percent) of the untreated quitters did neither. This, too,
suggest that members of the treated group experienced more
difficulties stopping than did the untreated quitters.

SEEKING HELP

People in trouble with drug abuse often seek assistance,
whether formally from social service agencies, treatment programs, or therapists, or informally from family and friends.
At the outset of our study we expected that those subjects
who got into trouble with cocaine use would probably avoid
formal sources of help in favor of informal ones. Most are
middle-class and the vast majority employed, so we assumed
that they would want to avoid the risk of stigma and that they
would have enough private resources (e.g., health insurance)
to avoid public agencies. Our data offer some support for this
view.

We asked all quitters whether they had sought any of
eight types of formal assistance (see Table 9.7). The most frequently mentioned services sought were mental health services (13.2 percent) and unemployment insurance (10.4 percent). In terms of the average number of services received,
treated respondents again got significantly more than the untreated (1.06 and 0.28, respectively). Less than one of five
untreated quitters reported that they had sought and received
such formal help, but more than three in five of the treated
quitters made such reports.

We also asked quitters about informal sources of help (e.g.,
family, spouse or lover, friends, employer, or other). Many

TABLE 9.7
Formal Help from Social Agencies:
Percentage of Total Quitters Answering Yes

While you were overcoming your coke use, did you ever seek and get help from any social agency, and if so, what kind?	Total Quitters (N = 106)	
Unemployment?	(11)	10.4%
Vocational training?	(3)	2.8
Disability?	(5)	4.7
Help for physical health?	(8)	7.5
Help for mental health?	(14)	13.2
Legal help?	—	
Financial help (welfare)?	(4)	3.8
Family or child care?	(4)	3.8
Other	(2)	1.9

Subsample	Mean Number of Yes Answers	Percentage Answering No to All 8 Questions	
Treated (N = 30)	1.06	(11)	36.7%
Untreated (N = 76)	.28	(62)	81.6

Note: F Test: 19.663; p = .0000.

more quitters availed themselves of such informal help; two of every five untreated but more than nine of ten treated respondents reported getting informal assistance (see Table 9.8). The most frequently mentioned informal sources were friends and family. Spouses and lovers were the third most frequently mentioned, followed by employers.

Compared to heroin addicts in a similar study (Waldorf, 1983), our heavy cocaine users generally sought and received less assistance of almost all types, especially from formal agencies. This is probably because the heroin addicts generally had been more criminalized and stigmatized, and had fewer private resources (education, jobs, insurance) than our respondents. In both studies, however, the untreated cases tended to

TABLE 9.8
Informal Sources of Help:
Percentage of Total Quitters Answering Yes

How about informal sources for help: Did you ever seek and get help from:	Total Quitters (N = 106)
Family?	(28) 26.4%
Spouse or lover?	(15) 14.2
Friends?	(36) 34.0
Employer?	(11) 10.4
Other (doctor)?	(2) 1.9

Subsample	Mean Number of Yes Answers	Percentage Answering No to All 5 Questions
Treated (N = 30)	1.93	(2) 6.7%
Untreated (N = 76)	.44	(46) 60.5

Note: F Test: 64.437; p = .0000.

use social service agencies far less than the treated. These differences are probably the result of several factors, not least the fact that in treatment, people often are referred to a variety of other agencies for services that treatment programs cannot provide. Recall, too, that our treated cases reported more problems than the untreated, so they may well have felt more need for assistance. Finally, our untreated quitters may be more self-reliant than the treated, for many were as reluctant to go to treatment programs as they were to seek other sorts of formal and informal help.

HARRY AND PATTY: AN EPILOGUE

Let us now return from the foregoing quantified, aggregate data to Harry and Patty, the two long-term users whose case histories we summarized earlier in this chapter. Recall that Harry, the lawyer, was a compulsive freebaser who used extremely large amounts of cocaine, experienced several crises because of it, and had a difficult time giving it up. Patty, the economist, on the other hand, shied away from the more direct mode of ingestion and remained a snorter, had few troubles because of her use, and was able to give it up rather easily. In Table 9.9 we summarize the answers that both gave to our structured questions about strategies and actions for quitting.

In what must be described as desperation, Harry tried geographic cures, changed his social circles, engaged in all four of the health actions, developed new interests, and got informal help from his wife, friends, and a doctor, in addition to two kinds of formal treatment followed by Cocaine Anonymous meetings. He took eleven of the twenty-seven quitting actions we asked about, and he succeeded only after a lot of heartache and several attempts. In contrast, Patty took only two actions, both to improve her health, and rather easily succeeded in quitting on her first attempt.

Both Harry and Patty used cocaine regularly over long periods, and neither had any trouble maintaining a supply of the drug (he had money and she was a dealer). What, then, can account for these differences? We were not privy to clinical data about possible physiological and psychological characteristics that could help explain the differences, but we can make two observations from our self-report data. First, it seems important that Harry and Patty differed in both the type and the pattern of their use. Harry was a freebaser and a heavy binger while Patty remained a snorter and a nipper. Mode of ingestion and style of use are clearly parts of the puzzle, but they also beg the question of *why* she remained a controlled snorter while he went off the deep end on freebasing binges.

Part of the answer may lie in our second observation, which centers on the use of the drug to deal with psychological problems. Harry admitted that he was insecure about his abilities and ambitions, and that he used cocaine to compen-

TABLE 9.9
Harry's and Patty's Actions to Quit

	Harry (Case #106)	Patty (Case #437)
GEOGRAPHIC MOVES		
Move to another city or state	No	No
Move to another neighborhood	No	No
Take a long vacation	Yes	No
Get out of town to avoid using	Yes	No
SOCIAL ACTIONS		
Make conscious efforts to avoid coke-using friends	Yes	No
Stop going to specific places where coke was being used, i.e., parties, bars, etc.	Yes	No
Seek new, non–drug-using friends	Yes	No
HEALTH EFFORTS		
Get more concerned with physical health	Yes	Yes
Change your eating habits	Yes	No
Start taking vitamins	Yes	No
Start a new program of physical conditioning	Yes	Yes
NEW INTERESTS		
Look for new interests	Yes	No
Get involved in sports	No	No
FORMAL ASSISTANCE		
Unemployment	No	No
Vocational training	No	No
Disability	No	No
Help for physical health	No	No
Help for mental health	No	No
Legal help	No	No
Financial help (welfare)	No	No
Family or child care	No	No
Other	No	No
INFORMAL ASSISTANCE		
Family	No	No
Spouse or lover	Yes	No
Friends	Yes	No
Employer	No	No
Other (doctor)	Yes	No

sate. Patty may have had her share of insecurities, but we got the distinct sense from our interviews that it was her style simply to charge ahead in life. No psychological problems surfaced in her accounts; she used cocaine because it felt good and was fun, not because she felt she needed it.

There is obviously more to their differences than we were able to ferret out of our interviews, and we will attempt further analysis in Chapter 10. But perhaps the existence of such differences is just the point: that two educated, middle-class individuals, both in their thirties, both with meaningful careers and families, both with regular access to cocaine, could show such variation in outcome. It may be that what is important here is that one of two people under such similar circumstances could use cocaine for years, not get into trouble, and quit easily by simply walking away from it; while the other became powerless over his drug use, almost watched his life go down the tubes, and found quitting to be an excruciating experience.

A Note on Drug Use after Quitting

As Harry's case suggests, quitting is often a long and arduous process in which slips are always possible. He and many of our other quitters made several attempts before succeeding. Relapse is generally considered an omnipresent danger in both Twelve-Step self-help groups (e.g., Phillips, 1990) and treatment circles (e.g., Marlatt and Gordon, 1985; Shaffer and Jones, 1989). Many studies have found high relapse rates, for example, among heroin addicts. Indeed, the old saying, "Once an addict, always an addict," is commonly taken as true, even by many addicts.[3]

We asked our quitters several questions about their post-cessation drug use, particularly about cocaine. In Table 9.10 we report the number of days that individuals used cocaine and the number of grams used since quitting. More than a quarter of all quitters had not used cocaine on any days since

TABLE 9.10
Illicit Cocaine Use Since Quitting, Treated and Untreated

I. Cocaine Use	Treated (N = 30)	Untreated (N = 76)	TOTAL (N = 106)
NUMBER OF DAYS USED SINCE QUITTING			
None	(16) 53.3%	(13) 17.1%	(29) 27.4%
1–5 days	(9) 30.0	(30) 39.5	(39) 36.8
More than 6 days	(5) 16.7	(31) 40.8	(36) 34.0
No answer	—	(2) 2.6	(2) 1.9
NUMBER OF GRAMS USED			
None	(16) 53.3	(13) 17.1	(29) 27.4
Less than 1 gram	(5) 16.7	(36) 47.4	(41) 38.7
1–2 grams	(4) 13.3	(26) 34.2	(30) 28.3
More than 2 grams	(5) 16.7	—	(5) 4.7
No answer	—	(1) 1.3	(1) 0.9
RANGE	0.2–8	0.2–10	0.2–10
MEDIAN	0.5 grams	0.7 grams	0.6 grams

II. (Treated only) After you left treatment, how long did you stay off cocaine?			(N = 30)
1 day			(1) 3.3%
4–12 months			(5) 16.7
13–24 months			(16) 53.3
25–48 months			(5) 16.7
More than 60 months			(3) 10.0

quitting. Another third had used on only one to five days, while an additional third reported using on six days or more. Put another way, nearly two-thirds of all quitters used cocaine on five days or less in the year or more since they had quit. In general, the treated respondents used for fewer days than the untreated. This is not surprising, given the stress placed on complete abstinence in virtually all treatment programs. Half of the treated cases did not use cocaine on any days, while this was true of only one-sixth of the untreated quitters.

We must note that these figures refer to postquitting time

periods of varying lengths. The minimum was 12 months, the maximum 108 months, and the median 23 months. To be categorized as a quitter, a respondent could not have used cocaine on more than four days in the year prior to our interview, or must have been completely cocaine-free.

The amounts respondents used after quitting were in most cases very small—dramatically less than they had been using regularly.[4] Of those who used cocaine after quitting, two-thirds used less than two grams total in the next year. Only five persons reported using more than that. Overall, 94.4 percent used two grams or less in the twelve months or more since quitting. The median total amount used by those treated cases who used at all after quitting was 0.5 gram, with one individual who had used 8 grams skewing that figure upward. The total median amount used by the untreated quitters was slightly higher at 0.7 grams.

Our last question about cocaine use was asked only of treated subjects. In a short section of questions about treatment experiences we asked, "After you left treatment how long did you stay off cocaine?" Half reported that they had not used cocaine for thirteen to twenty-four months after they left treatment, and another quarter had not used for twenty-five months or more. Taken together, four in five of the treated quitters had remained completely cocaine-free for more than one year after treatment.

One of the more gloomy prognoses for persons who quit abusing drugs is that while they may quit using their drug of abuse, they simply move on to other drugs or substitute one for another. Waldorf's (1983) previous research on recovery from heroin addiction, for example, showed that a sizable percentage of those who quit heroin used alcohol and marijuana as temporary substitutes to help them cope with cravings. We expected that our cocaine quitters, too, might have substituted other drugs.

We asked all quitters if, after quitting, they smoked more cigarettes, drank more alcohol, or started using other drugs that they were not using before. Among treated and untreated

TABLE 9.11
Drug Substitution: Percentage of Total Quitters
Answering Yes

During the period when you were stopping, did you:	Total Quitters (N = 106)
Smoke more cigarettes?	(29) 27.4%
Drink more alcohol?	(22) 20.8
Start using other drugs you weren't using when you used coke?	(18) 17.0

alike, only about one in four smoked more cigarettes immediately after quitting, and only about one in five drank more
alcohol (see Table 9.11).[5] Most drank less. To our surprise,
even fewer (17 percent) started using other drugs. Of the few
who did, a majority used only marijuana, which almost all
had used before and during their cocaine use.

With the exception of marijuana, roughly 90 percent of
our quitters did not use other illicit drugs after quitting. Only
a small number ever used amphetamines or opiates after quitting cocaine (percentages ranged from 6.6 percent to 12.7
percent), and only two people used these more than a few
times. Marijuana was the most frequently used illicit substance, more so among the untreated group. Nearly a quarter
of the quitters said they had not used marijuana at all since
quitting cocaine; most of this group had been to treatment.

These data on postcessation drug use are, on the whole,
encouraging. Those who underwent natural recovery processes were as likely to succeed as those who went through
formal treatment. While it is clear that our untreated quitters
used somewhat more cocaine and other drugs somewhat more
often than our treated quitters, the quantity and frequency
were by and large negligible and did not appear to have put
them at increased risk of relapse. Although it is likely that the
treated group used drugs less often because they had absorbed
abstinence values in the course of treatment, our interviews

suggest that rigid abstinence from all consciousness-altering substances is not a prerequisite for recovery. Among both our groups of quitters, occasional drug use (sometimes called "slips") was common, but for most this did not appear to be particularly consequential.

CHAPTER 10

MAKING SENSE OF CESSATION: A SYNTHESIS

Let us now try to put some flesh on the statistical bones supplied in Chapter 9. We have presented a good deal of quantitative data on why and how people quit using cocaine. But, aside from illustrative case histories, we were reporting mostly aggregate patterns of responses to questionnaire items. In this chapter, we will attempt to wring a more general sort of meaning from our subjects' accounts by culling core themes from the unstructured, in-depth portions of our interviews. Our central question is: for all the variation in use patterns and problems, and for all the contradictory tendencies observed among our respondents, what can we say about how cocaine users reassert control, pull themselves out of trouble, or stop using?

THE GENERAL CONTEXT OF CONTROL AND CESSATION

A Stake in Conventional Life

We have tried to remain as close as possible to our data, and to employ as often as we could in our interpretations the indigenous language of our respondents. However, at a certain point in our analysis we realized that one important piece of the puzzle was not explicitly discussed by the users. We came to see that simple phrases like "I couldn't afford it anymore," "It was messing up my work," and "My wife was getting pissed," contained an insight as profound as it was simple. As we have suggested in earlier chapters, what keeps users from going over the edge with cocaine, or allows many of them to climb back, is their *investment in their everyday lives*. This investment is so taken for granted that it rarely receives attention but, as Richard Flacks argues, human beings are fundamentally committed to their everyday lives, and for good reason:

> In addition to all those activities that are ultimately grounded in physical survival, everyday life is constituted by activity and experience designed to sustain one's self as a human being—to validate or fulfill the meaning of one's life, reinforce or enhance one's sense of self-worth, achieve satisfaction and pleasure or, negatively, to overcome distress, resolve problems, restore continuity, do duties so that the life one believes or expects one to have or to be entitled to can be lived. (1988, 2)

As a group, our respondents were a rather diverse lot, displaying a great variety of life-styles. In contrast to most other studies of drug users, especially heroin addicts, we interviewed people from all social classes—wealthy professionals and managers who lived in huge homes and drove expensive cars; middle-class, white-collar workers from the suburbs; solidly working-class people of nearly all ethnic groups; and people who were unemployed. Our respondents included Latino "homeboys," university students, welfare mothers, rock musicians, artists, drug sellers, professors, prostitutes, and a host of ordinary workers and citizens.

Despite their heavy cocaine use, few of these people had life-styles centered on cocaine. Most used a good deal of cocaine for a good number of years, but few were ever *merely* cocaine abusers. Further, neither their cocaine use itself nor its consequences stigmatized them as forever deviant or earned them the sort of label that Howard Becker has called (following Everett Hughes) a "master status" (1963, 32). For example, we interviewed a white female sales manager for a large computer company who used cocaine heavily for twelve years and continues to use. She worked hard throughout those years and attained prominence in her profession. Similarly, our black nightclub owner, cocaine seller, and entrepreneur used for fourteen years, but continued to build his business and sustain his family. These two did not let their lives become dominated by cocaine.

The majority of people in our sample worked regularly, maintained homes, and were responsible citizens. Most were more conventional than unconventional and did not see themselves as being particularly deviant or in any significant way distinct from other people they knew. Patty was a long-term user and part-time dealer, but more importantly she was a mother, a Girl Scout leader, and a professional economist. As with most of the others, her identity had many dimensions; "cocaine user" was not the defining one, or even an especially significant one. These people used cocaine, yes; but despite its pharmacological prowess, they rarely adopted a cocaine-centered life-style.

This evidence suggests that for most of our respondents, a commitment to their everyday lives gave them a stake in normalcy and bonded them to the conventional world. They placed a high premium on and sought to maintain their life-styles, and they appeared to resist moving toward other, more outlawlike life-styles. Their world was not organized like the street heroin-addict culture of "hustling, copping, and fixing." To us this fact has theoretical significance. When cocaine use conflicted with their commitment to conventional daily life, these users either reduced their use dramatically, abstained temporarily, or abandoned cocaine completely.

Previous studies of heroin addicts (e.g., Chein et al., 1964; Feldman, 1968; Waldorf, 1973) found that large numbers come from disadvantaged backgrounds, have little experience of regular work, and develop rather elaborate deviant identities and ideologies centered on "hustling, copping, and fixing." Early in their careers most street addicts are criminalized by society, and they adopt convict codes (Irwin, 1970) of morality. On top of heroin's powerful pharmacology, the addict life-style tends to keep addicts locked into the drug world and makes it rather difficult to abstain or to adopt more conventional roles (cf. Adler, 1985; Shover, 1985). There are, of course, cocaine users who also use heroin and heroin users who also use cocaine, and we suspect that many such people come to resemble heroin addicts and participate in heroin-using subcultures.[1] The vast majority of our respondents, however, neither inhabited such subcultures nor resembled such addicts.

One reason for this difference surely has to do with the middle-class backgrounds of most of our subjects. But what we have called commitment to conventional daily life is not simply a function of social class, for our working-class respondents had such a commitment, too—indeed, because their daily lives were often more economically difficult, perhaps a stronger commitment. Moreover, it is easy enough for affluent people to become unmoored and alienated despite high incomes. The point is, regardless of their formal social class or status, compared to most heroin addicts (at least those on the street), our respondents were enmeshed in lives that mitigated against excessive use. Even for those who went over the edge, the structure of their lives provided strong social-psychological incentives and resources for climbing back.

Identity Interests: Another Kind of Stake

Another dimension of commitment to conventional daily life seemed to push many troubled heavy users toward control or cessation. Just as they were invested in their lives, so too they were invested in the sense of self sustained by those lives. They had what might be called "identity interests," which they looked after in much the same way people look after their material interests.[2] For example, many of our respondents spoke in sad, regretful tones about some of their behavior while under the influence of cocaine. Their accounts were full of perceived gaps between their self-image and their behavior. Several pointed out that they knew they had to reduce use when they observed themselves engaging in what they called junkie behavior (e.g., meeting dealers late at night in strange places, growing agitated when a connection was late, hoarding supplies they had once willingly shared). One young, white, female snorter explained why she moved away from cocaine this way: "There's just somethin' in me that makes me want to do somethin' with my life that makes me stop. . . . There's somethin' in me that still knows that I can do a lot of things I want to do. I still have somethin' I'm striving for" (Case #569).

Put another way, their many asides about regrettable or embarrassing behavior suggested that they also had a stake in conventional identity—in being thought of by themselves and others as "regular citizens." These conventional identities served as yardsticks against which cocaine-seeking or -using behavior was often measured. Another young white woman, for example, told us why she decided to stop freebasing: "I like to go outside and socialize and run around and do things, and for a while I just didn't see any of my old self in my freebase self. It's a completely different person . . . not talking to anyone except for the heavy derelicts I was hangin' out with behind closed doors for four months" (Case #703).

In short, such desire to maintain one's sense of self or one's personal identity was an additional incentive for avoiding abuse, returning to controlled use, or quitting. Such stakes in conventional identity seemed to work hand in glove with the commitment to conventional everyday lives to form the social-psychological and social-organizational context within which control and cessation were possible. This phenomenon is noteworthy because it runs counter to so much recovery literature, which typically implies that *drugs* come to dominate identities and lives. This was certainly true in our most problematic cases, but for the bulk of our respondents, identities and lives usually dominated drug use.

The Transformation of the Cocaine Experience

In tandem with commitment to conventional daily life and identity, certain qualities of the cocaine high itself also help explain why most of our heavy users were able to avoid inundated, drug-centered life-styles. When users maintain controlled patterns of use, the effects of cocaine usually do not interfere with the normal tasks of daily living the way the use of other drugs can. Our respondents generally agreed that when cocaine is used ceremonially or in controlled ways it can be an exceedingly enjoyable experience. It provides a wide range of positive effects to those who use it in moderation: more energy, a certain intellectual focus, enhanced sensations, and increased sociability and social intimacy. Social, sexual, or recreational activities and work can be enlivened, and many respondents used the drug not only in pleasurable but also in productive ways. Sometimes even the most mundane tasks became more tolerable, even pleasurable, with "a little toot."

In many ways, however, these very qualities of cocaine encourage more and more use. As we noted in Chapters 2 and 3, the very qualities of the cocaine high that people value mean that they can find cocaine useful or pleasurable in an increasing number of activity spheres. Thus, within a relatively short time use can easily become a habit that insidiously develops a life of its own. Ceremonial weekend use can stretch quite easily into midweek nipping, and short, moderate binges can grow longer and heavier rather quickly.

But such protracted daily use or regular heavy binges slowly transform the *experience* of the cocaine high. Our respondents' accounts were full of comments about how, after "too much," cocaine use "stopped being fun." Such comments led us to the hypothesis that long-term patterns of abuse contain certain seeds of cessation. Most of our respondents who used cocaine heavily for long periods began to experience negative physical symptoms, and many of the original, sought-after pleasures began to diminish or disappear. After prolonged heavy use, the initial euphoria slowly and subtly became dysphoria. Instead of feeling a sense of well-being or exhilaration, users began to feel unwell and unhappy. Instead of feeling energetic and more alive, they began to feel lethargic, slow, or "overamped." Instead of feeling more enthusiastic about the events of one's life, one feels apathetic and blasé. At this point, more cocaine no longer served as a pick-me-up, but rather led many to feel less alert and even depressed.

Beyond changes in physical effects, excessive use also transformed social aspects of the cocaine high. If a person used the drug initially in pleasant social situations to enliven or extend sociability, as most of our respondents did, long-term heavy use often became a solitary and selfish activity that tended to isolate the user. Many who used it heavily moved away from other people, hoarded their supplies, or used alone. Many who were once pleased to share the good things in their lives (including cocaine) came to avoid other people so they would not feel obliged to share or, often more important in their "overamped" state, even to "deal with" others.

Similarly, many users initially found that cocaine enhanced their sex lives. But after extended periods of heavy use, sex usually became either tiresome or physically difficult to engage in at all (Macdonald et al., 1988). Many males who drifted toward heavy use experienced impotence even while their desire was undiminished. Many female heavy users felt insensitive and had trouble achieving orgasm. Thus, in the sexual sphere, too, the very high that initially pulled lovers closer was often transformed by excessive use into one that began to push them apart.

Our heavy users also noted psychological transformations. Under the influence of cocaine they initially saw the world as a pleasant, good place much like "the best of all possible worlds" described by Voltaire's Doctor Pangloss in *Candide*. But after protracted heavy use, the world seemed far less hospitable and paranoia increased. Some heavy users reported that they suspected everyone, hid from illusory enemies, spent hours peeking out of windows or looking around bushes for imaginary police officers or robbers. One heavy user/dealer became so paranoid during one binge that he hid for hours on the top shelf of his closet. After long stretches of heavy use depression often settled in as well. Some such users took more cocaine to help overcome the sodden, heavy feelings that dragged their emotions down. But more cocaine tended to intensify the original depression and quickly pull them into a spiraling downward cycle that fueled pain rather than pleasure.

These psychological transformations often accompanied the myriad physical, financial, workplace, and relationship problems we described in Chapter 8. Time and money, for example, were expended on cocaine, taking time and money away from other needs and interests, and adding stress to daily life. On top of this the central nervous system stimulation from the drug tends over time to frazzle nerves and make users edgy. This in turn can strain relationships with spouses or coworkers. Such negative consequences of protracted, heavy cocaine use accumulate and interact with each other, often resulting in a kind of stress multiplier effect. And the one thing users do not need when they have been ingesting large quantities of a strong stimulant is more stress.

As the cocaine high was transformed, the ratio of positive to negative consequences shifted and the scales were tipped toward the negative.[3] At such a point, many heavy users began to undergo considerable psychological pain and to question the rationality and desirability of continuing to use a drug that offered them so few of the pleasures that had prompted their use in the first place. At such a point, those with conventional stakes in jobs, homes, families, communities, and identities tended to find the resources and the resolve to abstain or quit. Those with fewer such stakes and social supports were more likely to feel indecisive and helpless to overcome cocaine's hold on them.

Taken together, our two themes of stake in conventional

life and identity, and transformation of the high, help explain both why so many people were able to use so much cocaine for so long without serious trouble, and why those who had trouble were so often able to pull themselves out of it. The argument boils down to this: after prolonged abuse, the cocaine high simply stopped being fun and started disrupting rather than enhancing the everyday lives and selves in which users were invested. In spite of cocaine's powerful reinforcements, most of our users cut back their use or periodically abstained ("laid off") in order to restore their balance, to protect careers, jobs, families, homes, and hobbies from disruption. All the normal roles these people assumed and all of the things they had worked for, material and otherwise, seemed to serve as a kind of social-psychological ballast[4] that kept most of them from being swamped by their cocaine use. When protracted, heavy cocaine use led to an accumulation of problems that threatened their stakes—especially after the very pleasure they originally sought had been transformed into pain—most cut back or made a move to quit. Although for most of our users it would be too much to say, as Alcoholics Anonymous and other Twelve-Step groups put it, that their lives had "become unmanageable," it is clear that the lives of many long-term heavy users did become increasingly difficult. And because those lives had meaning and value, these difficulties provided powerful spurs to cessation.

OTHER ASPECTS OF THE CESSATION PROCESS

Although disruptions of conventional life and identity along with various transformations of the cocaine experience moved many of our most problematic users to cut down or stop, others had more mundane motives for quitting. Some simply got bored with the constant high-energy state of the cocaine high or tired of the social scene surrounding it, and simply walked away. Others quit for situational reasons, like the cocaine seller who stopped selling for fear of arrest and did not want to use if he had to pay retail prices for questionable-quality cocaine. Events also push people toward quitting—for instance, breaking up with a spouse or lover who had supplied the drug, or episodes of severe physical effects. Recall, for example, Claude, who had no intention of quitting until he had a convulsion, but then realized that he could not keep using. A minority of our quitters, however, were not moved by the mundane, by ill health, or even by threats to their conventional lives; they suffered.

Struggles of the Damned: "Rock Bottom" and Despair

Some of our subjects fell into profound despair and experienced existential crises, which in the discourse of treatment and recovery are known as "rock bottom." In extreme cases these experiences include contemplations of suicide. Such states are similar to Kierkegaard's concept of despair (1941a and 1941b), a state in which individuals grow tired of what he called the aesthetic life (i.e., hedonism) and experience profound boredom and discontent. In Kierkegaard's formulation the only options then are death or a change to an ethical or religious life. In our more secular era, when such crises concern addiction, treatment clinicians and therapists are called instead of priests and ministers. But parallels remain, for Twelve-Step groups still insist that "recovering" people turn themselves over to the "higher power" or God in some form, and virtually all treatment programs insist on a kind of chemical chastity—abstinence from all consciousness-altering substances.

However, such despair was not common even among the quitters in our sample; most had been moved to stop using precisely to avoid these conditions. Such crises occurred far less frequently among our cocaine quitters than among a similar sample of former heroin addicts (Waldorf, 1983). In general, those who suffered existential crises or rock bottom states had made several attempts to stop using cocaine and had relapsed. After repeated failures they felt, in Alcoholics

Anonymous argot, "powerless over the drug." These respondents usually sought formal treatment of some kind, although a couple converted to fundamentalist religious communities that provided social support, structured their time, and offered ideological prescriptions for thought and behavior in much the same way many drug programs do. Typically, treatment was short-term—a week to a month of residential care, followed by regular aftercare and sometimes Cocaine Anonymous meetings.

Struggles of the Not-So-Damned: Commonsense Quitting

At the opposite end of the continuum were the quitters who stopped using without the help of treatment. Most of those we interviewed did not have severe, underlying psychological problems or other addictions. Stopping cocaine abuse was a surprisingly straightforward and relatively trouble-free process for them. However, most people we interviewed had a difficult time abstaining even temporarily if the drug was readily available. Users seemed to believe the adage, "If it's around, you'll use it." That is why quitters so often used social avoidance strategies and why sellers in particular had to stop selling to stop using.

Geographic moves and changes in social circles were the most common social avoidance strategies. A short vacation, trip out of town, or visit to a friend's house for a few days seemed to help many quitters, especially when combined with conscious efforts to avoid other users or social situations where cocaine had been used in the past. Such strategies seemed to work in part because very few quitters reported experiencing anything akin to the withdrawal syndrome observed with heroin or Valium addicts or alcoholics.[5] Untreated quitters did not report serious withdrawal symptoms like those described by some of our treated quitters. This could be because treated quitters felt more addicted, or because they learned in treatment to interpret their feelings as withdrawal, or both. The most frequently reported form of postquitting distress was feeling uncomfortable for a day or two, experiencing some mild depression, fatigue, or insomnia. For most untreated quitters, such feelings were never severe enough to seem unmanageable or seriously erode their resolve to stop using.

Whenever both members of a couple were involved in an abusive cocaine-use pattern, then both had to stop at the same time. If one member of the couple decided to continue to use while the other tried to quit, the quitter was usually lured back to his or her old drug-using pattern. In several instances marriages and relationships dissolved when one partner did not stop. One man, for example, decided to give up cocaine because of the impact his and his wife's use was having on their children. She had become a compulsive freebaser and begun to neglect the children. When he discovered that she had locked the children out of the house while she and another person freebased for hours he realized that the situation was out of control. He stopped selling, stopped using, turned his wife out of the house, and began to raise their two daughters on his own. Eventually, she joined Cocaine Anonymous and quit using, and the children now visit her regularly.

Unlike most heroin addicts, most of our heavy cocaine users did not have to make major changes in their lives to stop using cocaine. On the contrary, as we suggested in our analysis of stake in conventional life and identity, most were able to quit largely by *maintaining* continuity in their lives. They continued with their previous occupations, stayed in marriages, repaired relationships, maintained old friendships, and kept up their old routines, all without relapsing. When the user did not have other severe psychological or drug problems, cocaine use generally did not destroy or substantially disrupt life-styles or identities, so there was little need to reorganize one's life and indeed much value in maintaining the organization of one's life. For most, making minor changes in the daily round of activities did the job of eliminating cocaine.

Cravings

None of this is meant to imply that quitting is always easy or that those who quit without great suffering or treatment did not have to work at it. Most of our quitters experienced some cravings for cocaine after they quit, but for the most part they were able to manage such cravings. One woman told us that she felt cravings regularly, but usually just resisted them. On two occasions she bought cocaine but used only small portions of it (less than a quarter of the gram) and gave the rest away (Case #436).

Interestingly, several people who succumbed to cravings in the midst of quitting found that the experience was unpleasant, or that it brought on bad memories or negative associations. In this sense, the transformations of the cocaine experience noted earlier seemed to stay with quitters and help them stay clean. One man for whom two years of daily use had rendered the cocaine high a negative experience reported that his few ceremonial uses after quitting were unpleasant: "I just didn't enjoy the feeling anymore." After a few such uses, he lost all desire for cocaine. At least two people reported that after quitting the mere sight of cocaine nauseated them. Some quitters found such negative experiences useful in strengthening their resolve. A 34-year-old man who experienced an angina attack while using cocaine described his experience this way:

> I was psyching myself up into this state and every time I was doing this I knew I was getting sicker and sicker and that in fact helped me to quit. I just kept saying . . . if somebody was doing it, which was all the time when I was working at the police department or security work or whatever, . . . my stomach would turn. (Case #441).

Other quitters, after staying away from cocaine for some months, found that they could use it again in small amounts, ceremonially or on special occasions, and not feel threatened or even wish to continue using. During such instances many enjoy the drug but were conscious of its powers and were careful not to return to regular use. The strategy for most was to avoid *buying* the drug, for if they had a supply handy, they would tend to use it. If they went to a party and it was available they might use it and think nothing of it, but they would not keep supplies on hand.

Cravings were not in themselves threatening to most quitters. They realized that cravings would be transitory and that nearly any minor distraction would cause them to subside (Biernacki, 1986). Of course, new interests and activities often provided such distractions. In general, most of our quitters found cravings little different from the yearnings one might feel for an old lover—one feels the desire, but with time it subsides and one thinks of him or her less and less.

Back to Conventional Living

Even during long careers of heavy cocaine use, most of our respondents were able to integrate their drug use into their lives. Those whose lives were disrupted or threatened by cocaine use usually cut back, abstained for a time (see, e.g., Cohen, 1989), or quit. In most instances quitters had not lost their jobs or destroyed their identities, so they did not have to fashion new ones. Unlike many heroin addicts—who have to struggle to rebuild new lives and identities on their own or go to therapeutic communities where such rebuilding is required—most of our quitters found no need for major life-style changes. In general, most simply continued in their old occupations, families, friendship networks, and communities. As we suggested earlier, such continuity clearly served as a resource for quitters, just as commitment to daily life and identity kept most of the others from getting so far into abuse that they had to quit.

Some treated quitters did make major changes in their lives. A small number became treatment professionals or drug counselors. Their cocaine careers became integral parts of their new identities as "professional ex–cocaine addicts." These people tended to articulate abstinence ideologies, and were quick to acknowledge their past experiences with the drug. None of the untreated quitters adopted such occupational aspirations, and they were understandably more reticent to broadcast their past histories. They did not wish to risk stigma or jeopardize their jobs by revealing their pasts to persons who might not be tolerant or understanding. But in part their reticence was because "ex–coke addict" was simply not how they thought of themselves; their troubles with cocaine were no more integral to their identities after quitting than using cocaine was before.

We do not mean to suggest that stake in conventional life and identity is the only explanatory variable that separates use from abuse, or controlled users from addicts. Most of our respondents would agree that the kind of heavy cocaine use they engaged in cannot be sustained for long without taking some toll on finances, family, physical health, and so on. Furthermore, single explanations can never fully account for complicated social phenomena, and as we have shown, the processes of using and quitting are extremely complex. Indeed, we have presented case studies of individuals who seemed to have everything to lose and still went off the deep end with cocaine, just as others in our sample had less to lose and yet maintained control.

Having said this, however, we can also say that stakes in conventional daily life and identity remain important for any theory attempting to explain the broad patterns of use and abuse of cocaine. Alongside our controlled users we found many affluent and middle-class users who had at some point weathered serious problems with cocaine. Yet our life histories suggest that they did weather them; most found ways to resist the allure of cocaine when it interfered with their lives too seriously or too often. Our subjects are not unique; the latest NIDA surveys show that cocaine use is declining as more and more middle- and working-class cocaine users are, as one of our respondents put it, "figuring out that they've gotta cool it." We think this is occurring because the idea that "cocaine can mess you up" has become a part of the stock of knowledge *in the culture of users,* and they understand this warning as more than just the propaganda of prevention proponents (see Becker, 1967).

Our notions about stake in conventional life and identity are also linked to what Zinberg (1984) called "set and setting." His pioneering work demonstrated that there is more to a drug experience than the molecular interaction between the pharmacological properties of a substance and the physiological properties of the person ingesting it. Expectations (set) and situations (setting) influence users' interpretations of raw effects, and thus help shape the meaning and patterns of use. Our study has led us to believe that "set" may be usefully extended beyond users' psychological set or immediate expectations about a drug to include personality and character development. And we think "setting" should be understood in broader social-structural and cultural terms, not only as the social situation in which a drug is used.

For example, if we construe "stake in conventional life" broadly, it leads to an understanding of a setting that includes *life chances*—the distribution of both the ability and the opportunity to build and maintain conventional everyday lives *in which one can develop a stake.* Our respondents believed that they had reasonably good prospects in life, and their identities or senses of themselves reflected that. Similarly, their cocaine use and the problems associated with it occurred in a social-structural setting in which such beliefs were sustained by real possibilities. Such users under such circumstances seemed to get into trouble with cocaine less often and to "just walk away" from it more readily than many had believed possible.[6]

In contrast, cocaine use among the unemployed and the poor of America's inner cities appears to have more devastating consequences. This is the only group in which cocaine use is not decreasing at this writing. One reason, of course, is that the crack industry offers ghetto residents the possibility of more money than they would ever see in straight jobs, so there are huge economic incentives encouraging the crack trade (Bourgois, 1989; Williams, 1989). But we think another reason is that this dangerous new form of cocaine has developed in a social-structural setting in which there are increasingly fewer reasons to believe that conventional lives and identities are possible.

Other Approaches to Cessation

Most of the literature on the processes involved in stopping drug use employs concepts such as maturation, spontaneous remission, and recovery. We have used such terms in the past, but now prefer the term cessation because it avoids the connotations of psychological immaturity, disease, and illness implied by the other terms. "Cessation" also seems closer to the phenomenological experience of our subjects, who spoke of stopping rather than growing up or getting cured. Terminology aside, in this section we will compare the themes in our qualitative data on cessation and the sense we have tried to make of it to three related bodies of work.

The "Maturing Out" Hypothesis

The first research on the phenomena of cessation from illicit drug use was conducted more than twenty-five years ago by Charles Winick (1962; 1964). Reviewing records of known heroin addicts in the Federal Bureau of Narcotics, he observed that people over thirty-seven years of age had fewer arrests than those younger. This observation suggested that heroin addicts became inactive as they reached their mid-30s. Winick attributed this development to physical and psychological maturation and, borrowing a term from the delinquency literature, claimed that addicts "matured out" of addiction. Winick did not, however, conduct interviews with "matured-out" heroin addicts to find out why they were arrested less often; he just assumed the reason was that they had stopped using heroin. Winick's findings were replicated in the 1960s and 1970s by Snow (1973) in New York, and by McGlothlin in California (McGlothlin, Anglin, and Wilson, 1977), whose colleagues continued his work in the 1980s (Anglin et al., 1986; Brecht and Anglin, 1988). These scholars used age as the main index of maturing out and did not question the psychological implications of the term.

The notion that cessation of drug use was related to age was applied to marijuana users in the 1970s. But Henley and Adams (1973) rightly took the emphasis away from maturation when they found that cessation of marijuana among college graduates "appeared to be related not so much to aging per se but to entry, that most people generally make, into significant social statuses," like marriage and parenthood. Such a view is supported by four other studies of marijuana use (Brown et al., 1974; Sadava and Forsyth, 1977; Krohn et al., 1980; and O'Donnell et al., 1976).

Other researchers have questioned the psychological implications of the maturing out hypothesis, or the idea that drug use reflects immaturity. The first was O'Donnell's (1969) excellent book on a ten-year follow-up of 266 opiate addicts. He too found that abstinence from opiates most often occurred as addicts aged, but he concluded that their accounts offered no support for the maturation hypothesis. In a similar ten-year follow-up of 248 Chicano heroin addicts in Texas in the 1960s, Maddux and Desmond found that while some ex-addicts attributed their abstinence to maturity, the concept was insufficient to account for the variety of explanations they gave for quitting (Maddux and Desmond, 1980; Desmond and Maddux, 1980). One of the present authors reached the same conclusion about maturing out in a study of 201 heroin addicts, half of whom had received treatment.

A sizable number of untreated ex-addicts (roughly a third) described their recovery in terms that suggest maturation. . . . Despite the numbers who made such statements, we have misgivings about the general usefulness of the concept (maturing out) for two reasons: (a) we found six other discernable patterns of recovery which account for a greater number of our respondents than those who said they had matured, and (b) recent research on the developmental stages of adults suggest that there is no single phase (or age period) where maturation takes place, but several possible phases (Waldorf, 1983; see also Waldorf and Biernacki, 1981).

In addition to such equivocal support in the literature, we had our own reservations about the relevance of maturing out for our cocaine quitters. Most of our subjects began their cocaine use in their middle twenties and early thirties after they had left school. They were by all outward indications mature people when they began their cocaine use—homeowners, responsible parents, successful workers—and so cannot be said to have used cocaine because of immaturity. Also, in a group with a median age of 30, status changes such as marriage and parenthood probably were not as important as milestones of maturity as they might be for younger drug users. Thus, neither aging alone nor assumption of adult roles accounted for cessation among our respondents. Furthermore, we found no evidence in our in-depth interviews of any progression from immaturity and drug use to maturity and cessation. Indeed, the maturing out hypothesis smuggles into scholarship on drug use an unsupportable assumption about abstinence that is rooted in temperance-era moralism: that fully developed human beings do not desire to alter their consciousness with drugs. As noted earlier, we have found it more accurate to say that problems that often accompany heavy cocaine use accumulate and disrupt users' lives, and then they move toward quitting. Thus, they don't so much mature out (although many got wiser the hard way) as burn out.[7]

Drifting Out

We also explored David Matza's (1964) work on "drift" as a means of making sense of our data. While not a formal theory, the concept of drift was a breakthrough for under-

standing why many young people moved in and out of delin-
quent or deviant behavior. Contrary to conventional social
science wisdom at the time, Matza found that most delinquents did not reject conventional norms or values and were
not committed to any deviant ideology or way of life. They
were living in a circumstance (youth) that allowed them simply to drift between deviance and conformity.

For our purposes, drift is not so much a theory of cessation
as a sensibility about the phenomenology or lived experience
of commitment to a behavior. The concept suggests that many
delinquents, drug users, and others defined as deviant cease
their deviant acts simply because they drift back toward the
conventional ways that they had never really abandoned anyway. Thus, moving from cocaine use to cessation need not be
the result of existential crisis or of maturation. Of course, as
both the maturation hypothesis and our earlier chapters imply, such a drift back to the conventional sometimes occurs
when an individual's situation changes, as when he or she
moves to new statuses or takes up new responsibilities (e.g.,
marriage, parenthood, school graduation, employment, etc.).
The concept of drift has not been rigorously operationalized,
but it has been useful in qualitative studies on users of marijuana (Henley and Adams, 1973; and Brown et al., 1974) and
heroin. Waldorf's (1983) study of cessation among heroin
addicts, for example, found that many simply drifted away
from heroin without conscious effort, apparently never having been committed to the drug or to the life-style of an addict
(see also Blackwell, 1983).

In the present study, we explored drift indirectly by asking
our quitters if there had been a specific day on which they had
decided to quit and if they had made a conscious decision to
do so. As Table 10.1 shows, half of the quitters reported that
they decided to stop on a certain day. Treated quitters answered yes to this question significantly more often than untreated quitters.

Although Matza's concept of drift provided us with a useful sensibility about the tenuousness of many users' commitment to cocaine use, the responses in Table 10.1 do not offer

TABLE 10.1
Questions About Drifting, Treated and Untreated Quitters

I. *Was there a certain day on which you decided to stop using cocaine?*	*Treated* (N = 30)	*Untreated* (N = 76)	*TOTAL* (N = 106)
Percentage answering yes	(21) 70.0%	(34) 44.7%	(55) 51.9%
	[Chi Square = 4.53; significance: p = <.03]		
II. *Was it a conscious decision on your part to stop?*			
Percentage answering yes	(28) 93.3	(64) 84.2	(92) 86.8
	[Differences were not significant.]		

strong support for the idea that our quitters just drifted out of cocaine use. Half of our quitters had not decided to quit on a specific day (although most treated quitters did), but the vast majority of both treated and untreated quitters had made a conscious decision to stop. Our qualitative data suggest that some quit for rather mundane reasons (e.g., it was no longer fun or had become boring). But we suspect that most who had used regularly and for as long as our respondents had would not merely drift out of cocaine use. As we said in the last chapter, many were able to walk away from cocaine relatively easily, but most had to make a point of doing so. However, our respondents were among the heaviest users in the United States, and it is our hunch that many less serious users do drift out of regular use.

Natural Recovery

To date the most extensive analytic description of natural recovery appears in *Pathways from Heroin Addiction: Recovery without Treatment* by Patrick Biernacki (1986). After interviewing both treated and untreated ex-addicts, Biernacki postulated that heroin addiction consists of many facets—physical, psychological, and social. He concluded that immersion in the social world of addiction (a life-style centered on hustling, copping, and getting high) and identification with that world are important to recovery. Contrary to popular stereotypes, he found different levels of immersion and social identification; the prototypical street addict was only one of three types. The other two resembled Matza's drifting delinquents; they seemed either to be passing through the heroin scene without breaking ties with the conventional world, or they were only peripherally involved with heroin and had little commitment to either the conventional or the addict world.

The experience of recovery varied by the level of immersion and identification. Street addicts had a difficult time overcoming their addiction because so much of their lives hinged on the addict life-style and because they were excluded from conventional society. They typically had to experience rock bottom or some existential crisis before overcoming their addiction. Once they resolved to quit they remained stigmatized and had a difficult time finding a new social identity or a niche in society where they could function comfortably. As a result they often had trouble staying off heroin. The other two types had an easier time because their immersion and commitment to the life-style were tenuous or fleeting; some just walked away from heroin and simply resumed their conventional lives.

Unlike Biernacki's former street addicts, few of our cocaine quitters were deeply immersed in a drug-centered life-style. Those cocaine sellers who did not also maintain straight jobs seemed most deeply immersed, along with some young, working-class users who had little attachment to conventional work. But as we have noted, most of our working- and middle-class users did not function in life-styles or subcultures that supported cocaine use the way the heroin world does.

More often than not our quitters decided to stop using after concluding that the increasing negative effects they were experiencing, combined with the interaction of such effects with their lives and identities, simply made continued cocaine use undesirable. Under such conditions, many of our heavy users simply walked away from cocaine with little difficulty, often by using social avoidance strategies.

Yet, in contrast to Biernacki's immersed street addicts, most (particularly the untreated) had less difficulty remaining abstinent because they were neither stigmatized by nor estranged from conventional society. Thus, they had little need for major life-style changes.

Howard Shaffer and Stephanie Jones of the Center for Addiction Studies at Harvard Medical School extend research on natural recovery to cocaine addiction in *Quitting Cocaine* (1989). Like Biernacki's heroin addicts and most of our quitters, their respondents stopped using cocaine after protracted use without the assistance of treatment. They found three ideal-typical phases of natural recovery: "turning points" when addicts begin consciously to experience negative effects; "active quitting" when they take steps to stop using; and "relapse prevention" or "maintaining abstinence." These phases clearly resemble the cessation processes described by our most problematic users, particularly our treated quitters. Although many of our quitters did not report feeling the need for dramatically active quitting or rigorous relapse-prevention strategies, the essential elements of the process were similar.

Shaffer and Jones also postulate two types of quitters— those who experience existential crises, or "rock bottom quitters," and "structure builders." The first are similar to Biernacki's street addicts who became increasingly immersed in the heroin world and addict life-style to the point at which virtually all aspects of "normal life" disintegrated and they were moved to quit (see also Waldorf, 1973; Jorquez, 1983; Brill, 1972). Many of our treated quitters had reached similarly desperate straits. Structure builders, by contrast, are people who do not necessarily experience dislocation because of their cocaine use but who set about finding activities to take its place. As we noted in Chapter 9, many of our quitters undertook activities to help them quit that could be understood as structure building (e.g., developing new social, political, or athletic interests or changing social circles). Again, however, many had never let their cocaine use destroy existing structures and thus already had jobs, families, communities, and activities to focus on while quitting.

Finally, Shaffer and Jones describe two quitting styles among natural recoverers—those who quit "cold turkey" (quitting suddenly and completely) and those who "tapered" their usage. Our quitters included both of these polar types and others who fell in between or tried both methods in different combinations until they succeeded. Also, as we will show in Chapter 11, some members of our long-term, follow-up group tapered naturally over several years without ever actively quitting; they just didn't bother to use anymore. At the other extreme were a few who had to make not using a daily preoccupation. Two things are noteworthy here. First, most of the treatment and recovery literature regards this tapering style of cessation as a cruel delusion or a form of "denial," while both Shaffer and Jones and our study suggest otherwise. Second, most treatment programs insist that patients quit "cold turkey," and most treatment professionals assume that withdrawal sickness always occurs. Neither was the case for most of our quitters.

PART IV

CONCLUSIONS

CHAPTER 11

TEN YEARS AFTER: THE LONG-TERM IMPACTS OF COCAINE ON A SMALL NETWORK OF USERS

In 1974 and 1975, we spent several months observing and interviewing twenty-seven cocaine users in one of the first ethnographic studies of modern cocaine use (Waldorf et al., 1977; Reinarman, 1979). More than a decade later, when this study was funded by the National Institute of Drug Abuse, we were able to reobserve and reinterview twenty-one of the original twenty-seven users. This network of friends had been using cocaine for an average of three years by 1974, making them part of a new cohort of users who began their cocaine careers well before the so-called epidemic of the 1980s. The nucleus of the group was made up of two extended families, and the others were related through marriage or tied by high school friendship. All but one were white (one was Filipino), and roughly half were female. Their median age was then 26, the youngest a 16-year-old high school student and the oldest a 51-year-old insurance salesman. The majority were from middle-class backgrounds. About half were college graduates and several others were attending local universities at the time.

Most members of this network were seasoned drug users who used alcohol and marijuana regularly and had experimented with hallucinogens and a variety of other illicit drugs in the late 1960s and early 1970s. They considered cocaine a luxury drug at first, a treat to be shared with close friends, usually on some special occasion. Most were casual, controlled users, although four eventually used on a daily basis. At the time of our initial interviews most did not believe cocaine to be addictive, although they expressed respect for its abuse potential.

We concluded then that casual use was the norm among these users and that they experienced remarkably few negative effects. Contrary to popular beliefs, we found no evidence that cocaine was a universal aphrodisiac or that it led to crime or violence. The most recurrent negative effects were minor: nose irritations and short-term fatigue and depression following long nights of cocaine use, which usually included marijuana and alcohol ingestion as well. The four daily users in the group also reported occasional irritability and edginess, as well as some resulting disruptions in personal relationships, but none felt addicted or in danger of becoming so. From our current perspective we realize that our description would probably have been less sanguine had we studied the group for a longer time. We now know, for example, that several members subsequently had physical and psychological problems with the drug when they began to use it more heavily over a longer period.

In spring 1986 we began to relocate these people for follow-up interviews on the long-term impacts of cocaine use. We were able to find twenty-four of the original twenty-seven (88.8 percent) and to interview twenty-one of them (77.7 percent). Two of the original respondents had died—one of gunshot wounds during a heroin-smuggling scheme in 1975 and a second of lung cancer in 1977. One person refused to be interviewed; third parties reported that he has a successful law practice and no longer uses cocaine. Three respondents had left the area and lost contact with members of the group, so we were unable to locate or interview them.

In these follow-ups we used the same questionnaire and in-depth interview guide that we used with the main sample. We added questions to get this group to take us through each year since 1975, describing their use of cocaine and other drugs;

highlights of schooling, work, and career; family and spousal relationships; arrests and imprisonments; health problems; personal crises; drug treatment episodes; and general living situations. We then explored in detail the phases of their cocaine careers.

Many of the respondents continue to socialize with one another. Career and family constraints have limited the biweekly gatherings that characterized this group's social life in the 1970s, but children's graduations, birthdays, holidays, and marriages still bring many members together several times a year. We were able to attend some of these gatherings to observe the group and catch up informally on the changes that had occurred in the previous eleven years. The cast of characters (pseudonymous) and their living situations in 1975 and 1986 are listed in Table 11.1, followed by brief summaries of the long-term consequences of cocaine use on their lives.

CHANGES BETWEEN 1975 AND 1986

Family Life and Parenting

As for many of their peers, family and parenting concerns are of paramount importance to this group. Thirteen of the twenty-one people reinterviewed during 1985–86 are parents. Many expressed concern about what to tell their children about drugs and whether or not to reveal past and present drug use to them. The responsibilities of parenting were often cited as important factors in the decision to limit or curtail drug use, especially cocaine use, among parents in the sample.

Six of the respondents have been divorced, including two of the couples interviewed in 1974. One couple, Jake and Elizabeth, do not see cocaine use as having contributed to their marital problems. But Sebastian and Bridget both claim that Sebastian's cocaine and heroin use contributed to their divorce.

TABLE 11.1
Characteristics of Follow-Up Group

	1975	*1986*
Bridget	25-year-old graduate student/ waitress; single, no children	36-year-old therapist; homeowner; divorced, 2 children
Sebastian	27-year-old construction worker; single, no children	38-year-old limousine driver; divorced, 2 children; on methadone
Scorpio	28-year-old construction worker; married, 3 children	39-year-old construction worker; homeowner; married, 3 children
De De	22-year-old mail clerk/college student; single, no children	33-year-old retail manager/salesperson; homeowner; married, no children
Maria	24-year-old college student/phone operator; single, no children	35-year-old teacher; married, 1 child
Pat	20-year-old college student/truck driver; single, no children	31-year-old attorney; divorced, no children; remarried
Elizabeth	29-year-old law student; married, 3 children	40-year-old attorney; homeowner; divorced, joint custody of 3 children
"Cost Factor"	22-year-old construction worker; single, no children	33-year-old construction worker; single, no children
Gail	28-year-old college student/waitress; divorced, 2 children	39-year-old x-ray technician; homeowner; divorced, 2 grown children
Coco	22-year-old college student/waitress; single, 1 child	33-year-old bar manager; homeowner; single, 1 child
Bud	28-year-old rental-agency clerk; single, no children	39-year-old rental-agency manager; married, 2 children
Aggie	21-year-old college student/truck driver; single, no children	32-year-old owner of film industry service business; single, no children
Jake	29-year-old attorney (studying for the bar exam)/hotel clerk; married, 3 children	40-year-old attorney; homeowner; divorced, joint custody of 3 grown children

TABLE 11.1 (*Continued*)

	1975	1986
Ouspensky	25-year-old college student/postal clerk; single, 1 child	36-year-old postal clerk/poet; divorced, joint custody of 1 child
Alexander	16-year-old high school student; single, no children	27-year-old English language teacher; homeowner; single, no children
Lisa	20-year-old living on inheritance; single, no children	31-year-old bartender; single, no children
Milt	25-year-old mail carrier; single, no children	36-year-old small art-business owner; homeowner; married, 1 child
Deborah	20-year-old dental assistant; single, no children	31-year-old; homeowner; married, 3 children
Lynn	22-year-old college student; single, no children	33-year-old bookkeeper/apartment owner; married, no children
Kent	23-year-old rental-agency manager; single, no children	34-year-old executive in national corporation; homeowner; married, 3 children
Stephen	26-year-old graduate student/research assistant; single, no children	37-year-old college professor; single, no children

Note: All names are pseudonyms.

Health Problems

Few health problems were reported. Health concerns, however, were cited as reasons to limit or abstain from cocaine use. The most frequently reported problems were nasal conditions that included sniffles, postuse stuffiness, and occasional nose bleeds. Most experienced these conditions as mere inconveniences, but for Pat and Elizabeth they were troublesome enough to lead both to reduce their use of cocaine greatly. Only one respondent, Maria, reported a serious health problem. On one occasion she ingested seven grams of cocaine within twenty-four hours and consequently suffered convulsions. After this incident she reduced her use and quit altogether three months later when she became pregnant.

Work and Careers

Almost all the respondents who expressed career aspirations in 1975 were able to realize them. At that time, four respondents were in law school or planning to start, and by 1986 all had graduated, passed the bar examination (three of the four on the first attempt), and were in successful practices. Three others who planned professional or managerial careers realized those plans (therapist, executive, professor). The two respondents who used the most cocaine for the longest periods of time, Milt and Jake, were still able to reach their career goals. Lisa's and Sebastian's drug use inhibited their occupational attainments, and both have expressed dissatisfaction with their current jobs. As we have noted before, given the middle-class backgrounds of most of the respondents, the impact of cocaine use on career attainment may be more substantial for users with fewer socioeconomic resources and opportunities.

Arrest and Imprisonment

Aside from its being illegal, cocaine use had no association with crime among this group. Sebastian, who became an active cocaine seller, was arrested for drug sales and possession and convicted for possession. He served six months on a work furlough program in lieu of jail. Gail was arrested and convicted for driving under the influence of alcohol, but this occurred months after she quit using cocaine completely in January 1984. No one else had any encounters, drug-related or otherwise, with police.

More Dangerous Drugs and Modes of Ingestion

Most of these respondents started out snorting cocaine and stayed with that mode of ingestion. Five had injected cocaine between one and five times, and three had freebased or smoked crack one to five times. Only Sebastian injected cocaine more than a few times. He went on a twelve-month binge in 1982 while on a methadone maintenance program for a heroin habit he had been battling since his days in Vietnam. He stopped using cocaine entirely in 1983.

Most of those who had experimented with freebasing or injecting quickly returned to snorting. The consensus was that shooting and smoking were dangerous in that they could lead to compulsive use patterns which all sought to avoid. These users believed that shooting could lead to uncontrolled use, and that only junkies used needles, an identity far from their images of themselves. Freebasing quickly got the same kind of reputation among the group. Their observations of cocaine users who had started to "lose it" or abuse the drug in this form were interpreted as evidence of risk and of the desirability of safer modes of ingestion. Ouspensky, for example, enjoyed freebasing but now sticks to snorting.

> RESPONDENT: I knew these people before they were getting heavy into it [freebasing] and I could see how they were changing. And I saw how they couldn't see that or didn't want to see it, too. So there was a tragic element to it all but that's part of the play.
>
> INTERVIEWER: So do you think that kind of caused you to stop?
>
> RESPONDENT: Yes, to bail right out. (Case #907)

Most members of this group came of age in the 1960s. Historically, they had relied on each other and on personal experimentation to develop their knowledge and beliefs about drugs and their effects. In their youth, they had been barraged by horror stories about marijuana and LSD which were directly contradicted by their own experiences. It had become their practice, therefore, to observer others using drugs and often to try substances personally before making a judgment about the qualities and risks of a drug or mode of ingestion. As other researchers have suggested, one problem with education and prevention programs that exaggerate the dangers of drug use is that users may discount the information (see Becker, 1967; Weil, 1972; Reinarman, 1979; Rosenbaum, 1981). That is, warnings that fly in the face of the experiences of a user or trusted peers will tend to be perceived as hysteria or propaganda, thereby discrediting official sources of prevention information. Although it appeared that this practice of relying on user knowledge and discounting official warnings left them open to the use or abuse of cocaine, such folk knowledge and user culture also kept most of them from injecting and freebasing.

The Heroin Summer

One original respondent who began dating Bridget in 1974 was a fairly large-scale cocaine dealer who also imported heroin into San Francisco. The Smuggler, as we called him, was shot and killed in early 1975 by a partner who wanted to take over the Smuggler's business. Before he died the Smuggler had left ten ounces, or "pieces," of heroin in Bridget's house without her knowledge. We had met the Smuggler on the downswing of his career as a cocaine importer (see Waldorf et al., 1977). He began importing heroin in a desperate attempt to bolster a failing enterprise. He solicited investors who would put up money to purchase cocaine in Mexico and reap substantial interest. Gail invested $1,000 and was paid $1,500, and a second time $3,000 and was paid $4,000. She invested $3,000 again but then the Smuggler was killed.

In an attempt to recoup her investment, Gail and Bridget tried to sell some of the heroin the Smuggler had left behind. They also used some of the heroin themselves and within weeks eight more people in the group had tried it. Prior to that summer only two members of the group had ever tried heroin. Sebastian was a veteran who had smoked both heroin and marijuana in Vietnam. Milt had used once before with his older brother in his hometown on the East Coast. Others in the group were quick to try heroin, just has they had cocaine three or four years before.

But there was a difference that had to do with their user culture. Once they had tried cocaine, most came to view it as relatively benign. But heroin's reputation as the "heaviest of the heavy drugs" was confirmed by their own experience, so most stopped using it. Two months after their failed attempts to sell the heroin, Gail and Bridget dumped the remainder down the toilet. Bridget explained their decision this way: "Everyone, including myself, was getting into it too much. Jake and Sebastian were using the most and we felt responsible. We felt the only thing to do was to get rid of the source."

Only Sebastian, Jake, and Milt used heroin more than a few times. Sebastian and Jake began to cultivate other sources for heroin, one of which was Milt. Milt was working in an art gallery where one of the owners had access to heroin. All three began using together and each found others outside of the group with whom they began to use regularly. Knowing how the other group members felt about heroin, each attempted to hide his use, especially from their spouses or lovers, and this placed their heroin use out of the orbit of group norms.

Eventually all three became addicted to heroin. Milt was evicted from an apartment that he shared with two other group members in 1976 primarily because of his heroin use. He left the network at this point and moved to another county. Sebastian continued to use heroin and cocaine intermittently for several years before seeking treatment. Jake and Milt sought short-term treatment and did not use heroin again. They went on to develop satisfying careers as an attorney and an art gallery owner, respectively. Sebastian re-enrolled in a methadone maintenance program.

These three heroin users were the only members of the group who sought help for drug problems. Each believed he was addicted to heroin at the time and wanted to stop using it. In all cases their cocaine use had waned as a result of their involvement with heroin. Milt sought out a private therapist and after several months was able to discontinue heroin use totally. Jake took acupuncture treatments for three months and also saw a private therapist. At the follow-up Jake reported that he had used cocaine twice in the last two years (he used no cocaine at all from 1976 to 1984), and Milt reported that he uses cocaine very moderately, (one to two lines) one or two times a year. Sebastian stayed on a methadone maintenance and had not used cocaine or any other illicit drug in three years when we reinterviewed him. It must be noted that although all of these men admitted to a cocaine "problem" or "addiction," it is difficult to separate their abuse of cocaine from their abuse of heroin. We cannot say whether any of them would have developed an addiction to cocaine and sought treatment if they had used it alone.

LONG-TERM PATTERNS OF COCAINE USE

For nearly all the follow-up subjects, except the three heroin users who sought help, regular ingestion of cocaine over an eleven-year period did not result in a pattern of compulsive use or addiction. There was substantial variation in the quantity and frequency of use, lengths of runs, and effects experienced. Despite popular conceptions and inferences based on treatment populations, it does not appear that eventual addiction or dependence is the inevitable outcome of sustained cocaine use. Uncontrolled or heavy cocaine use is clearly possible,[1] but to judge from this group, so are continuous controlled use and return to controlled use. We found at least four different career use patterns.

Continuous Controlled Use

One-third (seven of twenty-one) of the group used moderately throughout the full eleven-year period. De De's experience with cocaine was typical of this group. At the time of the first interview she was a college student and a part-time mail clerk. Despite living on a tight budget, she used $10 to $25 worth of cocaine (a quarter gram) a week, primarily on the weekends so that it would not interfere with work or school. She continued in this fashion from 1975 to 1978. Some weeks she would not use at all and several times a year she might use more, especially if someone offered to share. In 1975, De De told us what she liked about the drug's effects: "I think coke makes you use your senses more. It's a very sensual drug. This makes your body feel good. . . . It makes you think. It just makes you feel good. It doesn't slow you down like weed. It stimulates you."

In 1978 she married and with her husband purchased a new home. The strain of a new mortgage coupled with her husband's very moderate pattern of use reduced her use even further. At follow-up, De De reported using an average of one-quarter gram a month. She and her husband regularly buy half a gram to celebrate their wedding anniversary, but otherwise her cocaine use is sporadic and never exceeds a quarter gram a month. Because her practice was to subordinate her use to budgetary and career constraints, and because her significant other was a very controlled user, De De, like others who fall into this type, never experienced any legal, social, or health-related difficulties as a result of her cocaine use. In 1986 she still reported enjoyment from her occasional cocaine use: "I do like the body feeling. . . . I like to describe it as 'everybody is pretty wonderful' when I'm on coke, you know. I have a good time and I'm willing to talk and fool around" (Case #902).

De De's continued positive view of cocaine and its effects was echoed by all others who had remained controlled users. What Weil calls "good relationships" with drugs tend to produce positive effects on users, and this pattern can be reinforcing (Weil and Rosen, 1983, 26). Cautious, moderate use, even over more than a decade, can allow users to have continuously positive drug experiences, and these seem to function as incentives to avoid abuse and the ill effects often reported by heavy users.

From Controlled to Heavy and Back to Controlled Use

At one time in their cocaine careers seven members of the group used large amounts during regular binges or used on a daily basis. All were able to maintain their jobs even during heavy use periods. The core difference between these heavy users and those who eventually quit entirely is that these people never allowed cocaine to become a major problem for them, nor did their spouses, employers, or friends view them as problematic users. For the most part they were able to keep their cocaine use under financial, physical, and social control. Their peak use period was between 1975 and 1981, and by the time of our follow-up interviews most were using less than a quarter gram a week. They appear to have found, as one put it, that "small amounts on special occasions is the best way to enjoy cocaine." At follow-up, this piece of folk wisdom had become accepted by virtually everyone as an important norm which, if followed, would maximize their ability to enjoy cocaine with minimal risks.

Pat's cocaine career illustrates the controlled to heavy to controlled pattern well. He began selling small amounts of cocaine and marijuana in college. The money helped finance his education and he enjoyed selling a drug that people saw as glamorous. Pat limited his cocaine use to his leisure hours, but his overall consumption gradually increased. He began to encounter some health problems that eventually caused him to reduce his use: "The main thing that I decided to quit for was because the physiological part. My nose really bothered me, more so than . . . other people . . . my problem was just more drastic. And it was not worth waking up in the morning and going through the process of two days of being miserable" (Case #942). Although Pat often refers to himself as a quitter because he no longer buys cocaine, we put him in this category because he does use small amounts on special occasions.

Controlled to Heavy Use to Abstinence

Five respondents used moderately for some time (five years on average), but then began to escalate their use to what they came to see as uncontrolled and detrimental levels. As a group they experienced the most cocaine-related problems of all

twenty-one follow-up subjects. At least two described themselves as "addicted" for at least a few months. Many experienced physical problems because of their use and, despite a
few frightening episodes, continued. They also felt substantial guilt over money spent, drugs stolen, and relationships
strained. Sebastian used the most and was the only shooter.
He injected twenty-eight grams a week for a year, a large
amount indeed. Unlike other members of the general sample,
he never went back to snorting once he had begun intravenous
injection.

These users were described by their fellows as the kind of
people who "took it to the max"; that is, took an activity
to extremes or did it at maximum capacity (e.g., working
eighteen-hour days; dancing until dawn; drinking until
drunk; snorting cocaine until the nose bleeds). While other
members tended to use cocaine largely "to keep the party
going a while longer," these users tended to use the drug all
night or until it was gone, sometimes for two days straight.
They often had trouble with other drugs like alcohol and
Valium, typically using them to balance the effects of cocaine
during heavy use periods.

Maria typifies this pattern. Between 1975 and 1980, she
used in a controlled fashion but sometimes felt the urge to
do more. In general, her use during this time was limited by
lack of access. In 1980 Maria's sister, Bridget, and several
friends began selling cocaine to supplement their incomes and
provide themselves with a less expensive supply. Increased
daily access to cocaine marked the beginning of problems for
Maria. Her consumption increased steadily and her husband,
family, and friends began to worry about her; some kidded
her about being a "coke hog." This was a very unfamiliar
identity for Maria, who had always been seen as kind and
gentle, and was one of the most moderate users in the network. Her family and friends stopped offering her cocaine and
Bridget eventually "cut her off" (refused to sell or give her
cocaine). Maria then began to steal cocaine from her sister
and her friends. Although she had never stolen anything be-

fore and felt terribly guilty, she couldn't help herself: "After a while of doing so much cocaine consistently, it gets to the point where nothing would get better and it didn't help. It felt worse but I still kept doing it" (Case #304).

Her heavy, uncontrolled use lasted for about eighteen months, the last six of which she spent trying to cut down. Maria stopped using, with little difficulty, when she discovered she was pregnant in 1983. She is now proud of having quit but ashamed of her past behavior. Since her daughter was born she has used two to three lines of cocaine on two occasions; both times were unpleasant and made her feel depressed. She had not used at all for eighteen months at the time of the follow-up interview.

From Controlled Use to Abstinence

Two of the women respondents, Lynn and Gail, fell into this category. They are not included in the continuous controlled use group because their pattern was unique. They stopped using entirely after nearly ten years of tightly controlled use without having experienced any serious cocaine-related problems. For them, cocaine was simply a pleasant way to prolong leisure activities. As Lynn said, "It would keep a party situation going on longer. If you are having a good time with your friends and you want to keep on having a good time with your friends instead of just letting the evening die, it would pick it right up again" (Case #908).

Both women used an average of a quarter gram of cocaine per week between 1974 and 1981. On minor binges once or twice a year, they might consume one gram in a week. Neither ever injected or freebased. Both reported that they drank more alcohol when they used cocaine to titrate its effects. Cocaine tended to make them edgy and nervous, and the alcohol "smoothed over" those effects. Gail expressed some worry over using "booze and coke" together "because when I stopped [using cocaine] I stopped drinking, and I was drinking a lot of times to take the edge off, so it was like a vicious cycle"

(Case #305). For both Gail and Lynn, the high was gradually transformed until they came to dislike the nervous, edgy side of the "coke buzz" that they once found stimulating. And neither liked the high costs. Gail recalled:

> I used to [get] really nervous and I didn't enjoy it. . . . I don't know if it was the quality of the stuff or what. It was really cut with a lot of speed and I just didn't enjoy it anymore at all. And it was expensive also and I realized how expensive it was and it wasn't as enjoyable as I thought, so I just stopped. (Case #305)

Gail has not used since 1981 and Lynn quit in 1984. Neither experienced any difficulty quitting, felt any withdrawal symptoms, or had to make any life-style changes. Their cocaine use never posed any problems for these women, but the combination of nervousness, increased alcohol use, expense, and (for Gail at least) declining quality, led them to abstain from further use. In fact, neither woman made any real effort to abstain, but merely allowed her cocaine use to atrophy. In contrast to Shaffer's and Jones's active quitters, Lynn and Gail did not so much quit as simply not bother to use anymore.

ONE CONTINUOUS HEAVY USER

The youngest member of the group, Lisa, did not fit any of the types discussed so far. She was the follow-up subject who most closely resembled the tragic figure of a compulsive cocaine abuser depicted in the media—locked into a downward spiral of long binges and concomitant family, economic, and health problems. In 1975, Lisa was already one of the heaviest users in the network. Here is how we described her then:

> Lisa, the "party girl," went on a coke binge for a solid year when she inherited a large sum of money in 1973. She generally lived with drug sellers so most of her cocaine was bought in large quantities. Often she would put up the money for large coke

buys that her dealer "old men" would sell. She told us of an instance when she was with five other people who used an ounce of cocaine in two days. At her high point she used 5 or 6 ounces [then $6,000 to $8,000 worth] in a month. (Waldorf et al., 1977)

Between 1975 and 1977, Lisa usually went skiing for one month a year, spent another month in Hawaii, and used cocaine only a few times. In 1978 she returned home, her inheritance depleted. She began working as a cocktail waitress and used in small amounts with other waitresses. She continued to work in nightclubs and bars, using more and more cocaine and drinking alcohol to counteract what she termed "the wired feeling." At our 1986 interview Lisa was working as a bartender and selling quarter grams of cocaine on the side. After eleven years, she was still snorting, drinking, and dancing with disaster, much to the dismay of the others in the network.

What Can Be Learned from Such Outcomes?

For most members of this small circle of long-term cocaine users, as for many heavy users in the larger sample, the tendency to escalate to abuse and addiction appeared neither inexorable nor inevitable. Cocaine was routinely available to them. Its use was hardly proscribed by abstinence norms or values. Most ingested it regularly and even went on occasional binges. Yet, in the end, most never came to use cocaine daily or abusively. All seemed to recognize that smoking crack or base and intravenous shooting offered more potent forms of the cocaine high, and they were not shy about admitting that they liked to get high. Yet, while several members flirted with these modes of ingestion, only Sebastian ever adopted one of them. For the others, the subcultural norms which allowed some kinds of use warned against others (Becker, 1967; Spotts and Shontz, 1985), and they knew that "too much of a good thing" would soon stop being fun and start disrupting their lives.

We are not saying that there were no risks in all of this. There is little question that uncontrolled cocaine use can lead to substantial social dysfunction and even shattered lives. Even among this small group of twenty-one long-term users, six experienced serious problems for at least short periods. The experiences of the remaining fifteen, however, suggest that a variety of other outcomes are possible, even after a decade of use (see Grinspoon and Bakalar, 1976; Erickson et al., 1987; Mugford and Cohen, 1988; Cohen, 1989; for similar findings on heroin users, see Zinberg, 1984; Hanson et al., 1985). Most of these people were from middle-class or upper-working-class backgrounds, but none started adult life with a silver spoon in his or her mouth. Yet, after years of cocaine use, each of the twenty-one was gainfully employed at the time of our follow-up, and, perhaps more telling, each of those who described educational and career aspirations in 1975 had attained them. Most own homes in one of the most expensive housing markets in the United States. All took risks and a minority experienced problems, but if the majority are any guide, long-term controlled use of cocaine need not entail wrecking one's life or even significant social dysfunction.

We also found little evidence among this group to persuade us that controlled use is impossible or even implausible, or that once control was apparently "lost," it could never be regained. Abstinence was the choice of some, but not of most. Only Sebastian felt that total abstinence was an imperative for avoiding abuse. The majority used cocaine for more than a decade, usually in a controlled fashion. One-third of these follow-up subjects had at one point escalated to daily use or abusive binges, but even they managed, without marked difficulties, to reestablish controlled, now mostly ceremonial use patterns.

As we argued in the last chapter, the desire for cocaine did not overpower users' concerns with family, health, and career. Instead, we found that the high value most of our users placed on these aspects of their lives militated against addiction. Paradoxically, even the value they placed on being able to *keep* getting high seemed to constrain abuse. As Bridget matter-of-factly explained to us, abuse is a self-evident evil because "if you do too much and blow it, then you can't do any more at all." Such group norms and informal social controls (the use pejoratives like "coke hog" and the refusal to sell or share with abusers, for example) pushed against the pharmacological and psychological forces that can pull people toward trouble (Becker, 1967; Zinberg, 1984).

Most of our respondents also successfully employed control strategies like limiting the times and spheres in which they used cocaine (not at work, only at night, never while pregnant, and so forth). Such strategies seemed to help them subordinate their drug use to the exigencies of daily life rather than subordinating their lives to their drug use. In fact the breakdown of such strategies served as warning signs to family and friends. When group members saw a fellow user expand the times and places of use, they ceased offering cocaine and started offering advice on stopping. Such practices were part of their user culture that seemed to help minimize abuse.

Such variations in long-term use patterns and outcomes suggest that "addictiveness" may by a property of neither personality nor pharmacology, apart from the personal and social resources of users, the social organization of their lives, and the cultural practices that shape the setting of use. Further research along these lines may help to identify the conditions underlying a range of outcomes that is far broader, and more hopeful, than either abject addiction or absolute abstinence. A deeper understanding of what makes such outcomes possible should be of value in both prevention and treatment efforts.

CHAPTER 12

COKE AND CULTURE

$W_{e\ set\ out}$ to describe in detail the cocaine-using practices and cocaine-related problems of 267 heavy users. In this final chapter we will review briefly our main findings and reflect upon what they might mean.

In summing up we must note again that our respondents were in some respects unusual. First, they were not a captive sample drawn from the most troubled users in jails, prisons, treatment programs, or from those who call help hotlines. Although most research on drug users is based on such samples, our respondents were drawn from the much larger population of cocaine users who have had no contact with such institutions. Second, we did not seek to study the nature and extent of cocaine use among the general population, for this strategy would have given us mostly respondents who merely experimented with the drug. Instead, we set out to find only those who had ingested substantial amounts over a sustained period and to interview them "in the wild," as they live and work. Thus, whatever our findings about the nature of cocaine use, abuse, or cessation, they must be understood as pertaining first and foremost to this group of heavy users in the community.

Further, we must restate a related caveat with respect to the social class of our respondents. Although our snowball sampling strategy allowed us to study cocaine users from a wide

range of groups, most of our respondents were solidly work-
ing- or middle-class, fairly well-educated, and steadily employed. This means that our research cannot necessarily tell us
much about, say, crack users among the poor or snorters
among the super-rich.

Becoming a Cocaine User

Nearly all our respondents first tried cocaine when it was
offered by a trusted friend. Cocaine use does not spread mys-
teriously from deviant strangers to virginal citizens, but rather
between otherwise ordinary folks who know each other. We
stress this obvious point because just as users inoculated each
other against "official" antidrug warnings, so too did they
serve as credible sources of informal, user-based warnings
about problems. Friends not only taught each other how to
use cocaine, they also taught each other about the risks of
doing so. The lessons learned by many of our respondents
seem to have become part of user lore (Becker, 1967; Zinberg
and Harding, 1982). We think this helps explain why cocaine
use has declined nationally.[1]

The second point about becoming a cocaine user is that a
few snorts will not do it. Many recent antidrug advertisements
have implied that a single dose of cocaine often kills or that
once you try it you will be hooked for life. The pharmacological determinism smuggled into such statements bears no relationship to our respondents' reports. Not only did we find
wide variation in initial effects, from subtle to stupendous and
positive to negative, but many users experienced no initial
effects at all. Most of our respondents had to *learn* the high;
that is, learn both to experience and then to appreciate the
effects of cocaine (cf. Becker, 1953). In the vast majority of
cases, it took several months of experimental or occasional
use before ingestion became frequent or regular. And most of
the roughly twenty-five million Americans who have tried
cocaine drop out well before their use reaches this stage.

Third, once use was initiated and the high learned, there was no uniform progression or pattern. Among our subjects we saw a continuum of use/abuse that included four relatively discrete use patterns or types of user: hogs, bingers, nippers, and ceremonial users. Moreover, there was considerable movement by individuals from one pattern or type to others— and not just in the direction of a downward spiral from experimental use to addiction. Although many users followed this often destructive path, we found at least as many who nipped and then binged and yet returned to nipping, and still others who became ceremonial users after heavy binge use or even after sustained abuse.

This heterogeneity of career patterns suggests possibilities for control that are too rarely acknowledged or studied. We stress this because about twenty-five million Americans have at least tried cocaine, and at least 90 percent of them used less cocaine less often than our respondents. So if controlled use is possible and addiction not inevitable even among our heavy users, then cocaine's image as the great scourge of the late twentieth century needs to be made more complicated.

CONTROLLED USE AND PROBLEMATIC USE

One of the findings that surprised us—and certainly one that some observers will see as controversial—concerns the existence of such controlled users. Cocaine is an alluring drug. It has many uses. It has become widely available. For all these reasons users often escalate their doses. But approximately half of our subjects sustained a controlled use pattern for periods ranging from a year or two to a decade. Our definition of "controlled use" is a pattern in which users do not ingest more than they want to and which does not result in any dysfunction in the roles and responsibilities of daily life. For example, use that results in any chronic, disruptive problems with health or work is not controlled. But in our definition, occasional nasal sniffles, irritability, or even weekend binges without proper eating and sleeping do not necessarily constitute loss of control any more than dehydration, headaches, and occasional nausea after nights of drinking constitute alcoholism.

Some observers consider *any* use of an illicit drug to be, by definition, "abuse." For them, the very concept of "controlled use" is an oxymoron. For us, this stance is a moral rather than an empirical one, although it is arguable that our attempt at a nonpejorative description of patterns of cocaine use has a tacit morality in that it fails to condemn. Similarly, most treatment professionals take it as Talmudic truth that once the use of a substance reaches abusive levels, the idea that one can cut back or return to controlled levels of use is at best an illusion born of denial and at worst a cruel hoax on a diseased individual. In fairness, clinicians may have sound practical reasons to avoid dwelling on the possibilities for controlled use. Many of our respondents fooled themselves into continued use and abuse by entertaining the idea that they "had it under control." Still, even among the heavy users we studied, many were able to maintain long-term control and others returned from abusive and compulsive levels to controlled use.

The other half of our sample did not always maintain controlled use. As our case study of Stephen in Chapter 7 illustrated, there is nothing necessarily permanent about a pattern of controlled use. While many long-term controlled users never escalated, Stephen taught us how even someone who had maintained moderate use for several years could drift into abuse. When his situation changed—more disposable income, more availability, more books to finish—so did his cocaine use.

The wide variability of use patterns, problems, and outcomes that we uncovered has made us wary about predictions and generalizations. We can, however, offer something of an ideal type of controlled user based on our observations, which does not do much violence to the empirical complexity of controlled use.

- Controlled users tended to be people who did not use cocaine to help them manage preexisting psychological problems, and did not also abuse other drugs, especially alcohol.
- Controlled users generally had a multiplicity of meaningful roles which gave them a positive identity and a stake in conventional daily life (e.g., secure employment, homes, families). Both of these factors anchored them against drifting toward a drug-centered life.
- Controlled users, perhaps because they were more anchored in meaningful lives and identities, were more often able to develop, *and stick to,* rules, routines, and rituals that helped them limit their cocaine use to specific times, places, occasions, amounts, or spheres of activity.

As we argued in earlier chapters, we found the factors of stake in conventional life and identity central for understanding both continuously controlled users and others who were able to reassert control. Such stakes seemed to keep their drug use from overtaking or "inundating" (Rosenbaum, 1981) their lives and identities. The fact that such social and social-psychological factors seem to mitigate against abuse and problems is hopeful insofar as it suggests that not everyone need fall victim to the worst that cocaine can offer. However, it also follows that those who have the least stake in conventional life may be at higher risk. We think this is one reason why the consequences of cocaine appear worse in Harlem than in Hollywood. Conventional lives and identities are not reducible to social class alone, but are clearly related to it. Clinicians are quick to point out that there is no shortage of affluent abusers and addicts who had "everything to lose." But middle- and upper-class people also have life chances and resources that make cocaine-related problems less disruptive in the long run than it so often is for, say, impoverished young people in America's inner cities.

Of course, a parallel point may be made about the capacities of families and communities to cope with members who are experiencing cocaine problems. We have suggested that the events going on in users' lives and the resources they have available influence cocaine use patterns and problems. The same may be said of the families and communities affected by cocaine problems. Although it was not the focus of our study, surely the prevalence of other problems and the availability of resources in families and communities also shape the consequences of heavy cocaine use.

We interviewed many respondents who at some point clearly lost control over their cocaine use. Those who were unable to maintain a controlled use pattern experienced problems of one sort or another, and these problems were often serious. As we noted in Chapter 8, both the most frequent and the most severe problems were reported by the heaviest users, especially those who employed the more direct modes of ingestion. In general, such problems fell along a continuum. Health problems, for example, ranged from the minor, transitory nasal irritations and nervousness reported by most to the severe problems of convulsions and angina reported by a small fraction.

There were surprisingly few differences between users and quitters with respect to the incidence or prevalence of problems. This suggests that the experience of physical health problems alone, for example, may not be a sufficient condition for cessation. Although quitters often cited health problems or concerns as a motivation for quitting, others reporting similar types and severity of such problems kept on using. Short of tossing up our hands and saying that some people are just more deeply addicted, we can draw two inferences here. First, the user's interpretation of cocaine-related problems appears more important than the mere presence of them. Such differing interpretations probably depend on the presence or absence of preexisting physical or mental health problems, on users' capacity to tolerate or manage problems, and on their ability to rationalize or deny their importance. All of these mitigating factors relate to other factors affecting the user's life.

Second, in attempting to understand the role cocaine-related problems play in cessation, it seems important to focus on the way that problems in different realms may interact and accumulate until a threshold of "trouble" is reached and the user makes an effective decision to cut down or quit. This threshold varied widely among respondents, especially since most reported both positive and negative effects of cocaine. As we argued in Chapter 10, it may be the ratio of positive to negative consequences that is important. Beyond this, cocaine-related problems typically interacted with and often exacerbated each other.

For example, financial problems often added stress to relationships, some of which were already strained by heavy cocaine use. About half our respondents reported difficulties having to do with the high cost of cocaine—users more than quitters, freebasers and shooters more than snorters. Horror stories depicting cocaine abuse as the direct and unequivocal cause of financial ruin are now standard fare in the media, and our worst case histories document in some detail the truth of such stories. But we also found that nearly half of our serious users managed to limit or control their use precisely to avoid financial strain.[2] This variation means that financial ruin is not an inevitable consequence. But even our controlled users would agree that cocaine can be, in more ways than one, a very expensive drug. And when these financial problems were added to other cocaine-related problems, many of our respondents cut back or quit.

Cocaine use also entailed work-related problems such as absenteeism, not working up to capacity, or strained relations with bosses or coworkers. A few users even lost jobs or quit school at least in part because of their abuse of cocaine. Here too, however, our data were mixed, for many of these same people reported that cocaine use had actually enhanced their productivity and work performance. Although many reported workplace problems at one point or another in their cocaine use careers, others had no cocaine-related difficulties at work. In the end, work problems, like sex and relationship problems, tended to be a function of how much was used, for how long, and in what ways.

What lessons can be drawn when some users have lots of problems, others have few or none, and still others go on using for years before problems occur? We set out to study heavy users and the problems they experienced, and we found no shortage of them. On the other hand, none of the many problems reported appear to be an inevitable consequence of even long-term use. At the very least, we can say that substantial and sustained cocaine use entails clear risks of problems in many spheres. But if we were asked whether any given user will experience any one or more of these problems, our candid answer would have to be "it depends." It depends upon the person and the personality. It depends upon the length and pattern of use. It depends upon the characteristics of the settings in which it is used. It depends upon the other problems in the person's life and the resources he or she has to deal with them.

CESSATION

Common sense suggests that the experience of cocaine-related problems should be a prime motivation for users to quit or curtail their use. For many this was true, but for others the cessation process was more complicated. Despite the fact that the greater the number of problems the more incentives a user had to quit, there are apparently no cocaine-related problems, no matter how severe—even angina—that in and of themselves always lead users to quit.

A significant minority of our respondents persisted in their cocaine use despite obvious and often serious negative effects. Again, the user's interpretation of the impacts of cocaine seems critical, for a problem or complex of problems that leads one user to quit immediately may not lead others to the same decision until later if at all. Our qualitative life-history data suggest that negative consequences are less likely to lead to cessation to the extent that cocaine is being used to deal with non–drug-related personal or psychological problems.

These data also suggest that serious cocaine users rarely have one, overarching problem which drives them to quit, but rather a complex of several problems that interact in unique ways within the context of users' lives. For some users such problems exacerbate each other as well as whatever other troubles the users are experiencing. When these interacting problems accumulated to the point where they seriously disrupted valued aspects of users' daily lives, most made some move to cut down, exert control, or quit.

Even this rather general proposition, however, does not fully account for all of the variation in outcomes we observed. Many of our users regulated their intake of cocaine so that such problems either never developed or did not accumulate to the point of disruption or unmanageability. Based on the kinds of data we could collect, we could not identify a magical "factor X" which all of our quitters reported and none of our users did. In fact, it is our hunch that attempts to find the sine qua non of cessation—the condition that is both necessary and sufficient to explain quitting—will be as futile as attempts to find a single cause of addiction. There may be as many routes to cessation as there are routes to addiction. We have pointed to some themes, but there were always exceptions.

We hope we have shed a bit more light on *how,* as a practical matter, users manage to quit. Here, too, we found great heterogeneity. A few of our respondents reminded us of the old saying of cigarette addicts: "Quitting is easy, I've done it a hundred times." One heavy user estimated that he had tried to quit forty times. In Chapter 9 we told the story of Harry, a compulsive freebaser who many times tried unsuccessfully to cut down or quit. It was only after failed treatment attempts, a wrecked car, and serious strain on his family and his law practice that a cocaine-induced health crisis propelled him into a long-term treatment regimen that worked. In our sample, however, this worst case scenario was not typical. More than half of our quitters were like Patty, who had made no previous attempts to quit and who, with varying degrees of effort and anguish, "just walked away" from cocaine and "never looked back." This was most likely to happen among untreated quitters, but nearly one-third of those who sought some formal treatment also reported no difficulty.

Given that our sample was designed to exclude all but very heavy users, we were pleasantly surprised by the relative ease with which so many managed to quit. Their strategies for doing so, moreover, were fairly commonsensical social avoidance techniques designed simply to put distance between themselves and the drug. Interestingly, while two in five sought new non–drug-using friends as a strategy, a majority did not; most had maintained such friends throughout their cocaine careers. As we noted, friends are a crucial part of getting into cocaine use and they also may be a crucial resource for getting out of it.

This formulation is so simple as to risk being branded "the painful elaboration of the obvious." Yet, the policy implications are not so obvious. Millions of dollars have been spent by the Partnership for a Drug-Free America, to cite just one example, on major media advertisements asserting that the best thing one can do for "cocaine addicts" is to cut them off, fire them from their jobs, and forbid them to continue to use cocaine if they wish to be treated as "normal." It may be true that some drug abusers need to be confronted in no uncertain terms.[3] However, our data suggest that users who are trying to quit are aided by friends who help them maintain or reaffirm their normality.

Jobs were another important resource for our cocaine quitters. Both friends and occupational roles reaffirm nondrug identities and bond people to conventional values and lifestyles. Indeed, we suspect that one reason why so many of our users could control their use and why so many quitters could quit is because they did not undergo identity transformation as, say, heroin addicts so often do. Friends and jobs to which users could return may be understood as identity resources and social anchors which could either keep people from getting swamped by cocaine use or help stabilize them again (Biernacki, 1986). Labeling, stigmatizing, or isolating drug users may push some to try to quit or to get help, and it seems to make nonusers feel good by symbolically reaffirming the supremacy of abstinence values (see Gusfield, 1963). But if our subjects are any indication, this strategy also risks robbing users of their ties to conventional life and confirming a deviant identity, which in turn make cessation less likely and continued use more likely.[4]

The complexity of our findings on use patterns, problems, and cessation make for a messy picture in which to see possible policy implications with respect to treatment. We know, however, that a significant minority of our quitters found it necessary and useful to seek formal treatment. We suspect that many other heavy users also have an excruciating time quitting, especially if they are without other resources. It seems to us clear, therefore, that if we as a society are serious about reducing cocaine problems, treatment programs of all types should be made available on request for all who want them. Too many people have struggled unsuccessfully with too many cocaine-related problems to leave cessation a matter of individual will, even if a surprising number manage with that alone.

It also seems wise to remember, however, that not all who desire to quit will want or even need formal treatment. Clearly the bulk of America's cocaine users are just that—cocaine users; they cannot be said to be sick or in need of treatment for mere deviant behavior alone, however much a public health strategy may be preferable to a law-enforcement one. But among our respondents who experienced problems and tried to quit, most did so without treatment. And we found no evidence that they were any less successful than the treated.

Virtually all treatment programs and Twelve-Step groups like Cocaine Anonymous demand adherence to an ideology of abstinence as the only answer for addictive disease. Yet, like the natural quitters studied by Shaffer and Jones (1989), few of our quitters found it necessary to abstain from all drugs in order to stay away from cocaine. Just as many of our subjects had returned to moderate controlled use after long periods of daily use or repeated binges, so did most of our quitters use alcohol, marijuana, and sometimes other drugs on occasion. Many even used cocaine in a ceremonial or special occasion manner after quitting without falling back into abusive patterns. We found no evidence that such people had more slips, relapses, or other problems than those who abstained.

We find it encouraging, even hopeful, that many quitters did not need treatment to stop successfully or to radically reduce their use to nonproblematic, ceremonial levels. Most of those in our sample who wanted to quit managed to do so. Although many had to work at it, most succeeded with far less difficulty than either they or we had imagined.

We discovered three factors which we think facilitate quitting. First, as we noted in Chapter 10, when cocaine use escalates to abusive levels, a gradual transformation of the cocaine experience tends to occur. What was experienced initially as euphoria often turns to dysphoria; stimulation can become depression; sociability can give way to isolation and paranoia, and so on. People use cocaine because it is pleasurable, because they find that it enhances their lives. So when long-term or heavy use comes to interact with their lives in such a way that the drug no longer has such effects, many will begin to turn away from it.

Second, the vast majority of our quitters reported at most minor withdrawal symptoms after quitting. Some reported cravings for cocaine, but these were most often seen as fleeting, transitory, and manageable. Very few reported anything like the severe physiological symptoms reported by alcoholics and opiate addicts. We think the relative absence of this painful, physical side of addiction helps account for why so many managed to walk away—and stay away—from cocaine.

Third, we found no cocaine life-style or any well-defined and all-consuming cocaine subculture like that found in most studies of heroin addicts. Our users typically had roles, responsibilities, and pursuits that they valued and from which they sustained a sense of self—what we have called stakes in conventional daily life and identity. When cocaine use or related problems threatened these, most in our sample either abandoned or substantially reduced their consumption. The cocaine scenes we saw and heard about were not like the heroin addict world, which furnishes sustaining memberships, networks, and a culture that often swallows users. The cocaine scenes described by our users were as varied as they were and seemed to be shaped by whatever circles of friends comprised them rather than by the form of drug use. Thus, movement away from cocaine use and toward cessation generally was not impeded by the hold or momentum of a cocaine subculture.

CULTURE AND POLICY

It is difficult at best to reach clear, concise conclusions in a study that found such variation in use patterns and outcomes. We have been forced by the complexity of the world we were rendering to use more qualifying language than a smooth writing style would dictate. We have often resorted to words like "some," "many," "most," and to the style of the proverbial "two-handed economist" ("on one hand, . . . on the other hand"). After grappling with these problems, we comforted ourselves with the idea that they do not result merely from our limitations as analysts or writers. Instead, we concluded that such variation and complexity are precisely the point.

We could find no evidence of a single, uniform career path that all heavy cocaine users ultimately follow. Progression from controlled to uncontrolled use is not inexorable. Like other studies of cocaine users in the community, ours found that controlled use is not impossible and that addiction to cocaine is not an inevitable outcome of even sustained use (see also Erickson et al., 1987; Mugford and Cohen, 1988; Cohen, 1989). A surprisingly large number of our heavy users experienced no serious social, psychological, or physical dysfunction as a result of their cocaine use. They continued to be

responsible parents, partners, workers, and citizens who remained "normal." Yes, they routinely violated drug laws, but
not because they were wholehearted deviants who utterly
rejected "straight" society. On the contrary, they knew they
were "normal" enough that using this drug, as opposed to that
one, simply did not make them lesser human beings. They
regulated their intake and "took care of business."

Having said this, it is incumbent upon us to reiterate the
risks. Not everyone in our sample was able to sustain such
control in the face of the reinforcements cocaine provides the
body and the brain, and the temptation to use more of it in
more spheres of life. Even the most careful and controlled
users we interviewed agreed that cocaine has clear abuse and
addiction potential. Almost all of our subjects knew people
who had gone too far with cocaine even if they themselves had
not. Some of them called this "addiction," others "abuse," and
still others had different names for compulsive use or loss of
control, such as "blowing it." Our sense is that for these users,
the various terms did not matter much. They knew trouble
with the drug when they saw it, and they had witnessed
firsthand more than enough problems to support such folk
understandings.

Thus, this study, like virtually all others of cocaine users
in the community, has documented both the well-publicized
problems that befall some users and the unpublicized possibilities for controlled, nonproblematic use. Ideally, we as a society could formulate and teach the principles and practices
users have developed to avoid problems and maintain control,
for we believe that these offer huge untapped potential for
harm reduction. However, such controlled use norms and
other informal social controls remain anemic; they have not
been allowed to become part of public discourse and culture.
Cocaine has been criminalized and scapegoated. When use
must be surreptitious, regulatory mechanisms are less likely
to be developed and disseminated. For bad reasons as well
as good, parents, schools, media, and government suppress
information about the possibilities and procedures for con-

trolled use. Thus, what one generation of drug users learns is difficult to transmit to the next. When social learning is impeded, the tragedies must be repeated. This is one reason why cocaine has caused problems for so many users in our society.

Having seen up close what kind of damage is possible from cocaine, we understand why well-intentioned parents and policymakers might not want to broadcast findings about controlled use. But as well-intentioned researchers, we cannot in good conscience hush up their existence in fear of facilitating the "denial" of some abusers or increasing the risks for some new users. For it is our contention that the considerable possibilities for exercising control over cocaine use can be seen as cultural resources that can facilitate personal capacities for control and social capacities for harm reduction (Becker, 1967; MacAndrew and Edgerton, 1969; Zinberg, 1984; Biernacki, 1986). If, for example, the only frameworks available in popular culture for interpreting one's drug-using behavior are addiction and abstinence, then the idea that one can and should exercise control can atrophy. Our interviews have convinced us that one important reason control was possible for so many is that they *believed* it was possible—believed that cocaine was not necessarily addicting, that it could and should be used in a controlled fashion. They had at least the beginnings of a *vocabulary of controlled drug use* with which to conceive and articulate normative expectations of controlled use.

We do not believe this potential for control can or should drown out what we have called the discourse of disease. Nor should the discourse of disease drown out the fact or the concept of controlled use; both concepts are alive and well in the social worlds of drug users.

Thus, there are good reasons for making the possibilities for controlled use a part of public policy debates right alongside findings of abuse and addiction.[5] Certainly America's understanding of its drug problems would be enriched by more research on the conditions under which such control is likely and unlikely. And we think law and public policy can only be improved by having to contend with such politically inconvenient scientific knowledge.[6]

Let us begin to practice what we preach. We can identify two distinct cultural "recipes" for individual responsibility from our users' accounts.

To minimize the likelihood of getting into trouble with cocaine: Make certain that you do not use cocaine every day. Use it only when you can rest the next day. Use it only in social situations and not to provide energy for essential tasks. Use only a prespecified amount. Make it a point not to have a regular supply around. Employ rules and rituals that restrict the amount used at one sitting and the number of spheres of life or activities in which it is used. Stick to ceremonial or special occasion social uses. Do not choose associates or activities with cocaine use in mind. Do not sell cocaine even to a few close friends. Do not use cocaine to "solve" problems or to compensate for shortcomings. And be sure to subordinate use of cocaine to the demands of daily life.

To get out of trouble with cocaine: Stop all sales of cocaine. Move away from social scenes in which cocaine is likely to be present. Take short vacations, change neighborhoods, stay with nonusing friends for a time. Publicly announce that you are quitting to give yourself some investment in staying away from it if only to avoid embarrassment. Maintain or renew relationships with non–cocaine-using friends. If your spouse or lover is using cocaine, get your partner to quit, too, or take a short break from the relationship. Begin a regular program of physical conditioning, not only to undo whatever damage cocaine has done but to substitute a new high. Do not exaggerate the difficulty of cessation. Some cravings are possible, but remind yourself that these are transitory and manageable because painful withdrawal symptoms are relatively rare. Take up new hobbies or pursue new interests to fill the void with other gratifying activities. If you need it, get help from friends, family, or treatment programs.

A Theory about Cultural Context

There are some threads of theory running through these conclusions that point toward a sociological perspective on drug
abuse. We have woven some of them into the fabric of earlier
chapters, but they bear explication here. These ideas amount
to two basic themes about the cultural context in which humans ingest drugs. First, at the micro level, pharmacology is
not destiny. As Zinberg (1984) and others have shown, the
interaction between the pharmacological properties of a substance and the physiological characteristics of a user accounts
for only part of a drug's effects. A sizable minority of our
sample experienced feelings of powerlessness or a loss of control over their cocaine use and often their lives. Yet even
among this uncontrolled group there was little evidence that
they would "do *anything*" to obtain their drug. Why? Not
because cocaine is not a powerful and reinforcing psychoactive substance, but because its powers are always *mediated by
users' norms, values, practices, and circumstances.*

No matter how seductive cocaine is, it is always ingested in
social contexts that shape how it is used and what its effects
are taken to mean by users. If users' drug-taking behavior is to
be understood, then the behavior's meaning to them, within
the context of their lives, is crucial. While most of our respondents abused cocaine on some occasions or at some
points in their careers, there was no lockstep escalation toward a sustained pattern of such abuse. The social organization of their lives cut against such risks; and most did not avert
their gaze from problems but often warned each other about
them. Clearly cocaine's pharmacological properties are capable of providing physiological and psychological sensations
that push users toward greater, more compulsive use. But to
elevate these properties to the status of supreme causal force is
to commit the fallacy of pharmacological determinism. Abuse
and addiction are not inevitable because pharmacological and
psychophysiological factors are not the only important variables.[7] As we said in Chapter 10, for example, after prolonged

heavy use, the actual felt effects of the high tend to be transformed, in part because of how they interact with the lives and identities in which users have a stake. Cocaine *feels* different, and is less reinforcing, when it is disrupting rather than enhancing one's life.

If our heavy cocaine users have demonstrated the dangers of cocaine, we think they have also demonstrated the dangers of drug determinism. They have taught us that beyond the drug itself, how users think about and behave toward drugs matter a great deal. Cultural norms matter. Subcultural practices matter. How closely we watch out for each other matters. The uses to which we put consciousness-altering substances matter. The personal and social resources of users matter. The value placed on productive daily lives matters. And, of course, the social distribution of *opportunities* for productive lives matters, for the absence of such opportunities is a large part of why there is so much crack use among the inner-city poor and why it has been so disruptive.

This brings us to our second, more macro-level point about cultural context. Pharmacological determinism is only one of the ideological mechanisms that exclude considerations of culture from the debate on drugs. The other is the presumption of pathology. By this we mean that virtually every politician, journalist, drug warrior, and moral entrepreneur speaks of our nation's drug problems as if no rational human being would want to get high. Of course, if pressed, most would admit that what they mean is, get high with illicit drugs. Conservatives are fond of speaking about illicit drug problems as if they were caused by the individual moral choices of pathological people. Liberals also talk this way but are apt to add that a pathological society also pushes people toward such irrational choices. Some in both camps speak of drug problems in terms of disease. But it is a rare, perhaps foolhardy, soul who speaks of drug users as people making rational choices.

We have learned from our respondents and from the history of drug use that what Mugford and Cohen (1988) call the "pathology paradigm" conceals far more than it reveals. First of all, as we said at the outset, there are no cultures and no epochs of history in which people did not ingest chemicals to get high. Indeed, as Siegel's insightful book, *Intoxication* (1989), shows, even animals seek out plants and fermented berries that will alter their consciousness. So it is not that people who get high are pathological, but rather it is alleged that people who get high with a substance defined as criminal by the state are pathological. The powers-that-be may have rational reasons for their categories; coffee is harder to abuse than cocaine. But the presumption of pathology is more a political claim than a scientific fact.

However pathological some drug abusers are or become, and however pathological our society is, it makes more sense to us to interpret most drug use with the presumption of pleasure-seeking (Mugford and Cohen, 1988). Whether we like it or not, a defining feature of advanced industrial societies—of modernity itself—is that human beings spend a large chunk of their lives and incomes consuming commodities for entertainment and pleasure. Unlike traditional, agrarian, preindustrial societies, modern, urban capitalist societies depend fundamentally for their economic survival on just such consumption. Business and even government massively promote this way of life. All citizens are encouraged, cajoled, and coerced to seek pleasure and entertainment through the consumption of commodities (Marcuse, 1964; Bell, 1976; Butsch, 1990). This is not only true of the "hardware" of social life like food and furniture, but increasingly of the "software"—spectator sports, movies, music, massage, video games, vacations, and amusement parks. And if we ask our fellow citizens why they do this, they tell us it is because they derive pleasure from it. Pleasure, in short, has become an utterable vocabulary of motive (Mills, 1940).[8]

In such a world, people who seek pleasure through the consumption of consciousness-altering commodities should not be thought of as coming from a different planet. In our peculiarly American version of modernity, a competitive, achievement-addicted, "Type-A society,"[9] cocaine's ability to make us feel empowered, euphoric, energetic, and ebullient fits our culture like a glove. If we want to know where people got the idea that they could take a chemical and change their mood, we will have to look beyond pathology. Recall, for instance, that the great rise in recreational drug use in the so-called cultural revolution of the 1960s was preceded by the pharmaceutical revolution. Drug companies and psychiatrists popularized the notion that we could take a pill and feel better long before Timothy Leary and psychedelic rock music came along. Bennett Berger (1981, 197) has argued more broadly that even before the 1950s, modern capitalist society had begun to socialize its citizenry to be aware of "the *induced* character of its own dissatisfied consciousness" and to believe it rational to seek more pleasurable and satisfying experiences. In short, whatever the risks of drug use, in our culture the consumption of drug commodities for entertainment and pleasure is not such a big jump from the norms of society. And to rail against the risks of this or that demon drug without understanding the ways in which our own culture makes drug use a thinkable and "do-able" thing is an abdication of analysis.

If we as a society underestimate the powers of such cultural components of our drug problems, then we overestimate the powers of cocaine and thereby risk contributing to the problems it can cause. If we as a society are truly interested in reducing the harm that drugs can do, rather than in the utopian and moralistic goal of abstinence, then we will have to open our analytic aperture more widely. We will have to examine more carefully how users themselves have developed practical procedures for regulating their use so as to minimize risk. And we will have to examine how all of us participate in and thus help constitute a culture in which the consumption of commodities for pleasure is so intrinsic that the consumption of drugs is commonplace.

APPENDIX

STUDY BACKGROUND, METHODS, AND SAMPLING

O*ur interest in* cocaine began in 1973. Cocaine was making a comeback, partly as a result of the reduced supplies of amphetamines beginning by the close of 1960s. As the negative effects of amphetamines became apparent, physicians stopped overprescribing them and federal agencies began to ban their use. Police were aggressively closing clandestine "speed labs," and many users became wary after experiencing problems. Cocaine began to fill the gap for people interested in stimulants, and smugglers met the demand (Brecher, 1972).

In 1973 we began to observe cocaine use in a small friendship network of largely middle-class men and women. Eventually we decided to undertake a short-term ethnography of the thirty-two users in this network who had regular associations with two families of sisters whom we called the "Austins" and the "Joyces" (the first was English in heritage, the second Irish). With a small grant from the Drug Abuse Council, an agency established by several foundations at the instigation of the Ford Foundation, we observed and interviewed this group for six months. We found recreational use and few problems the norm. The conclusions of this research were reported in more detail in Chapter 11 (see also Waldorf et al., 1977; Reinarman, 1979).

A few years later, Waldorf conducted a study for the National Institute on Drug Abuse (NIDA) on the social-psychological processes of recovery or cessation from heroin addiction which focused on addicts who had quit without treatment. At that time virtually nothing was known about untreated quitters; few clinicians and researchers believed they existed. Nevertheless, this study located and interviewed 101 untreated ex-addicts, documenting their strategies for cessation.[1] As public concern mounted over the rise in cocaine use and abuse, we proposed to NIDA that a study of heavy cocaine users who had quit, with and without professional assistance, would be timely. In 1986, NIDA awarded us a research grant to study cocaine cessation.

THE SAMPLE

During the two-year study we interviewed 267 persons, including a main sample of 122 current users and 106 quitters. Most chapters in this book describe this group. In addition to the main sample we have included two substudies. The first is a follow-up of the network we first interviewed in 1974–75. Ten of these follow-up interviews are also included in the main sample. The remaining eleven persons did not meet our criteria for inclusion in the main sample (see below). A second substudy consists of fifty-three interviews with persons who primarily freebased or smoked crack during the period of their heaviest use (Chapter 6). Of this group, twenty were quitters and twenty-five were present users at interview. An additional eight freebasers were interviewed but did not qualify for inclusion in the main sample.

METHODS OF LOCATION

With few exceptions (Erickson et al., 1987; Chitwood and Morningstar, 1985; Siegel, 1982; Smart et al., 1984), cocaine researchers usually study treatment populations because they are convenient to locate and consist of extreme users. This has been the case with other drug research as well (Waldorf, 1980) and has made it difficult to generalize from the findings. As a result most of our knowledge of cocaine users come from extreme cases and therefore may not apply to the majority of users.

We tried to avoid this problem by utilizing social networks of present and past cocaine users to locate subjects. Sociologists call this method chain referral or snowball sampling, a type of purposive sampling (Biernacki and Waldorf, 1981; Watters and Biernacki, 1989). We began our interviews among the people we originally studied in 1974–75. We also interviewed a number of other present and past cocaine users. After all interviews we asked respondents if they knew other users or quitters who might agree to be interviewed.

The project staff also recruited and trained a number of specific people to assist us in locating and interviewing black and Latino users, women, freebasers, special occupation groups, college students, and gay men. Most of these interviewers were current or ex–cocaine users who had access to other networks of users and quitters. For example, we trained an intelligent, outgoing Latino "homeboy" (a barrio or neighborhood youth) who located homeboy cocaine users. Another very social ex-user knew a large network of people who worked in Silicon Valley (the heart of the computer industry near San Jose), and he recruited a number of users from the ranks of technical and managerial workers. A white surfer who was a controlled user knew a network of freebasers in an affluent, North Bay town. He interviewed twenty-six users, most of whom were middle-class blacks. A black rock musician joined the study for six months and located twenty-four persons from his networks; they were mostly white. We also recruited a particularly bright and conscientious undergraduate who had close contacts with university students, many of whom lived in a dormitory notorious for drug use. She interviewed fifteen young users there. Using contacts developed by the principal staff and these selected interviewers, we were able to penetrate several diverse networks of present and past users. We went to some lengths to locate women and minorities so as to have a reasonably representative sample.

CRITERIA FOR EXCLUSION AND INCLUSION

The general focus of the study was cocaine, so we did not want to confound our findings by including subjects with other drug problems. Therefore we used a screening interview to exclude persons with recent histories of problems with alcohol or other drugs. Anyone who had used four or more ounces of distilled spirits (or the equivalent in wine, beer, or any combination) per day for at least sixty days in a row within ten years was excluded. We also excluded anyone who reported using any opiate, methamphetamine, or barbiturate daily for two weeks or more within a ten-year period prior to the interview. Persons who were in treatment, prisons, jails, or other institutions were also excluded, as were people on probation or parole who are usually required to submit to urine testing. Because one of the principal aims of the study was to learn about cessation, we sought to avoid people who were under external pressure to stop using cocaine; i.e., those who had not undergone a coercion-free period when they might have stopped using.

Our criteria for inclusion specified both amount and length of cocaine use in the hopes of tapping the most serious or heavy users. Any person who used an average of two or more grams of cocaine per week for at least six months, or who used any amount daily for at least twelve months, was included. These twin criteria were devised to tap the full range of possible use patterns.

Most of the people we interviewed used cocaine in greater amounts for longer periods of time than our criteria specified. Of those who used 2 or more grams a week for at least 6 months, the median number of months they used such an amount per week was 11.9. One long-time seller had used 2 or more grams per week for ten years. Cocaine use during the peak period of use for our subjects was high; the median average amount used was 4.6 grams a week for a median peak period of 2.8 months, which is higher than that in most previous studies. The range of cocaine use during the peak period was 1 to 56 grams per week, with fourteen persons reported using 28 or more grams a week at peak.

To be considered eligible as quitters, respondents had to be cocaine-free or have drastically reduced their use to less than four single occasions in the twelve months prior to the interview. These were the minimum criteria, but the median number of months clean (cocaine-free) or in reduced patterns was twenty-three months, and nearly a quarter (23 percent) of the quitters reported that they had stopped for four years or more.

Our twofold criteria for quitters—to be clean or using at dramatically reduced levels—were based upon our early experiences with the long-term follow-up respondents. When we began to reinterview them, we learned that most of the quitters in this group did not hold abstinence values. In short, they did not believe that they could never use cocaine at all once they had stopped heavily using or abusing the drug. Most believed that they could use cocaine on occasion and not return to heavy use, and they generally lived by those standards. They typically neither bought cocaine nor sought it out. However, if they were at a party and someone offered them cocaine they might take it, enjoy the experience, and forget about it. In general, they were not threatened by single instances of cocaine use and did not return to any pattern of regular use.

We defined "treated quitters" as any person who had made three or more visits or spent three or more days in any recognized drug-treatment program (i.e., detoxification, hospital, private psychotherapy, Cokenders, Cocaine Anonymous, etc.). Very few of our untreated quitters went to treatment at all; only two reported that they had ever sought formal help. Treated quitters usually did not view casual or occasional cocaine use in the same way as our untreated quitters did.

Twenty-two of our thirty treated cases were clean and believed that they should remain completely cocaine-free. Untreated quitters did not learn such values, although they did learn from their own experiences and those of friends and associates that they should not abuse the drug.

Most treatment programs are based on some version of the disease concept of alcoholism and drug dependency, which holds that all people with the disease must remain utterly free of all consciousness-altering substances forever. In this belief system, any "slip," even an occasional "snort," puts the former abuser on a slippery slope to relapse and disaster. As researchers, however, we did not feel that we had to impose such treatment standards—particularly when large numbers of our untreated cases had drastically reduced their use from regular binges or daily use to one or two "lines" per year and were maintaining legal and productive jobs, meeting family responsibilities, raising children, making house payments, and so forth. We found no evidence that these lives were threatened by occasional cocaine use.

Description of the Sample

A typical member of our sample is a white man, 30 years old, raised as either a Catholic or a Protestant but no longer particularly religious, with at least one year of college, and working at a white-collar job. This subject is typical in a statistical sense but our sample contained a lot of variation. Nearly two out of five (39.1 percent) of our respondents were women (see Table A.1). The youngest member of our sample was 18 years old and the oldest 53. We excluded minors from the study because they would require parental permission to be interviewed. To get parental permission we would have had to inform parents that the study was about drug use, and we did not want to compromise young respondents with their parents. The median age of our respondents was 30.5 years; quitters were somewhat older on average (mean=32.9 years) than present users (mean=29.9 years).

TABLE A.1
Demographic Characteristics of Present Users and Quitters

	Users (N = 122)	Quitters (N = 106)	TOTAL (N = 228)
AGE			
Range	18–53 years	18–50 years	18–53 years
Median	28.1 years	34.0 years	30.5 years
SEX			
Female	(42) 34.4%	(47) 44.3%	(89) 39.0%
Male	(80) 65.6	(59) 55.7	(139) 61.0
ETHNICITY			
Black	(24) 19.7	(12) 11.3	(36) 15.8
Latino	(15) 12.3	(5) 4.7	(20) 8.8
White	(76) 62.3	(88) 83.0	(164) 71.9
Other	(7) 5.7	(1) 0.9	(8) 3.5
EDUCATION			
Range	4–26 grades	6–21 grades	4–26 grades
Median	13.0 grades	14.2 grades	13.2 grades
Grades 4–11	(12) 9.8%	(11) 10.4%	(23) 10.1%
High school graduate	(39) 32.0	(12) 11.3	(51) 22.4
Some college	(44) 36.1	(36) 34.0	(80) 35.1
College graduate	(27) 22.1	(47) 44.3	(74) 32.5
MARITAL STATUS			
Married	(23) 18.9	(22) 20.8	(45) 19.7
Living with lover	(21) 17.2	(23) 21.7	(44) 19.3
Other	(78) 63.9	(61) 57.6	(139) 61.0
RELIGION REARED IN			
Catholic	(49) 40.2	(36) 34.0	(85) 37.3
Protestant	(38) 31.1	(38) 35.8	(76) 33.3
Jewish	(19) 15.6	(10) 9.4	(29) 12.7
Other	(5) 4.1	(2) 1.9	(7) 3.1
None	(11) 9.0	(20) 18.9	(31) 13.6
OCCUPATION			
Managerial and professional	(14) 11.5	(12) 11.3	(26) 11.4
White-collar	(48) 39.3	(52) 49.1	(100) 43.9
Skilled working class	(22) 18.0	(15) 14.2	(37) 16.2
Unskilled working class	(13) 10.7	(4) 3.8	(17) 7.5
Housewife	(4) 3.3	(2) 1.9	(6) 2.6
Student	(6) 4.9	(12) 11.3	(18) 7.9
Unemployed	(8) 6.6	(9) 8.5	(17) 7.5
Illegal occupations	(7) 5.7	—	(7) 3.1

In keeping with the known ethnic composition of cocaine users in the United States, seven in ten of our respondents were white. However, we were able to interview a reasonably diverse ethnic mix of other respondents—15.8 percent black, 8.8 percent Latinos, and 3.5 percent "other," largely Asians and Native Americans. On average, our subjects were fairly well educated; more than two-thirds (67.5 percent) had attended college, although the range of education is wide. Our least educated respondent left school in the fifth grade and our most educated was a university professor who held two Ph.D. degrees. Quitters reported slightly more formal education than users—a median of 14.2 years as compared to 13.0 years for present users.

Compared to other studies of drug users, we interviewed a high percentage of people in middle-class and upper-middle-class occupations. This is in keeping with the champagne image of cocaine. More than two in five held white-collar jobs, while one in eight were in professional or managerial positions (five attorneys, four university professors, one dentist, one optometrist, and a number of corporate executives). One female executive earned $80,000 a year working for a multinational corporation, drove a $30,000 Porsche, and had used cocaine for twelve years. However, nearly one in four respondents (23.6 percent) were in skilled and unskilled working-class occupations, and one in fifteen were unemployed. A similar percentage were college students, and a small number worked in illegal occupations (seven persons or 3.1 percent), usually drug sales.

Only one in five were married at the time of the interview, and another one-fifth lived with lovers or partners. The remaining three-fifths were neither. About one in four (27.2 percent) had minor children living in their household.

USE OF DRUGS OTHER THAN COCAINE

In the early stage of our interviews we asked a battery of questions about the illicit drug use of our respondents to get some idea of the range and frequency with which they used drugs other than cocaine. Twenty-eight different drugs were listed and each person was asked how often they had used each. We asked quitters about the time periods before and after they quit (or radically reduced their use) of cocaine. Each answer was coded according to seven different frequencies ranging from never to more than one thousand times.

Most respondents were experienced drug users. Nearly three-fourths said that they had used marijuana more than a thousand times in their lifetimes (see Table A.2). Given our exclusion criteria, regular use of opiates was rare. About half said they had never used heroin, while the majority of those who had used heroin and other opiates had done so on less than ten occasions. To our surprise, more people reported having used opium and Percodan or codeine at least once than reported using heroin. We had expected that large numbers might report having used some form of amphetamines because, like cocaine, they are central nervous system stimulants. A majority had used these drugs, although most on less than fifty occasions in their lifetimes.

After marijuana and cocaine, the most frequently used illicit drug was LSD. More than four out of five had used LSD at least once, and a quarter (25.8 percent) more than fifty times. One of the least frequently used drugs was PCP; less than half had ever used it and only 3 percent had used it more than fifty times.

Our data on most recent drug use for present users was more straightforward. For this group we asked a series of questions about cocaine and other drug use in the week prior to our interview. Of our 122 current users, more than two-thirds had used in the previous week (see Table A.3). The median number of days they had used in that week was 1.6; only five persons (5.9 percent) had used on all seven days. The median amount used was just over half a gram; the range was 0.25 to 11 grams. In Chapters 10–12 we noted the tendency for users to reduce their intake when cocaine began to wear on other aspects of their lives. These data support this idea in that a large percentage of our present users had reduced their use

TABLE A.2
Lifetime Frequency of Illicit Drug Use by Subsample, by Percentage

Drug	Never	1–10	11–50	51–1,000	>1,000
			Number of Times Used		
MARIJUANA					
Users (N = 122)	—	1.6%	3.3%	20.5%	74.6%
Quitters (N = 106)	—	1.9	4.7	22.6	70.8
Total (N = 228)	—	1.8	3.9	21.5	72.8
LSD					
Users	13.9	29.5	32.8	23.0	0.8
Quitters	14.2	30.2	27.4	26.4	1.9
Total	14.0	29.8	30.3	24.6	1.3
METHAMPHETAMINES					
Users	27.9	33.6	18.0	17.2	3.3
Quitters	34.9	23.6	20.8	14.2	6.6
Total	31.1	28.9	19.3	15.8	4.8
PILL AMPHETAMINES					
Users	23.8	21.3	23.8	27.0	4.1
Quitters	21.7	17.9	24.5	30.2	5.7
Total	22.8	19.7	24.1	28.5	4.8
HEROIN					
Users	46.7	37.7	9.0	5.7	0.8
Quitters	50.0	26.4	13.2	8.5	1.9
Total	48.2	32.4	11.0	7.0	1.3
OPIUM					
Users	29.5	52.5	14.8	3.2	—
Quitters	33.0	50.9	10.4	5.7	—
Total	31.1	47.8	16.2	4.4	—
PERCODAN/CODEINE					
Users	38.5	32.0	9.8	17.2	2.5
Quitters	41.5	29.2	12.3	13.2	3.8
Total	39.9	30.7	11.0	15.3	3.1
QUAALUDES					
Users	22.1	39.3	21.3	14.8	2.5
Quitters	19.8	34.0	28.3	17.9	—
Total	21.1	36.8	24.6	16.2	1.3
VALIUM					
Users	25.4	32.0	19.7	20.5	2.5
Quitters	21.7	28.3	20.8	23.6	5.7
Total	23.7	30.3	20.2	21.9	3.9
PCP					
Users	54.1	33.6	9.0	1.6	1.6
Quitters	55.7	37.7	3.8	2.8	—
Total	54.8	35.7	6.6	2.2	0.9

TABLE A.2 (*Continued*)

	Never Used Any Opiate	Never Used Any Amphetamines
Users	9.0%	14.9%
Quitters	15.1	16.3
Total	11.8	15.6

from peak period levels. The median amount used at peak period was 4.9 grams a week, or about eight times as much as was used during the week prior to the interviews. Moreover, the data support the notion that cocaine-using careers do not follow a straight line progression of increased consumption. Respondents' use often oscillated, and many were able to exercise sufficient control to reduce their use substantially or to abstain for varying periods.

Arrest History

One of the most striking findings, considering how often our respondents used illicit drugs, was how few had ever been convicted of crimes. After an early review of responses to a

TABLE A.3
Cocaine Use in Previous Week, Users ($N = 122$)

Now let's talk about your coke use last week.	
I. How many days did you use [cocaine]?	
Median number of days:	1.57
Percentage who used on 0 days:	(38) 31.1%
Percentage who used all 7 days:	(5) 4.1
II. How much did you use (in all)?	
Median grams:	0.6
Range:	0.25–11.0

TABLE A.4
Arrest and Prison History by Subsamples

Arrest/Prison History	Users (N = 122)	Quitters (N = 106)	TOTAL (N = 228)
EVER ARRESTED AS JUVENILE	(32) 26.2%	(25) 23.6%	(57) 25.0%
Range	1–23	1–6	1–23
Median	1.0	1.0	1.0
EVER ARRESTED AS ADULT	(55) 45.1	(40) 37.7	(95) 41.7
Range	1–10	1–18	1–18
Median	1.0	1.0	1.0
EVER CONVICTED AS ADULT	(28) 23.0	(26) 24.5	(54) 23.8
Range	1–7	1–11	1–11
Median	1.0	1.0	1.0
DRUG POSSESSION			
Arrest	(27) 22.1	(16) 15.1	(43) 18.9
Conviction	(12) 9.8	(12) 11.3	(24) 10.5
EVER INCARCERATED AS JUVENILE	(16) 13.1	(10) 9.4	(26) 11.4
Median days	4.0	7.0	6.0
EVER INCARCERATED AS ADULT	(28) 23.0	(22) 20.8	(50) 21.9
Median days	6.6	3.0	6.0
Modal days	1.0	1.0	1.0

question about the number of months spent in jail or prison, we had to revise the coding category from months to days (Table A.4). Our previous research on other drug users (particularly heroin users) had led us to expect long and complicated jail or prison histories. Such was not the case with these respondents; only one in five (22 percent) had ever been incarcerated in jail or prison, and then for very short stays (the median stay was six days, but the modal stay was a single day). The exception was a former heroin addict who had spent years in prison and was a very problematic freebaser at the time of our interview.

Three out of five of our total sample had never been arrested as adults on any charge; less than one in four had any adult conviction. This suggests that sustained cocaine use, at least for this sample, did not entail immersion in a criminal life-style or subculture. The fact that our respondents generally were fairly well educated and steadily employed surely helps account for this. However, the prevailing wisdom about cocaine use holds that any sustained pattern of use usually leads to the loss of legitimate opportunities and a propensity toward criminal involvement. Thus, our data suggest that such a trajectory is far from inevitable.

These respondents broke drug laws against possession and, often, sales regularly, but only one in five had ever been arrested as an adult for drug possession and only about half of those were ever convicted. Similarly, only one in twenty was ever arrested for drug sales and less than half that number convicted. Such low drug sales arrests were surprising because, as we noted in Chapter 5, many users become involved at some level in distribution. Two of five (40.4 percent) reported that they had sold at least some cocaine on some occasions during their drug-using careers. Furthermore, this may be a low estimate because we asked few questions about sales, our primary interests being use and cessation.

NOTES

Chapter 1

1. *Time,* Sept. 22, 1986, p. 25.

2. All potential respondents who reported in our screening interviews that they had used enough alcohol, opiates, barbiturates, or amphetamines to be considered an alcoholic or an addict were excluded. See Appendix for details.

3. Although the war on drugs (especially cocaine) continues to widen at this writing, the incidence and prevalence of cocaine use as measured in national surveys by NIDA has been declining since 1987. Moreover, while "cocaine-related" emergency room episodes and deaths monitored by DAWN continued to increase after we completed our study, some preliminary data suggest a decline by the end of 1989. Secretary of Health and Human Services Louis W. Sullivan reported a 20 percent decline in emergency room episodes and deaths in the fourth quarter of 1989 (*New York Times,* "Medical Emergencies for Addicts Are Said to Have Dropped by 20%," May 15, 1990, sec. A; see also "Cocaine Epidemic Has Peaked, Some Suggest," *New York Times,* July 1, 1990, sec. A, and "U.S. Says Hospital Statistics Show Use of Cocaine May Have Peaked: Cocaine-Related Hospital Visits Drop Again," *New York Times,* Sept. 1, 1990, sec. L).

4. The one exception we know of are the Inuits of the Northern Territories, who could not easily grow grapes or grains or psychoactive plants, and who used no psychoactive drugs until white explorers brought them alcohol.

5. Some readers may question whether such a methodological stance is biased toward the "deviants'" view. Perhaps it is biased, but surely no more so than the dominant methodological stance, which

presupposes the pathology of drug users. Howard Becker is instructive on this point: "What we are presenting is not a distorted view of 'reality,' but the reality which engages the people we have studied, the reality they create by their interpretation of their experience and in terms of which they act" (1963, 174).

Chapter 2

1. Freebasers and crack users were different on this score. Many did report an immediate desire for another hit on the pipe. See Chapter 6.

2. Cohen's study of recreational cocaine users in Amsterdam found that an "ever increasing dose is a rarity when we look at careers of longer than five years" (1989, 40). Indeed, like many of our subjects, more than four-fifths of Cohen's users regularly abstained for one month or longer, in part to avoid just such escalation (see also Erickson et al., 1987; Mugford and Cohen, 1988).

3. To their credit, the authors of the DSM-III-R avoid specifying how often a user must use a drug to qualify as dependent or addicted. The same cannot be said for a recent report by the staff of the U.S. Senate Committee on the Judiciary (1990) on what the authors claim are "hard-core cocaine addicts." This report uses its alarming new estimates of the number of such "addicts" to advocate for the laudable goals of deemphasizing casual or experimental users as targets of national policy and increasing the number of available treatment slots. The authors argue that the NIDA Household Surveys underestimate the number of "hard-core addicts" in the United States by a factor of 2.5 because they miss users in jail or treatment or who are homeless. However, the report repeatedly defines hard-core cocaine addicts as persons who report using (or are estimated to use) cocaine once a week (or more). Neither methodological nor evidentiary justification is offered for this fundamental assumption, on which all the core claims of the entire report rest: that use of cocaine [How much? How often? For how long? By what mode of ingestion? Of what purity?] once per week or more constitutes "addiction."

4. The same point may be made about drinking practices and problems. A person who drinks routinely, alone, and in the morning is more likely a problem drinker or an alcoholic than another who drinks a greater quantity of alcohol at cocktail hour with friends.

Chapter 3

1. We observed that positive comments about cocaine and sex that referred to one point in a cocaine-use career did not preclude negative comments about cocaine-related sexual problems or dysfunction during later stages. See Chapter 8.

2. Contrary to what one would expect from all the recent attention being given to crack-using mothers, this woman gave birth to a healthy, robust boy who weighed more than nine pounds. While she clearly took risks by freebasing during her pregnancy, she also ate well and availed herself of good prenatal care. Unlike crack users who live in impoverished circumstances, she had the resources to provide good medical care and diet.

3. This interview was conducted by a committed feminist who had to control her occasional urges to criticize the respondent about the way he spoke of women.

Chapter 4

1. For a more detailed analysis of workplace use and workplace problems, as well as a critique of the many wild claims about how much illicit drug use costs American businesses, see Reinarman, Waldorf, and Murphy (1988). An earlier version of some of the material in the beginning of this chapter was first published there.

Chapter 5

1. Reuter's (1990) interviews with cocaine dealers reveal that most make far less money than the figures routinely cited in media accounts. For further comparisons, see another recent study of drug dealing, particularly crack dealing among gangs, by Skolnick et al. (1989).

2. As Max Weber might have seen it, cocaine dealing amounts to the spirit of capitalism without the Protestant ethic. If he were writing about the world of our sellers he might have used the title, "The Pleasure Ethic and the Spirit of Capitalism."

3. This hierarchy is similar to the one we described in the mid-1970s (Waldorf et al., 1977) and that is described in Patricia

Adler's fine book about high-level cocaine selling in southern California, *Wheeling and Dealing* (1985). There were, however, a few differences. First, crack was not sold in San Francisco or southern California when these earlier studies were conducted and was only beginning to emerge when we started this research, although crack's precursor, freebase, was made and smoked by users. Second, Adler distinguishes between ounce dealers who cut or diluted their product and those who did not, but this distinction was not as clear in our interviews. Third, we found part-ounce dealers and middlemen, which Adler did not classify separately.

4. Respondents who mentioned that they engaged in sales were analyzed separately to see if they differed from mere users. We found no statistically significant differences in terms of ethnicity, mode of ingestion, or treatment experience. Sellers were slightly younger than other users on average and somewhat more likely to have had an adult arrest for drug possession (though not for sales), but these differences were not statistically significant. The one significant difference was that sellers on average used more cocaine at their peak period—5.2 grams vs. 4 grams per week.

5. Mugford and Cohen (1988), in a similar study of recreational cocaine users in three Australian cities, also found a tendency toward different styles of use by gender. Their female respondents were less likely to seek out the drug, and more likely to receive it as a gift, use it socially, and be mindful of the consequences of use on others.

6. Terry Williams (1989), in his study of a crew of young crack sellers in Manhattan, found that most of his subjects knew they could not use crack and still be successful sellers. While crack was considered bad for business by his "cocaine kids," they still snorted powder cocaine.

Chapter 6

1. One can smoke powdered cocaine (cocaine hydrochloride), but its vaporizing point is approximately 180 degrees centigrade, whereas cocaine in base form vaporizes at about half that temperature.

2. The ether method of cooking cocaine to produce freebase is said to be a "hassle" because, above and beyond its flammability,

ether is sometimes difficult to obtain, because it is another ingredient that must be measured and mixed, and because its odor is detectable.

3. Freebasers who prepared their own base reported using ratios of cocaine to baking soda that varied from one-to-one to three-to-one. However, precooked crack as sold on the streets generally contains more bicarbonate and other "cuts" or impurities. Several respondents mentioned using Double-Up (a commercially available solidifier and adulterant), lidocaine, or even the soft drink 7-Up in the extraction process. There were also reports of "prop" or "bunk" crack which contained little or no actual cocaine (e.g., "chips" of glycerine soap or candle wax, or even compressed pieces of bread). Moreover, even if done properly and with no "cuts," the bicarbonate method of cooking does not yield as pure a rock as the ether method because it does not "free" the cocaine base from all adulterants (McDonnell, Irwin, and Rosenbaum, 1990).

4. In this chapter we often refer to both "freebasers and crack users" without distinguishing between the two. There are differences, but, given that the high and the compulsive use patterns described below are identical and that both types of smokable cocaine are now made by the bicarbonate of soda method, we often speak of the two as a set or interchangeably. It should be noted, however, that most of the respondents in this subsample considered themselves "basers" and did not buy crack on the street, although some used crack some of the time and others used it most of the time.

5. The notion that set and setting are crucial influences on the social construction of drug effects has been developed by Becker (1953; 1967), Zinberg (1984), and Weil (1972).

6. The noun "jones," from heroin addict argot, means an addiction or, in this case, a strong craving characteristic of addiction.

7. The authors are grateful to field interviewer Douglas McDonnell for his insights on this point.

8. The cessation process for the entire sample, basers and snorters alike, is described in Part IV.

9. The one exception was nasal irritations, which most snorters reported experiencing at one time or another, but which did not affect freebasers and crack users. In fact, both snorters and shooters remarked that one advantage of smoking was that it did not "fuck up your nose" or leave you with "holes in your arms."

10. Cheung, Erickson, and Landau (1991) reported on a

community-based sample of crack users in Canada among whom use was often "infrequent"; less than one-third were continuous compulsive users. Interestingly, most users recognized the risks of crack and acted accordingly to limit both their own frequency of use and the popularity of crack by spreading word of its dangers in user folklore. This suggests, ironically, that the very addictiveness of crack can mitigate against addiction, or, more generally, that culture mediates pharmacology.

11. E.g., Goldstein et al. (1989) offer a sophisticated empirical analysis of the relationship between crack and homicides in New York City. They found that in 1988, 74 percent of all New York's "drug-related homicides" and 85 percent of all "crack-related homicides" were "systemic," that is, they stemmed from "the exigencies of working or doing business in a black market" rather than from either the economic compulsivity of addicts or the psychopharmacological effects of the drugs. Interestingly, of the thirty-one drug-related homicides that were determined to be psychopharmacological, crack accounted for only three (< 10 percent), while alcohol accounted for twenty-one (67 percent).

Chapter 7

1. These will be more fully explored in Chapter 12, after we have discussed cocaine abuse and related problems.

2. On this point, see especially Becker (1967), who demonstrates that user lore on how to use LSD properly led to a clear decline in LSD-induced psychotic episodes; Zinberg (1984), who develops the same sort of theoretical insights independently in research on heroin and other drugs; and more recently Shaffer and Jones (1989), who further develop the notion of informal social controls and show why they have had limited success in mitigating cocaine abuse.

3. Examples abound in antidrug advertisements such as those of the Partnership for a Drug-Free America. In one recent full-page ad in major newspapers across the country, readers are told that "monkeys with unlimited access to cocaine self-administer until they die." Then the ad's narrative makes the great leap: "Like monkey, like man." The authors neglect to point out that the monkeys, unlike most humans, were unnaturally caged and given no other stimula-

tion—precisely to obtain this sort of result. Thus, even if one could safely extrapolate from animal behavior to that of humans, which is fallacious on its face, humans do not generally allow themselves unlimited access to cocaine and live in cages without other stimuli. Ironically, the same ad goes on to admit that cocaine users "run a 10 percent risk of addiction" (*San Jose Mercury News,* Aug. 2, 1990, sec. D).

Chapter 8

1. See Reinarman, Waldorf, and Murphy (1988, 48–58) for a critique of public discourse on the presumed but unsubstantiated link between cocaine use and productivity, absenteeism, etc. Indeed, while our data support the idea that cocaine abuse entails at least some such costs to American business, the only formal estimation study repeatedly cited in support of such claims (Harwood et al., 1984) measured *neither* cocaine use nor productivity.

2. Some couples reported adapting to these difficulties by engaging in increasingly diverse sexual practices, e.g., oral sex, masturbation, use of mechanical devices. For a more detailed description of the sexual effects of heavy cocaine use, see Macdonald et al. (1988).

Chapter 9

1. There were no statistically significant differences in these patterns of responses by treatment status, gender, ethnicity, or mode of ingestion.

2. Shaffer and Jones report the same point in their study of cocaine quitters on the East Coast: "seeing coke meant doing it" (1989, 146).

3. However commonsensical this saying appears to be, it is not necessarily true. The number of addicts who recover naturally has been underestimated because of the predominance of research on treatment populations (see, e.g., Waldorf and Biernacki, 1977, 1981; Waldorf, 1983; and Shaffer and Jones, 1989). Moreover, the saying, "once an addict," can be a self-fulfilling prophecy insofar as it continually stigmatizes those attempting to recover and mitigates against the assumption of nonaddict roles and identities (Biernacki, 1986).

4. As a check on the veracity of our respondents and the validity of our data, we asked all interviewers to judge whether respondents were high at the interview and whether any signs of drug use were observable. Our interviewers reported that six (5.7 percent of the quitters) were high at the interview, all on marijuana, and that in an additional nine interviews (14.2 percent) there were signs of drug use, all marijuana except for one crack pipe.

5. More than twice as many quitters drank *less* after quitting. Our in-depth interviews suggest that this is probably because so many drank more than usual during heavy cocaine use in order to come down from the high.

Chapter 10

1. In contrasting our sample with typical heroin addict samples, we do not wish to imply that there is no diversity among heroin users. While most research is done on captive samples of heroin addicts in prisons or treatment programs who tend to be homogeneously poor, other heroin users and addicts have more diverse characteristics. See, e.g., Zinberg (1984) and Hanson et al. (1985).

2. For an extended analysis of identity interests, particularly of the way they mediate material or class interests, see Reinarman (1987).

3. We are indebted to Dan Gilbarg for the notion of "ratio of consequences." See also Shaffer and Jones (1989, 150–57).

4. "Ballast" is used here metaphorically. It is a nautical term meaning the weight placed in the bottom or the keel of a sailboat to provide stability, to keep it from being capsized by wind or waves.

5. In their review of the literature, Busch and Schnoll (1985, 291) note that "until recently there was a consensus in the literature that dependence was unlikely because of the lack of physical withdrawal." Some clinicians have now redefined withdrawal in more psychological terms to suit the malaise that sometimes follows cessation of heavy cocaine use. But as we noted in Chapter 3, despite some reports of discomfort, mild depression, or transient craving, very few of our respondents reported anything akin to (physical) withdrawal as traditionally defined.

6. Set and setting are also related to what we have called the transformation of the cocaine high or experience. For if a drug's

effects are never merely physiological and pharmacological, it follows that when a drug is disrupting one's life its effects will actually feel different.

7. In fairness, our study may not be the best test of the maturing out hypothesis. More systematic studies of young crack users, for example, might show more support. However, the sheer passage of time ensures that one is older when one quits than when one beings cocaine use, and we have no reason to believe that maturity rather than accumulating troubles will account for cessation. A true test would have to employ a noncircular, truly value-neutral definition of maturity and show that cocaine quitters were more "mature" than a control group of users of the same age and background.

Chapter 11

Acknowledgment: Earlier versions of this chapter were presented at the annual national meeting of the Society for the Study of Social Problems in New York in August 1986 and published in the *British Journal of Addiction* (Murphy, Reinarman, and Waldorf, 1989).

1. As elsewhere in this book, we define "heavy" use of cocaine as regular use of an average of at least two grams per week for at least six months, or daily use of any amount for one year or more. It should be noted that most of our respondents reported occasional binges of heavy use, but these were generally of short duration (e.g., typically a weekend or two, occasionally a week or two). In order to be classified as having a heavy use pattern, a respondent must have reported *sustained* use at the above levels. Unlike the main sample, however, for this follow-up we defined "controlled" or "regulated" use more narrowly as that which caused no social dysfunction, and which was never daily or never exceeded a quarter gram a week.

Chapter 12

1. See, for example, the latest NIDA surveys (1989) and preliminary data on more recent declines in "Medical Emergencies for Addicts Are Said to Have Dropped by 20%," *New York Times,* May 19, 1990, sec. A; "Cocaine Epidemic Has Peaked, Some Say,"

New York Times, July 1, 1990, sec. A; and "U.S. Says Hospital Statistics Show Use of Cocaine May Have Peaked: Cocaine-Related Hospital Visits Drop Again," *New York Times,* Sept. 1, 1990.

2. Like many of our respondents, Cohen's (1989) recreational cocaine users in Amsterdam usually limited their use to avoid financial problems. One in four (25.7 percent) abstained periodically for a month or more for financial reasons, and half (50 percent) had a rule that cocaine use was inappropriate after a certain level of expenditure per month.

3. For a frightening example of what can happen when this logic is taken to extremes, see Trebach (1987, ch. 2) on "tough love" totalitarianism.

4. On the importance of identity resources in quitting heroin use, see Biernacki (1986). He makes a cogent case that the old axiom "once a junkie, always a junkie" can be a self-fulfilling prophecy. Yes, the risk of relapse is real, but conventional roles, friends, and identities clearly help users stay straight. Thus, to the extent that labeling limits users' ability to maintain conventionality, it increases the likelihood that they will remain within or be drawn back toward illicit drug scenes. This logic is at the core of the relatively successful "normalization" drug policy of the Netherlands, which has consistently tried to keep drug users inside rather than outside the societal "tent." If all bonds to conventional society are not broken, then users are more likely to be exposed to controlled users and nonusers and to be persuaded that they can and should deal with their problems, control their use, get help, or quit (see Cohen, 1989; and Van Vliet, 1990).

5. See Ron Roizen's (1987) perceptive history of the controlled drinking controversy. Even with a licit drug like alcohol, findings showing the possibility that alcoholics might learn how to drink in a controlled manner have been suppressed as heresy.

6. The term "politically inconvenient scientific knowledge" is Howard Becker's (personal communication). On the need for greater flexibility and finer distinctions among types of use and users in law and public policy, see Bakalar and Grinspoon (1984).

7. Shaffer and Jones (1989, 149) reached much the same conclusion: "Cocaine quitters reveal that addiction does not reside in drugs. It resides in human experience. A substantial number of cases of natural recovery from cocaine, alcohol, opiates, and tobacco all serve to remind us that, in spite of the physiological dependence that

may be one consequence of drug use, addiction is not inevitable."
For a similar and compelling argument that addiction does not exist
independent of life context and is not inevitably progressive and
diseaselike, see Stanton Peele (1989).

8. For much of this argument about modernity and pleasure, we
drew upon and are indebted to Stephen Mugford and Phil Cohen
(1988).

9. We are indebted to Shaffer and Jones (1989) for the idea of a
"Type-A society" having an affinity for stimulants like cocaine.

Appendix

1. The findings of this study were reported in four articles (Waldorf, 1983; Waldorf and Biernacki, 1981; Biernacki and Waldorf,
1981; and Waldorf and Biernacki, 1977) and a book (Biernacki,
1986).

REFERENCES

Adams, Edgar H., Ann J. Blanken, Lorraine D. Ferguson, and Andrea Kopstein. 1989. Overview of selected drug trends. Paper prepared for Division of Epidemiology and Prevention Research, National Institute on Drug Abuse, Rockville, Md.

Adams, E. H., and J. Durell. 1984. Cocaine: A growing public health problem. In J. Grabowski, ed., *Cocaine: Pharmacology, Effects, and Treatment of Abuse,* 9–14. NIDA Research Monograph no. 50. Rockville, Md.: National Institute on Drug Abuse.

Adler, Patricia A. 1985. *Wheeling and Dealing: An Ethnography of an Upper-Level Drug Dealing and Smuggling Community.* New York: Columbia University Press.

Adler, Peter, and Patricia A. Adler. 1983. Shifts and oscilations in deviant careers: The case of upper-level drug dealers and smugglers. *Social Problems,* 31:195–207.

Akers, Robert L., Robert L. Burgess, and Welden T. Johnson. 1968. Opiate use, addiction and relapse. *Social Problems* 15:459–69.

American Psychiatric Association. 1987. *Diagnostic and Statistical Manual of Mental Disorders.* 3d ed., rev. Washington, D.C.: APA.

Anglin, Douglas M., M. L. Brecht, J. Arthur Woodward, and Douglas G. Bonett. 1986. An empirical study of maturing out: Conditional factors. *International Journal of the Addictions* 21:233–46.

———. 1987. Conditional factors of maturing out: Personal resources and preaddiction sociopathy. *International Journal of the Addictions* 22:55–69.

Ashley, Richard. 1975. *Cocaine: Its History, Uses and Effects.* New York: St. Martin's Press.

Bakalar, James B., and Lester Grinspoon. 1984. *Drug Control in a Free Society.* Cambridge: Cambridge University Press.

Becker, Howard S. 1953. Becoming a marijuana user. *American Journal of Sociology* 59:235–42.

———. 1963. *Outsiders: Studies in the Sociology of Deviance.* Glencoe, Ill.: Free Press.

———. 1967. History, culture, and subjective experience: An exploration of the social bases of drug-induced experiences. *Journal of Health and Social Behavior* 8:162–76.

Bell, Daniel. 1976. *The Cultural Contradictions of Capitalism.* New York: Basic Books.

Berger, Bennett M. 1981. *The Survival of a Counterculture.* Berkeley: University of California Press.

Biernacki, Patrick. 1986. *Pathways from Heroin Addiction: Recovery without Treatment.* Philadelphia: Temple University Press.

Biernacki, Patrick, and Dan Waldorf. 1981. "Snowball sampling: Problems and techniques of chain referral sampling. *Sociological Methods and Research* 10:141–61.

Black, Donald. 1983. Crime as social control. *American Sociological Review* 48:34–45.

Blackwell, Judith Stephenson. 1983. Drifting, controlling and overcoming: Opiate users who avoid becoming chronically dependent. *Journal of Drug Issues* 13:219–36.

———. 1985. Opiate dependence as a psychophysical event: Users' reports of subjective experience. *Contemporary Drug Problems* 12:331–50.

Bourgois, Phillipe. 1989. In search of Horatio Alger: Culture and ideology in the crack economy. *Contemporary Drug Problems* 16:619–49.

Brecher, Edward M. 1972. *Licit and Illicit Drugs.* Boston: Little, Brown.

Brecht, Mary Lynn, and M. Douglas Anglin. 1988. Conditional factors of maturing out: Legal supervision and treatment. Los Angeles: Department of Psychology, University of California.

Brill, Leon. 1972. *The De-Addiction Process.* Springfield, Ill.: Charles C. Thomas.

Brower, Kirk J., and M. Douglas Anglin. 1987. Adolescent cocaine use: Epidemiology, risk factors, and prevention. *Journal of Drug Education* 17:163–80.

Brower, Kirk J., Robert Hierholzer, and Ebrahim Maddahian. 1986. Recent trends in cocaine abuse in a VA psychiatric population. *Hospital and Community Psychiatry* 37:1229–34.

Brown, James W., Daniel Glaser, Elaine Ward, and Gilbert Geis.

1974. Turning off: Cessation of marijuana use after college. *Social Problems* 21:527–38.

Busch, Katie A., and Sidney H. Schnoll. 1985. Cocaine: Review of current literature and interface with the law. *Behavioral Sciences and the Law* 3:283–98.

Butsch, Richard, ed. 1990. *For Fun and Profit: The Transformation of Leisure into Consumption.* Philadelphia: Temple University Press.

Cahalan, Don. 1970. *Problem Drinkers.* San Francisco: Jossey-Bass.

Chein, Isidor, Donald L. Gerard, Robert S. Lee, and Eva Rosenberg. 1964. *The Road to H.* New York: Basic Books.

Cheung, Yuteh W., Patricia Erickson, and Tammy Landau. 1991. Experience of crack use: Findings from a community-based sample in Toronto. *Journal of Drug Issues* 21:121–40.

Chitwood, Dale D., and Patricia C. Morningstar. 1985. Factors which differentiate cocaine users in treatment from nontreatment users. *International Journal of the Addictions* 20:449–59.

Cohen, Peter A. 1987. Cocaine use in Amsterdam in non-deviant subcultures. Paper presented at International Council on Alcohol and Addictions Congress, Lausanne, Switzerland, June.

———. 1989. *Cocaine Use in Amsterdam in Non-Deviant Subcultures.* Amsterdam: University of Amsterdam.

Coser, Lewis A. 1972. *Sociology through Literature,* 2d ed. Englewood Cliffs, N.J.: Prentice-Hall.

Desmond, David P., and James F. Maddux. 1980. Religious programs and careers of chronic heroin users. In Russell Faukenberry, ed., *Problems of the '70s, Drug Solutions for the Eighties: Proceedings of the National Drug Abuse Conference.* Lafayette, La.: Endac Enterprises Print Media.

Diamond, Edwin, Frank Acosta, and Leslie-Jean Thornton. 1987. Is TV news hyping America's cocaine problem? *TV Guide,* Feb. 7, 4–10.

Drug Abuse Warning Network (DAWN). 1987. *Trends in Drug Abuse Related Hospital Emergency Room Episodes and Medical Examiner Cases for Selected Drugs, DAWN 1976–1985.* Rockville, Md.: National Institute on Drug Abuse.

Duster, Troy. 1970. *The Legislation of Morality.* New York: Free Press.

Erickson, Patricia G., E. M. Adlaf, G. F. Murray, and Reginald G. Smart. 1987. *The Steel Drug: Cocaine in Perspective.* Lexington, Mass.: Lexington Books.

Erickson, Patricia G., and Bruce K. Alexander. 1989. Cocaine and addictive liability. *Social Pharmacology* 3:249–70.

Erickson, Patricia G., and Glenn F. Murray. 1989. The undeterred cocaine user: Intention to quit and its relationship to perceived legal and health threats. *Contemporary Drug Problems* 16:141–56.

Feldman, Harvey W. 1968. Ideological supports to becoming and remaining a heroin addict. *Journal of Health and Social Behavior* 9:131–39.

Flacks, Richard. 1988. *Making History: The American Left and the American Mind.* New York: Columbia University Press.

Freud, Sigmund. 1974. Uber coca [1884]. In R. Byck, ed., *Cocaine Papers,* 49–73. New York: Stonehill Publishing.

Gay, George R., and Charles W. Sheppard. 1973. Sex-crazed dope fiends: Myth or reality? *Drug Forum* 2:125–40.

Gay, George R., John A. Newmeyer, Michael Perry, Gregory Johnson, and Mark Kurkland. 1982. Love and the Haight: The sensuous hippie revisited: Drug/sex practices in San Francisco, 1980–1981. *Journal of Psychoactive Drugs* 14:111–23.

Geertz, Clifford, 1973. *The Interpretation of Cultures.* New York: Basic Books.

———. 1983. *Local Knowledge: Further Essays in Interpretive Anthropology.* New York: Basic Books.

Gilbarg, Daniel. 1988. Understanding cocaine use: A ratio of consequences model. Northeastern University, Boston, unpublished paper.

Gold, Mark S. 1984. *800–Cocaine.* New York: Bantam Books.

Gold, Mark S., and K. Verebey. 1984. The psychopharmacology of cocaine. *Psychiatric Annals* 14:714–23.

Gold, Mark S., Arnold M. Washton, and Charles A. Dackis. 1985. Cocaine abuse: Neurochemistry, phenomenology, and treatment. In N. J. Kozel and E. H. Adams, eds., *Cocaine Use in America: Epidemiologic and Clinical Perspectives,* 130–50. NIDA Research Monograph no. 61. Rockville, Md.: National Institute on Drug Abuse.

Goldstein, Paul J., Henry H. Brownstein, Patrick J. Ryan, and Patricia A. Bellucci. 1989. Crack and homicide in New York City, 1988: A conceptually-based event analysis. *Contemporary Drug Problems* 16:651–87.

Grinspoon, Lester, and James Bakalar. 1976. *Cocaine: A Drug and Its Social Evolution.* New York: Basic Books.

Gusfield, Joseph. 1963. *Symbolic Crusade: Status Politics and the American Temperance Movement.* Urbana: University of Illinois Press.

Hanson, Bill, George Beschner, James Walters, and Elliott Bovelle, eds. 1985. *Life with Heroin: Voices from the Inner City.* Lexington, Mass.: D. C. Heath.

Harwood, H. J., et al. 1984. *Economic Costs to Society of Alcohol and Drug Abuse and Mental Illness: 1980.* Report to the U.S. Alcohol, Drug Abuse, and Mental Health Administration. Research Triangle Park, N.C.: Research Triangle Institute.

Henley, J. R., and L. D. Adams. 1973. Marijuana use in post-college cohorts: Correlates of use, prevalence patterns and factors associated with cessation. *Social Problems* 20:514–20.

Inciardi, James. 1987. Beyond cocaine: Basuco, crack and other coca products. *Contemporary Drug Problems* 14:460–92.

Irwin, John K. 1970. *The Felon.* Englewood Cliffs, N.J.: Prentice-Hall.

Jaffe, Jerome. 1985. Drug addiction and drug abuse. In L. Goodman and A. Gilman, eds., *The Pharmacological Basis of Therapeutics,* 7th ed., 532–601. New York: Macmillan.

Jekel, J. F., D. F. Allen, H. Podlewski et al. 1986. Epidemic freebase cocaine abuse: Case study from the Bahamas. *Lancet* 8 (479):459–62.

Jellinek, E. M. 1952. Phases of alcohol addiction. *Quarterly Journal of Studies on Alcohol* 13:673–84.

Johnston, L. D., J. G. Bachman, and P. M. O'Malley. 1984. *Highlights from Student Drug Use in America, 1975–1984.* Rockville, Md.: National Institute on Drug Abuse.

Jorguez, James S. 1983. The retirement phase of the heroin-using career. *Journal of Drug Issues* 13:343–65.

Kierkegaard, Søren. 1941a. *The Sickness unto Death.* Walter Lowrie, trans. Princeton, N.J.: Princeton University Press. Originally published in 1843.

———. 1941b. *Fear and Trembling.* Walter Lowrie, trans. Princeton, N.J.: Princeton University Press. Originally published in 1843.

Kozel, Nicholas J., and Edgar H. Adams, eds. 1985. *Cocaine Use in America: Epidemiologic and Clinical Perspectives.* NIDA Research Monograph no. 61. Rockville, Md.: National Institute on Drug Abuse.

Krohn, Marvin D., Lon Lanza-Kaduce, M. Radosevich, and Ronald

L. Akers. 1980. Cessation of alcohol and drug use among adolescents: A social learning theory. Paper presented at the Annual Meeting of Society for the Study of Social Problems, New York, August.

Langer, S. Z., and M. A. Enero. 1974. Cocaine: Effect of in vivo administration on synaptosome uptake of norepinephrine. *Journal of Pharmacology and Experimental Therapeutics* 191:431.

Levine, Harry Gene. 1978. The discovery of addiction: Changing conceptions of habitual drunkenness in American history. *Journal of Studies on Alcohol* 39:143–67.

————. 1984. The alcohol problem in America: From temperance to alcoholism. *British Journal of Addiction* 79:109–19.

————. 1990. Temperance cultures. Paper presented at the Society for the Study of Addiction seminar, Substance Misuses: What Makes Problems, Windsor, England.

————. Forthcoming. *Drunkenness and Civilization.* New York: Basic Books.

Lindesmith, Alfred R. 1947. *Opiate Addiction.* Evanston, Ill.: Principia Press.

Macdonald, Patrick T. 1986. Cocaine use and abuse: An empirical test of competing theoretical models. Ph.D. thesis, University of California, Santa Barbara.

Macdonald, Patrick T., Dan Waldorf, Craig Reinarman, and Sheigla B. Murphy. 1988. Heavy cocaine use and sexual behavior. *Journal of Drug Issues* 18:437–55.

McDonnell, Douglas, Jeanette Irwin, and Marsha Rosenbaum. 1990. Hop and hubbas, a tough new mix. *Contemporary Drug Problems* 17:145–56.

McGlothlin, William H., M. Douglas Anglin, and Bruce D. Wilson. 1977. *An Evaluation of the California Civil Addict Program.* NIDA Services Research Monograph Series. Washington, D.C.: U.S. Government Printing Office.

McGrath, Mike. 1989. Crack City USA. *East Bay Express,* May 19, 13–23.

Maddux, James F., and David P. Desmond. 1980. New Light on the maturing out hypothesis on opiate dependence. *Bulletin on Narcotics* 32:15–25.

Marcuse, Herbert. 1955. *Eros and Civilization.* Boston: Beacon Press.

———. 1964. *One-Dimensional Man: Studies in the Ideology of Advanced Industrial Society*. Boston: Beacon Press.

Marlatt, G. A., and J. R. Gordon, eds. 1985. *Relapse Prevention: Maintenance Strategies in the Treatment of Addictive Behaviors*. New York: Guilford Press.

Matza, David. 1964. *Delinquency and Drift*. New York: John Wiley and Sons.

Mills, C. Wright. 1940. Situated actions and vocabularies of motive. *American Sociological Review* 5:904–13.

Mody, C., B. Miller, and H. McIntyre. 1988. Neurologic complications of cocaine abuse. *Neurology* 38:1189–93.

Mugford, Stephen, and Phil, Cohen. 1988. *Drug Use, Social Relations, and Commodity Consumption: A Study of Recreational Cocaine Users in Sydney, Canberra and Melbourne*. Report to the National Campaign Against Drug Abuse. Canberra: Australian National University.

Mule, S. J. 1984. The pharmacodynamics of cocaine abuse. *Psychiatric Annals* 14:724–27.

Murphy, Sheigla, Craig Reinarman, and Dan Waldorf. 1989. An 11-year follow-up of a network of cocaine users. *British Journal of Addiction* 84:427–36.

Murphy, Sheigla, Dan Waldorf, and Craig Reinarman. 1991. Drifting into dealing: Becoming a cocaine seller. *Qualitative Sociology* 13.

Murray, John B. 1986. An overview of cocaine use and abuse. *Psychological Reports* 59:243–64.

Nadelmann, Ethan. 1989. Drug prohibition in the United States: Costs, consequences, and alternatives. *Science* 245:939–46.

National Institute on Drug Abuse (NIDA). 1986a. Data from the Drug Abuse Warning Network: Annual Data, 1985. Statistical Series I, no. 5. Washington, D.C.: NIDA.

———. 1986b. National household survey on drug abuse, 1985. Rockville, Md.: NIDA, Division of Epidemiology and Statistical Analysis.

———. 1989. National household survey on drug abuse: 1988 population estimates. Rockville, Md.: NIDA, Division of Epidemiology and Prevention Research.

O'Donnell, John A. 1969. *Narcotic Addicts in Kentucky*. Public Health Service Publication no. 1881. Washington, D.C.: U.S. Government Printing Office.

O'Donnell, John A., Harwin C. Voss, Richard A. Clayton, Gerald T. Slotin, and Robin G. W. Room. 1976. *Young Men and Drugs: A Nationwide Survey.* NIDA Research Monograph no. 5. Rockville, Md.: National Institute on Drug Abuse.

Peele, Stanton. 1989. *Diseasing of America: Addiction Treatment Out of Control.* Lexington, Mass.: D. C. Heath.

Petersen, Robert C. 1977. Cocaine: An overview. In R. C. Petersen and R. C. Stillman, eds., *Cocaine: 1977,* 5–15. NIDA Research Monograph no. 13. Rockville, Md.: National Institute on Drug Abuse.

Petersen, Robert C., and Richard C. Stillman, eds. 1977. *Cocaine: 1977.* NIDA Research Monograph no. 13. Rockville, Md.: National Institute on Drug Abuse.

Phillips, Joel L., and Ronald D. Wynne. 1980. *Cocaine: The Mystique and the Reality.* New York: Avon Books.

Phillips, Mary Dana. 1990. Breaking the code: Toward a lexicon of recovery. Paper presented at the Kettil Bruun Alcohol Symposium, Budapest, Hungary, June.

Preble, Edward, and John H. Casey. 1969. Taking care of business: The heroin user's life on the street. *International Journal of the Addictions* 4:1–24.

Reinarman, Craig. 1979. Moral entrepreneurs and political economy: Historical and ethnographic notes on the construction of the cocaine menace. *Contemporary Crises* 3:225–54.

———. 1987. *American States of Mind: Political Beliefs and Behavior among Private and Public Workers.* New Haven and London: Yale University Press.

Reinarman, Craig, and Harry G. Levine. 1989. Crack in context: Politics and media in the making of a drug scare. *Contemporary Drug Problems* 16:535–77.

Reinarman, Craig, Dan Waldorf, and Sheigla Murphy. 1988. Scapegoating and social control in the construction of a public problem: Empirical and critical findings on cocaine and work. *Research in Law, Deviance, and Social Control* 9:37–62.

Reinarman, Craig, and Mary Dana Phillips. 1991. The politics of self-control in postmodernity: The "twelve-step" movement and advanced capitalist culture. Paper presented at the Conference on Contemporary Social Movements and Cultural Politics, Center for Cultural Studies, University of California, Santa Cruz, March 22–24.

Reuter, Peter. 1990. *Money from Crime: The Economics of Drug*

Dealing, no. R–3894. Santa Monica, Calif.: The Rand Corporation.

Robins, Lee N., J. E. Helzer, M. Hesselbrock, and Eric Wish. 1979. Vietnam veterans three years after Vietnam. In Leon Brill and Charles Winick, eds., *Yearbook of Substance Abuse.* New York: Human Sciences Press.

Roizen, Ron. 1987. The great controlled drinking controversy. In Marc Gallanter, ed., *Recent Developments in Alcoholism,* 5: 245–79. New York: Plenum Press.

Room, Robin G. W. 1978. Governing images of alcohol and drug problems. Ph.D. diss., University of California, Berkeley.

———. 1983. Sociological aspects of the disease concept of alcoholism. *Research Advances in Alcohol and Drug Problems* 7:47–91.

Rosenbaum, Marsha. 1981. *Women on Heroin.* New Brunswick, N.J.: Rutgers University Press.

Sadava, S. W., and R. Forsyth. 1977. Turning on, turning off and relapse: Social psychological determinants of status changes in cannabis use. *International Journal of the Addictions* 4:509–28.

Scharse, Robert. 1966. Cessation patterns among neophyte heroin users. *International Journal of the Addictions* 1:23–32.

Schneider, Joseph. 1978. Deviant drinking as disease: Alcoholism as a social accomplishment. *Social Problems* 25:361–72.

Seeley, John R. 1962. Alcoholism is a disease: Implications for social policy. In D. J. Pittman and C. R. Snyder, eds., *Society, Culture, and Drinking Patterns,* 586–93. New York: John Wiley and Sons.

Shaffer, Howard J., and Stephanie B. Jones. 1989. *Quitting Cocaine: The Struggle against Impulse.* Lexington, Mass.: Lexington Books.

Shover, Neal. 1985. *Aging Criminals.* Beverly Hills, Calif.: Sage Publications.

Siegel, Ronald K. 1982. Cocaine smoking. *Journal of Psychoactive Drugs* 14:277–559.

———. 1984. Cocaine smoking disorders: Diagnosis and treatment. *Psychiatric Annals* 14:728–32.

———. 1985a. New patterns of cocaine use: Changing doses and routes. In Nicholas J. Kozel and Edgar J. Adams, eds., *Cocaine Use in America: Epidemiologic and Clinical Perspectives,* 204–20. NIDA Research Monograph no. 61. Rockville, Md.: National Institute on Drug Abuse.

———. 1985b. New patterns of cocaine use: Changing doses and routes. In Nicholas J. Kozel and Edgar H. Adams, eds., *Cocaine Use in America: Epidemiologic and Clinical Perspectives.* NIDA Research Monograph no. 61. Rockville, Md.: National Institute on Drug Abuse.

———. 1989. *Intoxication: Life in Pursuit of Artificial Paradise.* New York: E. P. Dutton.

Skolnick, Jerome H., Theodore Correl, Elizabeth Navarro, and Roger Rabb. 1989. *The Social Structure of Street Drug Dealing.* Sacramento: State of California, Department of Justice, Bureau of Criminal Statistics.

Smart, Reginald G., Patricia G. Erickson, Edward M. Adlaf, and Glenn F. Murray. 1984. Preliminary report on a study of adult cocaine users: Patterns, problems and perspectives. Toronto, Ontario: Alcoholism and Drug Addiction Research Foundation.

Smith, David E., Donald R. Wesson, and Michael Apter-Marsh. 1984. Cocaine and alcohol-induced sexual dysfunctions in patients with addictive disease. *Journal of Psychoactive Drugs* 16 (4):359–61.

Snow, Mary. 1973. Maturing out of narcotic addiction in New York City. *International Journal of the Addictions* 8 (6):921–38.

Spotts, J. V., and F. C. Shontz. 1985. A theory of adolescent substance abuse. *Advances in Alcohol and Substance Abuse* 4:77–81.

Stall, Ron, and Patrick Biernacki. 1986. Spontaneous remission from the problematic use of substances: An inductive model derived from a comparative analysis of the alcohol, tobacco, and food/obesity literatures. *International Journal of the Addictions* 21:1–23.

Sutherland, Edwin, and Donald R. Cressey. 1978. *Criminology.* Philadelphia: Lippincott.

Thompson, Edward P. 1971. The moral economy of the English crowd in the eighteenth century. *Past and Present* 50:76–136.

Trebach, Arnold. 1987. *The Great Drug War.* New York: Macmillan.

U.S. Senate. Committee on the Judiciary. 1990. *Hard Core Cocaine Addicts: Measuring—and Fighting—the Epidemic.* Washington, D.C.: U.S. Government Printing Office.

Van Dyke, Craig, and Robert Byck. 1982. Cocaine. *Scientific American* 24:128–42.

Van Vliet, Henk. 1990. Separation of drug markets and the normalization of drug problems in the Netherlands. *Journal of Drug Issues* 20:463–71.

Verebey, K., and M. S. Gold. 1988. From coca leaves to crack: The effects of dose and routes of administration in abuse liability. *Psychiatric Annals* 18:513–20.

Waldorf, Dan. 1973. *Careers in Dope*. Englewood Cliffs, N.J.: Prentice-Hall.

———. 1980. A brief history of illicit drug ethnographies. In Carl Akins and George Beschner, eds., *Ethnography: A Research Tool for Policy Makers in the Drug and Alcohol Fields*. Rockville, Md.: National Institute on Drug Abuse, Services Research Branch.

———. 1983. Natural recovery from opiate addiction: Some social-psychological processes of untreated recovery. *Journal of Drug Issues* 13:237–80.

Waldorf, Dan, and Patrick Biernacki. 1977. Natural recovery from opiate addiction: A review of the incidence literature. *Journal of Drug Issues* 9:281–90.

———. 1981. Natural recovery from opiate addiction: Some preliminary findings. *Journal of Drug Issues* 11:61–74.

Waldorf, Dan, Sheigla Murphy, Craig Reinarman, and Bridget Joyce. 1977. *Doing Coke: An Ethnography of Cocaine Users and Sellers*. Washington, D.C.: Drug Abuse Council.

Washton, Arnold M., and Mark S. Gold. 1984. Chronic cocaine abuse: Evidence for adverse effects in health and functioning. *Psychiatric Annals* 14:733–43.

———. 1987. Recent trends in cocaine abuse: A view from the national hotline, "800–COCAINE." *Advances in Alcohol and Substance Abuse* 6:31–47.

Washton, Arnold M., Mark S. Gold, and A. L. Pottash. 1984. Survey of 500 callers to a national cocaine helpline. *Psychosomatics* 25:771–75.

Watters, John K., and Patrick Biernacki. 1989. Targeted sampling: Options for the study of hidden populations. *Social Problems* 36:416–30.

Weil, Andrew. 1972. *The Natural Mind*. Boston: Houghton Mifflin.

Weil, Andrew, and Winifred Rosen. 1983. *From Chocolate to Morphine: Understanding Mind-Active Drugs*. Boston: Houghton Mifflin.

Williams, Terry. 1989. *The Cocaine Kids: The Inside Story of a Teenage Drug Ring.* Reading, Mass.: Addison-Wesley.

Wilson, William J. 1987. *The Truly Disadvantaged: The Inner City, The Underclass, and Public Policy.* Chicago: University of Chicago Press.

Winick, Charles. 1962. Maturing out of narcotic addiction. *Bulletin on Narcotics* 14.

———. 1964. The life cycle of the narcotic addict and of addiction. *U.S. Bulletin on Narcotics* 16 (1).

Zinberg, Norman E. 1984. *Drug, Set and Setting: The Basis for Controlled Intoxicant Use.* New Haven and London: Yale University Press.

Zinberg, Norman E., and Wayne M. Harding. 1982. Control and intoxicant use: A theoretical and practical overview. In Zinberg and Harding, eds., *Control over Intoxicant Use: Pharmacological, Psychological and Social Considerations.* New York: Human Sciences Press.

Zinberg, Norman E., W. M. Harding, and M. Winkeller. 1978. A study of the regulatory mechanisms in controlled illicit drug users. In K. Blum, S. J. Feinglass, and A. H. Briggs, eds., *Social Meanings of Drugs: Principles of Social Pharmacology.* New York: Basic Books. Also in *Journal of Drug Issues* 7(1977): 117–33.

Zinberg, Norman E., W. M. Harding, S. Stelmack, and R. A. Mablestone. 1978. Patterns of heroin use. *Recent Developments in Chemotherapy of Narcotic Addiction: Annals of the New York Academy of Sciences* 311:10–24.

INDEX